Public Admin

Public Administration
CASES IN MANAGERIAL ROLE-PLAYING

Robert P. Watson
Florida Atlantic University

New York San Francisco Boston
London Toronto Sydney Tokyo Singapore Madrid
Mexico City Munich Paris Cape Town Hong Kong Montreal

Vice President/Publisher: Priscilla McGeehon
Senior Acquisitions Editor: Eric Stano
Senior Marketing Manager: Megan Galvin-Fak
Production Manager: Charles Annis
Project Coordination, Text Design, and Electronic Page Makeup: WestWords, Inc.
Cover Design Manager: Nancy Danahy
Cover Designer: Keithley and Associates
Manufacturing Buyer: Al Dorsey
Printer and Binder: The Maple-Vail Book Manufacturing Group
Cover Printer: Lehigh Press, Inc.

Library of Congress Cataloging-in-Publication Data

Public administration : cases in managerial role-playing / [edited by] Robert P. Watson.
    p. cm.
  Includes bibliographical references.
  ISBN 0-321-08552-3
  1. Public administration—Case studies.   I. Watson, Robert P.
JF1351 .P815 2001
351—dc21
                                          2001038540

Please visit our website at www.ablongman.com

ISBN 0-321-08552-3

MA–04 03 02 01

10 9 8 7 6 5 4 3 2 1

Remembering Donald A. Martin, Jean Hoffman Watson, and Austin Watson

CONTENTS

PREFACE

Case studies are useful pedagogical tools. Cases expose students to a mix of theory and practice. They offer the opportunity to participate in discussions, debates, or projects pertaining to the subject matter. And through cases, the student is often able to better relate to the material being presented. *Public Administration: Cases in Managerial Role-Playing* integrates all these elements of learning through a series of role-playing scenarios that present students with a realistic view of what it is like to manage public agencies, programs, and employees.

The goals of the book include stimulating interest in the field of study and practice of public administration and offering readers tools and insights that will prepare them to be better managers. The book features contemporary, realistic cases of typical managerial problems administrators face in both the public and nonprofit sectors. By giving students the opportunity to role-play a manager in the case who is confronted by a dilemma and must make a decision, the student is able to "walk in the shoes" of a public administrator and thereby get a taste of what it is like to work as a manager in a government or nonprofit agency. As is often the situation in the real world, the problems posed in the cases are such that no obvious, single, or simple solution presents itself. The student-role-player must consider an array of complex and interrelated factors and multiple courses of action in deciding how to respond to the situations in the case. Such are the themes of the book: public administration is a challenging endeavor defined by uncertainty and complexity. And decision making in the public and nonprofit sectors is rarely a straight-forward act; rather, it is a process that involves consideration of a host of interrelated political, ethical, legal, and other factors.

Beyond offering cases that simply present the facts surrounding a managerial dilemma, the *Case Analysis* approach employed in the book encourages students to analyze the sources of the problems at hand, possible courses of action, consequences of their decision, and a host of political, ethical, legal, and other factors comprising the macro-environment in which the act of administration occurs. This model is designed to foster critical thinking and group discussion about the issues and problems in the cases and to promote comprehensive but realistic analysis as a tool of and precondition to decision making. To assist the student in approaching the cases and understanding the Case Analysis model, the book opens with a brief discussion of how students can use this approach when analyzing the cases and performing the role-playing scenario.

The case studies contained in the book cover the central tasks of the practice of public administration and major areas of the field of study, including organizational behavior, management, personnel administration, budgeting, ethics, program planning, and evaluation. The cases reflect common managerial dilemmas set in a mix of local, state, and federal government agencies as well as nonprofit organizations. Each case is suitable for pre-professional, entry-level, and mid-career learners, and students do not need a technical understanding of the issues covered to understand the cases. The cases are written with a generalist audience in mind. Both undergraduate and graduate students should find the cases valuable. An attempt was made to produce cases that are both challenging yet entertaining, and complex yet highly readable. Teachers should find the cases short enough to be used as in-class assignments. At the same time, enough background information on the issues of the case exists to capture the complex nature of public administration.

Another feature of the book that teachers and students should find attractive is the interdisciplinary nature of the cases. The authors of the cases represent an array of scholars from such disciplines as public administration, political science, economics, sociology, psychology, social work, and criminology, and the contributors bring backgrounds from academia, research, and the "real world" to their writing. They therefore offer a range of perspectives on the subject, yet the authors share the common perspective of presenting management and decision making in the public and nonprofit sectors as occurring under conditions of uncertainty, complexity, and a host of political, ethical, and environmental constraints.

The cases are organized into six sections, each section corresponding to a major theme in public administration. An essay opens each of these sections. These introductory essays provide a brief overview of the important concepts pertaining to the topic at hand and pose questions to guide the student in approaching the ensuing topical area and corresponding cases. The cases were designed with learning in mind. At the beginning of each case the reader will find a short overview of the agency in which the case is set and a list of the major characters in the case, both in boxed format. This background information should make the process of following the storyline even easier. Each case closes with a few discussion-oriented questions and a list of useful sources for further reading.

I would like to thank those reviewers who provided feedback on the manuscript for this book in its various stages of development:

William Chappell, Columbus State University

Denise Scheberle, University of Wisconsin - Green Bay

Robert Blair, University of Nebraska at Omaha

Warren Campbell, California State University

David W. Sink, University of Arkansas at Little Rock

Joseph Ohren, Eastern Michigan University

Charles W. Washington, Florida Atlantic University

I hope the cases bring to life for you the challenging, important, and rewarding endeavor we call public administration. Enjoy the book!

Robert P. Watson

THE CASE ANALYSIS APPROACH

WHY CASE STUDIES?

The case study is a popular and useful learning and training tool found in many disciplines, including public and nonprofit administration. It offers the advantage of taking concepts that might otherwise seem vague and complex and presenting them in an accessible and comprehensible format. Cases devoted to public administration offer the student the opportunity to examine either actual or realistic events in government and thereby gain exposure to how public and nonprofit sector agencies operate. When the cases are written in such a way that they involve the reader in the decision-making process, students also gain applied learning experiences and are better able to relate the lessons of the exercise with their own experiences.

The *Case Analysis* approach used in this book mixes theory and practice by permitting readers to apply concepts of administration to realistic situations. This is possible because the cases are based on the everyday experiences of managers and those dilemmas commonly found in public agencies. Each case also poses ethical questions and considerations for the reader and is set in an environment composed of an array of highly political and complex issues and problems. Faced with making a decision about these problems, the reader is encouraged to think critically about problem solving, decision making, and the challenge of managing public agencies, programs, and employees.

WHY ROLE-PLAYING?

For each case in the book, the reader will be asked to role-play a central character in the case and make a decision that addresses the problem(s) at hand. This offers the reader the opportunity to participate in the learning process and gain insights into the work of public administrators as well as an appreciation for the challenging, complex nature of public administration.

As is often the situation in the real world of government and nonprofit organizations, however, no single or obvious decision—or even a best course of action—presents itself to the manager. Rather, numerous potential courses of action exist. So too are multiple forces acting and interacting to frame the complex problems present in the cases. Through the role-playing process, students are exposed to such facets of decision making and managing in the public and nonprofit sectors in a way that might not be possible by simply studying the theories of public administration or reading textbook discussions of the topics. Role-playing allows students to practice what they learn, to think critically about and discuss the problems at hand, and to hone management skills they will need in their careers.

WHY CASE ANALYSIS?

The *Case Analysis* approach expands on the conventional notion of a case study by incorporating not only an approximation or description of an event but by offering portrayals of realistic events that are designed to introduce the reader to such characteristics of administration as uncertainty, complexity, and compromise. The cases that follow cover the central tasks involved in management and the major areas of the fields of study including organizations, management, personnel administration, budgeting, ethics, program planning, and evaluation. They are drawn from and are applicable to local, state, and federal government as well as the nonprofit sector and are designed for pre-profession, entry-level, and mid-career managers and both undergraduate and graduate students.

The Case Analysis approach requires an analysis of the facts, problems, actors, stakeholders, courses of action, and possible outcomes pertaining to the case. Secondly, the decision-making framework of the Case Analysis approach involves the analysis of political and ethical factors both impacting and resulting from the decision. As such, more than simply presenting facts, these cases are designed to encourage analysis, raise questions, and promote group discussion about the complexities of being a manager.

STEPS IN THE CASE ANALYSIS

The cases in this book hope to foster comprehensive analysis of administrative problems and thoughtful, informed decision making; yet they are also intended to be realistic scenarios of the act and art of management. Unfortunately, perfect textbook illustrations of how one should manage or make decisions are often at odds with the reality of the practices of street-level managers. For instance, rarely do managers have the time, resources, knowledge, and information required to comprehensively assess the situation, explore all possible courses of action, and make the ideal decision. More often than is suggested in textbooks, decisions are made based on gut instinct or a "quick and dirty" analysis of only the most apparent factors.

Therefore, the Case Analysis approach attempts to offer a compromise between textbook and reality. The approach blends what is referred to in the literature as the "rational-comprehensive" (textbook) and "incremental" (realistic) models of public administration. The former approach to managerial decision making is based on unrealistic assumptions such as administrators having every detail of the issue at their command—full and accurate information; ample time; and the necessary resources and expertise to make the best decision. As such, it is in practice, unattainable. Yet it serves as a goal in which to aspire for an ideal approach to decision making. On the other hand, the incremental model, while realistic in its emphasis on the need to compromise and on decision making under imperfect conditions, is, however, also unacceptable in practice. It is unacceptable because it embraces the possibility of accomplishing only small or incremental adjustments on the past and, in the words of scholar Charles Lindblom, who studied the decision-making models, incrementalism simply "muddles through."[1] Although it might be more practical and politically feasible, such an underachieving approach should neither be the goal of management nor means by which future managers are trained. The Case Analysis approach blends the two models by employing the characteristics of compromise, complexity, and realism of the incremental model, yet aspiring to the most informed and comprehensive decision model possible.

There are seven steps involved in Case Analysis. To facilitate the analysis of the case, its dilemmas, and subsequent decision-making process, it is recommended that the reader prepare a written *case brief* for each case. The student encountering a case on administrative issues and problems for the first time may have difficulty understanding the precise facts of the case, as the issues and problems are often very complex and interrelated. Even the most experienced analysts and government managers find it helpful to prepare a written overview or brief of the salient points of the case. As such, it is good practice to prepare written briefs not only as students studying cases but as managers faced with decisions.

The format for a case brief is offered in the sample below. It is recommended that the reader first identify the case title at the top of the page and list each of the seven steps involved in the Case Analysis in a brief of approximately one or two pages. Remember, the case brief is not a comprehensive assessment of the case but merely a tool that should only include the most important points that will aid the reader in making decisions about the case. Therefore, answers to each of the seven steps need not be written as full sentences. Short bullets will suffice.

SAMPLE CASE ANALYSIS BRIEF

Title of the Case

1. Facts:

   ◆ List the pertinent facts
   ◆ Focus on the what, where, when, and why of the case

2. Issues:

   ◆ List the primary problem and issue
   ◆ List any secondary or related problems and issues
   ◆ Identify the sources or causes of the problems/issues

3. Actors:

   ◆ Name, Title
   ◆ Name, Title, etc...
   ◆ Identify any important traits of the actors that could shed light on the decision-making process

4. Analysis:

- ◆ Identify the resource and formal/legal constraints and issues
  (staff and budgetary resources, rules and regulations, responsibilities of the job, …)
- ◆ Identify the ethical constraints and issues
- ◆ Identify the political constraints and issues
- ◆ Attempt to identify any unknown or unforeseen constraints and issues

5. Group Analysis:

- ◆ In small groups, discuss step four
  (consider having each group member role-play a different actor in the case and/or different community or interest group impacted by the issue and course of action.)
- ◆ If conflict arises in the group, consider suitable approaches to conflict resolution, cooperation, and coordination

6. Courses of Action:

- ◆ Consider precedents or paradigms/models to guide the decision
- ◆ List three possible courses of action and develop criteria to rank them

7. Decision:

- ◆ Select and recommend a course of action
- ◆ Provide a short overview of the decision and rationale/justification for it

THE CHALLENGE OF THE PUBLIC SECTOR

With almost five million employees working in the federal government and another fifteen million workers on state and local government payrolls, the *public sector* of society is both a major employer and major force in the United States. Government touches nearly every facet of our lives. Consider, for instance, an average day in the life of an average person. Let us call her Jane Q. Citizen.

Jane awakens each morning to music on her alarm-radio that is played by a radio station that must be licensed by the Federal Communications Commission. The company that built Jane's alarm-radio had to adhere to an array of governmental regulations while manufacturing the alarm clock and licensing requirements on the sale of the unit. The public water supply enables her to bathe in the morning. Afterward, she eats a breakfast of foods tested, inspected, and regulated by public agencies such as the Food and Drug Administration, topped off by a glass of juice from oranges grown by Florida farmers receiving government subsidies and protection from rival international producers. The roads on which Jane drives to work were built with public money and managed by the state Department of Transportation; her car includes seat belts and a shatter-proof windshield, both required by law. Jane is legally able to drive her car to work because she obtained a driver's license from the state, which also registered her automobile and furnished her tags. Had she not driven, she could have used the public transportation system made available by municipal and county governments.

Jane works in a building originally approved for development by a local government planning and zoning board, monitored during construction by a building inspector, examined by the fire marshal, and deemed safe by occupational safety and health standards. Even the elevator she rode to her job was certified by a government inspector. At work, Jane is protected from discrimination and unfair labor practices by an assortment of statutes, but pays part of her income in taxes for such protections. And the list goes on and on and on.

Some of the work performed by private businesses pertains directly or indirectly to government. For instance, many large defense contractors such as General Dynamics are private enterprises, yet they build and furnish weapons and supplies for the U.S. military. So, while both the company and the employees can be classified as belonging to the *private sector,* a good portion of their sales and production processes are in the direct service of government. This is known as *privatization*, the process whereby public services such as building missiles, operating correctional centers, and collecting trash are undertaken by private enterprises for government. Such *"contracting out"* of public services occurs at all levels of government. Likewise, numerous businesses, consultants, and law firms owe their existence directly to government. For instance, a firm that conducts environmental impact assessments of large-scale development projects, such as airports, performs a service that is mandated by law and does it because of government policy.

Given the pervasiveness of government in society, public administrators end up performing nearly every type of job imaginable. Behind every regulation, inspection, and certification, as well as every road, prison, and court, is a government employee. These public programs and services are provided within a broad array of settings, by a number of different types of agencies, and in response to a host of problems. Indeed, many people work for government, but even those who do not still feel the presence of government in their daily lives. Managing public agencies, programs, and personnel is a challenging and important endeavor.

The Rise of the Administrative State

This was not always the case, however. When George Washington assumed the presidency in 1789, the federal government consisted of only five departments: state, war, treasury (developed as a congressional agency), the attorney general, and the postal service—all staffed by a small number of employees. So how did government grow from such modest beginnings to the massive size it is today? There are numerous theories that attempt to explain the growth of government over the course of U.S. history. These include (1) majoritarian preference, whereby new roles for government and, thus, the growth of government was sanctioned by the wishes of the majority of the citizenry, (2) the growing complexity of modern society, which necessitated new challenges for government and increased activism by government, and (3) the interest by public agencies in self-promotion and self-preservation, which resulted in budgets that are expanded beyond necessary levels by beneficiaries, bureaucrats, and legislators, and public programs that are rarely terminated regardless of their usefulness.

The growth of government in terms of size and function also appears to be a byproduct of crisis and social upheaval. Historically, periods of social and economic turmoil and threats to national security have been followed by an expansion of the functions of government directly in response to new demands created by changes in society. As such, the analogy of a *staircase* can be used to depict the growth of government over time, whereby periods—at times a few years, at other times a few decades—of relatively no change in the nature of governance are punctuated by sudden, dramatic expansions in government. The flat base of the staircase upon which one steps represents the static periods with no significant new directions in governance. The expansion—the rise to the next step in the staircase—is triggered by crisis. In other words, the growth of government has not been linear or gradual, but sporadic yet continual.

From the founding of the nation until the post-Civil War era, the nature of governance in the United States was passive and, for many decades at a time, remained largely unchanged with few profound new directions in governance. The size of government remained small. All that changed, however, in the late nineteenth century with the coming of the American *Industrial Revolution*, the first major event in U.S. history that sparked a fundamental change in the practice and size of government. The combination of technological advancements and the rise of the entrepreneurial spirit led to the assembly line and mass production process, which changed the way products were produced and marked the country's emergence as an industrialized state. Corresponding to this was a shift in the composition of the population, brought about by migration from rural areas to rapidly growing, new cities of farmers displaced by technology. Such rural flight and waves of immigrants produced the necessary labor base for new factories. As a result, the largely agrarian and rural character of the country had, by the close of the 1800s, been transformed into an increasingly urban society.

The sudden experience with urbanization and industrialization produced some unintended and harmful side effects, such as overcrowded cities with unsafe housing, dangerous factory work conditions, abusive child labor practices, rampant political corruption, and inadequate public infrastructure. The inadequacies were in the form of a lack of essential services like fire and police protection, hospitals, roads, sanitation systems, and a safe public water supply. In response to these problems, a series of government agencies, programs, and services were established, thus expanding the role and size of government. Known as the *Progressive Movement*, the early part of the twentieth century saw government become involved in protecting child labor, regulating meat and food production, preventing monopolistic and collusive business practices, and providing adequate municipal services and public infrastructure. The Industrial Revolution and subsequent Progressivism ushered in a new era of government activism and, with it, a need for more professionally trained, competent public administrators to manage these programs and services.

The second era that initiated a fundamental expansion of the role and size of government came in the late 1920s and early 1930s with the *Great Depression*. Because of over-speculation on Wall Street, risky business and financial practices, and other factors, the stock market collapsed in 1929 and, in its wake, thousands of businesses and banks failed. With at least one in four Americans unable to find work, the country was experiencing perhaps its worst economic crisis. The election of Franklin D. Roosevelt as president in 1932, with his promise of a *New Deal* for the country, resulted in the creation of dozens of new agencies and programs. Roosevelt's experiment involved an expansion of government into new realms like economic management. This was accomplished by assisting struggling banks and businesses, regulating the cost and pricing practices of private enterprise, and promoting such employment-generating initiatives as the Works Progress Administration, Civilian Conservation Corps, and Tennessee Valley Authority, where the unemployed were put to work in the service of public projects. The New Deal also saw the public sector involved in providing a social safety net for the less fortunate and economically disadvantaged through the creation of social welfare programs and, in 1935, the social security program.

The third major period in the expansion of the nature and scope of government occurred in the 1960s. The turbulent decade of the 60s saw the birth of several social movements, including the civil rights movement led by the Reverend Martin Luther King Jr., the "second wave" of the women's movement, which was launched in 1963 with the publication of *The Feminine Mystique* by Betty Freidan, the consumerist movement headed by the activism of Ralph Nader, and, sparked by Rachel Carson's groundbreaking 1962 book, *Silent Spring*, the environmental movement. A period of social revolution, the 60s and early 70s witnessed further social change at the hands of the free speech movement, the peace movement and protests of the Vietnam War, and the counter-culture of "free love" and drugs. The result was that, through the 1960s and 1970s, numerous social and regulatory agencies were created and government began in earnest the promotion of civil rights and liberties for all its citizens. President Lyndon B. Johnson launched his *Great Society* program in an attempt to alleviate poverty through such social programs as Medicare, Medicaid, food stamps, and numerous other services for the needy which, according to some, ushered in the modern "welfare state."

As a result of these historical periods, the function of government was expanded to include economic management, regulation of commerce, promotion of social equality and justice, and attempts to mitigate poverty. With the expansion of public programs and services, not only were more public administrators needed, but the importance of the government employee in society was enhanced. This growth in the functions government performed is reflected in the size of government in terms of the number of government employees. The public sector has become a leading employer. In many communities around the country, especially smaller, rural communities or those that serve as home to military bases, the government is the largest employer in town and, with such a high percentage of the workforce on the public payroll, the government has become the economic engine of those communities. With so many programs and such sizeable payrolls, not only does the government employ many of its citizens, but the federal budget has grown accordingly. For instance, the federal budget for fiscal year 2001 was a whopping $1.8 trillion, which accounted for roughly 19 percent of the country's GNP.[1] Yet, employees of state and local governments comprise the far majority of all public employees.

The Federal System

A defining characteristic of public management is working with other units of government and functioning within a system composed of levels of government. This is a product of *federalism*, whereby the national, state, and local governments exist and share power. Other countries such as Canada and Germany have federal systems, as opposed to the United Kingdom or France, both of which have unitary systems where a central government is *the* legal entity. Federalism by definition distributes power and authority among different levels of government, with each government having its own jurisdiction. The U.S. Constitution is the supreme legal code of the land, and it grants specific powers to the federal government, such as the responsibility for external affairs of the country and national security. Yet, the Constitution reserves other powers for the states, while still other responsibilities such as dealing with crime and welfare are shared between governments. Here, the concept of *interdependence* is a primary element of federalism. Another defining characteristic is *complexity*, if not confusion, as the Constitution does not spell out in detail the exact powers of each governmental unit and the specifics of one government's relationship to another.

The exact parameters of *intergovernmental relations* (IGR) are thus hard to pinpoint, as are the jurisdictional boundaries, responsibilities, and powers between governmental units. Even though the federal government would appear to be the dominant level of government, all levels of government have grown in size and scope of their functions, although recent decades have witnessed far greater growth at the local level (municipalities, counties). As such, several different government agencies might have a role in delivering a certain public program. This means a manager might have to *share authority* with other agencies or governments. Accordingly, the jurisdictions of governmental units often overlap, and the relationships between them are continually evolving.

A common model for understanding the relationship between governments has been to depict IGR as a "layer cake" with the federal government representing the top layer; states serving as the larger, middle layer; and local governments serving the most numerous and broadest—but lowest—level of the tiered cake. However, such a model is too simplistic and inaccurate in its view of orderly, non-overlapping, and independent relations between governments. A more accurate depiction of IGR as a "marble cake" has been offered by Morton Grodzins and Daniel J. Elazar.[2] Here, the functions of government are mixed together in terms of roles, clientele, and goals, much as the blending swirls of a marble cake.

But even the marble cake analogy fails to capture the true character of IGR.[3] In addition to the three-tiered view of federal, state, and local governments, there are numerous other governmental units such as special districts like water, school, sewage, and health, public utilities, that do not fit neatly into a characterization of public or private entities, and councils of governments such as cooperative planning commissions. The federal government provides *grants-in-aid* to state and even local governments and governmental units engage in *revenue sharing* in the joint delivery of public services. Add to this the proliferation of think tanks, nonprofit social organizations, and public/private partnerships between business and government that are a part of the policy process and the interdependence and cooperative nature of management in the public sector becomes a central characteristic. Public managers must be prepared to work within a context of intergovernmental relations.

Who are Public Administrators?

Technically, public administrators are those individuals working in a managerial capacity in government; managing the people, programs, resources, and budgets of the public sector. However, the term can also apply to any public employee, whether they work in a managerial capacity or not. As such, forest service rangers, firefighters, correctional officers, and public school teachers are public administrators.

Public administration includes the academic and scholarly study, profession, and practice of governance. While the work of managing government is the *practice* of public administration, the *study* of the subject can be found in college courses, graduate degree programs, and scholarly journals that focus on public administration. Organizations comprised of public managers and those organizations and individuals dedicated to the study and development of public management form a *profession* of public administration. Numerous organizations such as the American Society for Public Administration, the International City/County Management Association, and the American Planning Association are devoted to furthering the profession.

Because public administration is both a multi-disciplinary field of study and a practice that, as was previously mentioned, involves such a wide array of jobs and tasks, it is difficult to arrive at a simple definition. Indeed, scholars in the field have struggled long and hard with the definitional dilemma, and it would appear that an accurate and inclusive, or an all-encompassing, definition that captures the essence of public sector management and the core values of public administration remains to be identified. Among the host of definitions offered by authors of textbooks on public administration are:

1. "Public administration is the use of managerial, political, and legal theories and processes to fulfill legislative, executive, and judicial government mandates for the provision of regulatory and service functions for society as a whole or for some segments of it."[4]
2. "Public Administration is the production of goods and services designed to serve the needs of citizens/consumers."[5]
3. "The practice of public administration involves the dynamic reconciliation of various forces in government's efforts to manage public policies and programs."[6]
4. "Public administration: The process by which resources are marshaled and then used to cope with the problems facing a political community."[7]
5. "Public administration is centrally concerned with the organization of government policies and programs as well as the behavior of officials (usually non-elected) formally responsible for their conduct."[8]

Fortunately, an assessment of the definitions offered in leading books on the topic contain some commonalities that permit us to gain a better understanding of the nature of just who public administrators are, and what it is that they do. For instance, Richard Stillman II[9], identifies the following list of common themes found in most definitions and textbooks:

1. A public setting.
2. The executive branch of government.
3. The formation and development of programs and policies.
4. Implementation of programs and policies.
5. Service to citizens, the community, and country.
6. The behavior of government officials and agencies.

Another way to study public administrators and determine just who can be called public administrators is to consider a demographic profile of government employees. A profile of the typical federal employee in Table I reveals some interesting findings.

Profile of Government Employees

"The Typical Federal Civilian Employee"

Age: 45.9 years
Length of Service: 16.9 years
Educational Level: 40.2% have bachelor's degree
Sex: 55.3% male, 44.7% female
Minority: 30% (17.7% Black, 6.5% Hispanic, 4.4% Asian/Pacific Islander, 2.1% Native Amer.)

Source: Office of Personnel Management, 2000

It is apparent that the public sector is more integrated than the private sector, with women and ethnic minorities comprising proportionately a larger percentage of government employees than what is found in most businesses. Moreover, women, African Americans, and Latinos make up a larger percentage of those serving in administrative positions in government than the percentages present in the private sector. Such findings affirm the existence of the principle of *representative bureaucracy*. In a democracy it is incumbent upon government to be truly representative of all the people, not only in elected offices but by reflecting in its non-elected ranks the character and content of the public. Public administrators are found in every state, community, and among all classes, races, and segments of American society, reflecting the rich tapestry that is the United States.

Another way to ponder the question, "Who are public administrations?" is to consider what it is that public administrators do. In answering such a question, it might be more beneficial to attempt to determine what it is they do *not* do, as managers in the public sector perform nearly every type of function—from technical to scientific to financial—that can be found in society. In recognizing the diversity of tasks performed by public managers, The National Association of Schools of Public Affairs and Administration, an accrediting entity that works with scholars and university programs in public administration, recommends that university programs in the discipline cover such divergent topics as (1) the political, social, and economic environment of the public sector; (2) the management/administrative process; (3) public policy and policy analysis; (4) analytical tools needed to administer public programs; and (5) organizational behavior in order to accurately capture the range of the field.

Public Versus Private Management

A common characterization of government employees—or bureaucrats—is that they are less efficient and less effective in their work than employees in the private sector. This perception is popularized in the media, cartoon strips, late-night comedy skits, and on film. It is so pervasive that it is hard to find someone that does not accept the "fact" of government inefficiency. Even the term *bureaucratic* has a negative connotation, implying excessive red tape, inefficiency, redundancy, impersonality, and other institutional attributes incongruent with productivity, quality, and customer service. Bureaucrats have become the scapegoats for nearly any ailment facing society. Politicians even run for office on platforms promising to reform government and reduce the size and power of the "evil" bureaucracy.

It must be conceded that many studies have confirmed the existence of problems in public sector productivity. Part of the rationale behind privatization is that private enterprise can accomplish tasks more efficiently and effectively than government. However, such comparative assessments do not always tell the full story. Charles Goodsell[10], a professor at Virginia Tech, takes issue with the foregone conclusion that business outperforms government. Dubbing it the "great falsehood about government," Goodsell maintains that U.S. bureaucracy compares favorably with the performance of governments around the world and even with the private sector in the United States. In short, in spite of widespread criticism, negative stereotypes, and a concession that bureaucracy could do better, Goodsell concludes that government actually works. Moreover, studies comparing the performance of the public sector with the performance of the private sector do not reveal the whole truth, in that the duties performed by the two sectors are often incomparable. The views of government as inefficient and ineffective often come from unfounded stereotypes, the media, and biased authors, which tend to depict government and public employees solely in negative ways or focus on the exception rather than the rule, which for government is usually equivalent to that found in the private sector. If one considers many of the tasks performed by government, it would appear that society asks the impossible of government. Many public endeavors are inherently complex and difficult to remedy, which might explain the poor performance of government in many assessments.

The inherent nature of the public sector precludes such comparisons, in that comparing the two sectors might be the classic case of trying to compare apples to oranges. The functions that government undertakes, for instance, differ dramatically from those found in the private sector. Likewise, the underlying principles and objectives of public sector programs are unlike those of the private sector. For example, while private businesses operate to make a *profit* and pursue market objectives, efficiency, and economy, the government provides services for the *people* according to universal notions of accommodation, assistance, and equity. While it is possible for businesses to pursue straightforward goals of efficiency when producing hamburgers, automobiles, or tennis rackets, it is another matter entirely for government, which provides such items as roads, police protection, and a system of justice. Where efficiency in the pursuit of profits might define the modus operandi for Ford, Nike, or Taco Bell, such narrow, monetary factors are not at the forefront of national security, public education, or environmental protection.

Indeed, output measures in the private sector such as effectiveness (measuring the accomplishment of objectives) and efficiency (do outputs exceed inputs) are easy to assess. In government there is often no standard performance measure. To make matters more difficult, some of the tasks undertaken by public administrators might never be fully accomplished, such as eradicating homelessness, assuring equality of opportunity to all Americans, preserving natural resources from degradation, or protecting consumers from dangerous and fraudulent business practices. Therefore, managers of public programs must consider non-economic factors in decision making, as opposed to their peers in the private sector who make decisions based foremost on profits.

The choices the political system confronts reflect this complexity and lack of clear-cut economic measures: Does one fund AIDS research or a new defense system? Food labeling requirements or trails in national parks? Childhood vaccinations or agricultural supports? Government seeks to *both* save such endangered species as the whale *and* support indigenous cultures like those native to Alaska. Yet, how does one decide what constitutes the correct decision when the native peoples of Alaska claim the right to continue their cultural practice of killing endangered whales? It becomes clear that in the public sector, decisions cannot be based solely on which program costs the least or is most efficient in operation.

At one level, it would appear that the public and private sectors are similar. The core managerial tasks—managing budgets, resources, and personnel—and the basic details that define management are somewhat similar. But, the objectives and rationale underlying the management function are quite different, and an argument can be made that the managerial task is much more difficult in the public sector than in the private sector. Graham T. Allison[11] echoes this dilemma in a famous article where he stated that public and private management can be compared and are alike, but are alike only "in all unimportant respects." The similarities, according to Allison, exist in the general day-to-day functions of managers such as planning, budgeting, reporting, and staffing. But, while these "micro-level" similarities might exist, management in the two sectors is different at the "macro-level." Here, there are striking differences in the time perspective of decisions, length of service, measurements of performance, presence and role of the media, legislative and judicial impact, career system, and other factors.

Grover Starling also identifies several significant differences between management in the two sectors.[12] Managers in the public sector have different purposes, structures, incentives, and settings, all of which contribute to a more demanding and challenging task. There are other differences between the public and private sectors, including the extent of managerial freedom and discretion enjoyed by managers and level of pay, which in equivalent situations, usually favor the private sector. While government lacks direct exposure to the free market and competition, and thus the natural incentives to improve productivity, there is usually far more public and media scrutiny as well as legal constraints placed on public operations, both of which might present difficulties for government managers.

Regardless of their accuracy or legitimacy, the many arguments that the public sector is less efficient and effective than the private sector undermine government's ability to fulfill its mission. Such widespread beliefs—founded or unfounded—jeopardize the public's confidence in its government. It also presents a problem for public administrators in that such a negative environment makes it hard to attract and retain quality employees. So too might public employees suffer from poor image and morale problems owing to the hostility directed at them by the public. It is thus significantly more difficult to manage public programs and agencies than some equivalent task or program in the private sector. Given the inherent difficulties associated with public administration, government needs highly capable individuals willing to accept challenges.

THE MANAGERIAL PERSPECTIVE

The task of management is complex. The volumes that have been written on management serve as testimony to that fact. University courses, executive training programs, and "how to manage" workshops by self-proclaimed management "gurus" still wrestle with the challenges of managing people, programs, resources, and organizations. Unless one can assemble a team of highly motivated experts and predict all events and obstacles that will occur, it benefits managers (and those who will become managers) to prepare for the challenges of management and hone their abilities, skills, and familiarity with the nature of managing. This book is dedicated to the latter point and presents the task of public management within several frameworks or environments.

1. All managerial actions occur within, and must consider the existence of, a highly political environment. Managing public agencies, programs, and employees is neither a value-free act nor one removed from the realities of the body politic.
2. Public administrators must consider a wide range of community, legal, and resource constraints, all part of a complex and dynamic environment within which the management function occurs.

3. Being a public administrator brings with it the charge to function according to high ethical standards. Accepting the public trust means functioning in a way that serves the public interest and is accountable to the public.

4. Perhaps the function that most separates managers from those working in a non-administrative capacity is the task of decision making, the core function of management and a task set before the readers of the cases in this book. The task of decision making is further complicated by attempting it in accordance with the three aforementioned environments of management.

The managerial perspective focuses on the "big picture," or the ability to see the forest in spite of the trees. While a certain proficiency in the details or technical aspects of the matters under consideration is necessary, it is also important to understand the environment within which the task of management takes place. Successful managers know that there is no single "best way" to manage and that there exists no proven formula for successful decision making. Certainly, the task of management is as much an art as it is a science. Of course, there are helpful rules, models, and approaches for one to follow that are tried and battle tested in the trenches by street-level managers. But, regardless of the lack of attention afforded to it in management training programs and textbooks, many managers believe there is a non-scientific side or approach to management, one that is based more on gut instinct and experience than scientific approaches. A response to either the models and theories of management or the "school of hard knocks" approach to management is to "practice" the science, and art, of management through the use of case studies and role-playing.

Managing in a Highly Political Environment

The field of study of public administration has struggled with an identity crisis and a lack of consensus among scholars attempting to identify the nature of the practice and direction the discipline should follow. Early scholars searched for an elusive set of principles of administration and their present-day colleagues ponder self-identity for the field. One of the problems facing many of the early studies of public administration was that they ignored the political realities of the task of managing public programs and agencies. Indeed, the profession was born in the late eighteenth century as an apolitical, neutral service and early scholars responded by advocating a *politics-administration dichotomy*, whereby public administrators were not to be involved in politics and were free from political pressures. This influenced subsequent scholarship and training, both of which neglected the political environment in which public administrators work. What is seen as a purely administrative function still involves politics and, even though it is now widely accepted that politics is an inescapable part of public administration, the age-old question of the relationship between the two and the resulting dilemmas remain.

Managing public programs and agencies is an inherently political endeavor, as the task does not exist in a vacuum. For example, politics is encountered in such everyday acts as making decisions about scarce resources, responding to initiatives and mandates from elected officials, exercising discretion, and discerning out of legalistic vagueness the intent of lawmakers and judges. Managers must be sensitive to politics because of the presence of public hostility to government and negative images of public administrators, the influence of powerful special interests, and the political gaming of elected officials (especially on sensitive issues and during election years). This does not mean that managers must place politics above their responsibility to perform their job, but it is beneficial for managers to consider the political ecology of public administration.

The term *ecology* comes from the Greek word "oikos," which means home or living place. Ecosystems are characterized by the interdependence of living things and achieving balance within a complex organic system. The study of ecology is not restricted to biology, as social scientists borrow from the approaches of their colleagues in the natural sciences. The ecology perspective is quite applicable to the study of organizations, especially organizations in the public sector, as the environment within which a public administrator functions is complex and influences decisions and outputs. The task of management in government agencies is inextricably linked to many other aspects of the organization and interacts with the larger political system. Rarely are managerial problems independent of other problems. Public administrators must be cognizant of this environment and learn to function within such a setting.

Ethical Considerations: A "Right Way" of Managing?

Public administration is not value free. Administrators deal on a regular basis with social values, moral dilemmas, and decisions regarding sensitive interpersonal relations. The problem is that there is not always agreement as to what constitutes ethical and unethical behavior. For instance, in judging the actions of employees, managers, and agencies as ethical, a variety of competing value systems come into play, from one's personal sense of morality to public codes of ethics. Even the act of judging the consequences of one's action is an exercise in relativism, as the consequences might be considered from the vantage point of oneself, one's clients, the department or agency, or society in general. Any action could therefore be judged according to different standards.

If one accepts the notion that those working in the public sector must be held to a higher standard, then it is necessary for public administrators to not only manage ethically but to foster an ethical climate within their agency. But the question about how to determine what constitutes ethical behavior remains. Here, ethical behavior can be distinguished from simply following rules. Agencies have rules and standards of conduct, but codes of ethics transcend notions of legalism, whereby a rule is "right" simply because it is a rule. Public administrators are rarely afforded the luxury of a simple and all-encompassing code of ethics to guide behavior. Managing public programs and services where the rubber meets the road, one encounters vagueness in and limits to stated rules. Often the guidepost for ethical behavior transcends day-to-day rules, as in the case with the higher ideals of democracy such as principles of openness and public accountability. Ethical considerations and dilemmas are built into each case in this book and the reader faces the challenge of determining the ethical course of action.

"The Buck Stops Here": Decision Making

Making decisions is perhaps the primary task of managers. Decision making is complicated by the host of forces, complexities, and unknown variables that exist in an already highly political and ever-changing environment. Managers face internal and external forces in making decisions, including competition for resources from other public agencies and pressures from clients and interest groups. Decision makers in the public sector also face a situation described by Gerald Garvey[13] as having "over-determined problems," whereby there are too many conditions impacting the decision and not too few.

The act of decision making implies selecting from various options. Those that study the decision process generally identify five stages in the process: (1) identification of the problem, (2) data collection and analysis, (3) the actual decision, (4) communication and implementation of the decision, and (5) evaluation of the impacts of the decision.

The aforementioned approach offers a simple and useful model to keep in mind when reading the cases in this book. Public sector managers will encounter a wide variety of problems. However, in many instances it is still possible to identify some generic types of problems and corresponding "tried and tested" solutions to these problems. Additionally, as part of the problem identification step, it is helpful to attempt to understand the *causes* behind the problem so that the action decided upon does not end up addressing the *symptom* rather than the root cause of the problem. Once the causes of the problem have been identified, the manager should identify relevant facts and gather data that will inform the decision process. It must be recognized that there are often limits to the amount of facts and data that can be gathered due to insufficient time, resources, and information. Managers also commonly consult with those around them—experts and their employees—in gathering and examining the facts surrounding the issue.

In making the actual decision, managers employ an array of approaches and styles, from the highly technical and those relying on statistical methods to off-the-cuff or gut-level decision making. One of the more common analytic approaches to decision making is *cost-benefit analysis*, whereby in a time of resource scarcity, it is necessary to weigh the potential costs against the potential benefits of a particular course of action. Costs and benefits can be measured in many ways. For instance, there are direct and indirect costs (sometimes called "externalities") and benefits, as certain programs might have "spillover" effects unintended by the original course of action. These are hard to anticipate. The cost-benefit approach requires managers to consider several questions such as: Who should benefit and who actually benefits? What is the value of the benefit? Who should pay for the costs? Does the value of the benefit outweigh all the possible costs? Costs can be computed according to more than simply a monetary measure. This includes such costs as a loss of time, impacts to the natural environment, displacement of individuals, quality of life measures, and an array of "unforeseen" costs.

Decision analysis is another method employed by managers. Rarely is there one possible course of action available to the decision maker. Consider, for instance, a program labeled A that benefits twenty people, whereas another program labeled B has a one-third chance of benefitting sixty people, but it might not work at all and no one will benefit. Which program, A or B, should be selected? On the other hand, suppose program B will benefit sixty people, but harm ten, whereas program A will not harm anyone but will only benefit twenty people. What course of action should be pursued? Decision analysis often incorporates probability, logic, and *decision trees*. A decision tree allows the manager to anticipate the possible consequences of each action and include that in the decision process by plotting an alternative course of action depending on the outcome of each previous decision.

Charles E. Lindblom[14], Yale economist and well-known scholar, offers a model with two basic approaches to making decisions. The first approach is termed the *rational-comprehensive* approach. This textbook or "root method" approach considers every single aspect of the matter and assumes the manager understands and pursues clearly-stated goals, has full and accurate information on which to base the decision, identifies and ranks alternative options, foresees all the consequences of the course of action, and has the requisite amount of time, resources, and talent in which to make and accomplish the action. The byproduct of this process is, theoretically, that the optimum decision will be selected. Yet, studies have shown that managers do not always follow rational, linear models of decision making. Nor do they always function in an orderly manner, first clarifying their goals, assessing options and consequences of each possible initiative, and selecting the optimum course of action based on complete and accurate information. So, in practice, this model is usually relegated to textbooks.

Lindblom describes a more realistic process he deems *incrementalism*, a process involving decisions and actions based on "successive limited comparisons." Actions thus amount to small steps or mere incremental departures from the past or existing arrangement. A realistic model, incrementalism is also a model of political compromise that accepts the existence of multiple goals, unforeseen constraints, and numerous complex forces acting in the decision-making environment. Other burdens like limited time, limited expertise, limited resources, and limited information regarding the nature of the problem further constrain managerial decisions and actions. As such, often the decisions made by public administrators are not the best or ideal courses of action.

This latter approach is not always preferable in that such decisions are rarely comprehensive or maximizing in nature. Rather, Lindblom sees such courses of action as merely "muddling through." However, the rational-comprehensive model is usually unrealistic, so it is equally limited. As such, the administrator is left to seek a balance between the two approaches in what amounts to a *bounded rationality*, which considers *some* (but not all) options and consequences, attempts to account for unforeseen conditions, yet works within the existing scope of time, resources, and expertise, and tries to move toward the organization's goals through the decision. This latter approach will be used in the role-playing exercises in the book.

Part I

Managing Public Organizations and Employees

THE CHALLENGE OF BUREAUCRACY FOR MANAGERS

Bureaucracy. The very term conjures images of excessive red tape, poor service from unresponsive and uncaring employees, and organizations that are resistant to change. Indeed, ask someone to define bureaucracy and most likely you will get a laundry list of negative characteristics that describe organizations that are inefficient and ineffective. Although organizations of all sectors and missions are bureaucratic in one sense of the word or another, bureaucracy is commonly equated with the executive branch of government, government employees, and government itself. It is true that some public sector agencies have suffered from being rule-laden, self-serving, and frustratingly slow to react. Not surprisingly, countless reform initiatives have sought to remedy such problems.

One of the first to study systematically the formal structure of organizations was Max Weber (1864–1920), a German sociologist and social scientist who defined the characteristics of bureaucracies.[1] Weber studied a wide variety of organizational systems including the ancient Chinese civil service, early Roman administration, military and church organizations, and other systems of administration. What he found was that commonalities existed across all organizations such as hierarchical structures, written rules, established jurisdictional responsibilities for members of the organization, a division of labor into such areas as line, staff, and management, and specialization of job tasks.

In spite of the negative connotations of bureaucracy and the best efforts of reform-minded politicians, bureaucracy appears to be the predominant format for organizations—public, private, and nonprofit. It is also a source of power and authority. Regardless of the fact that bureaucracy is perhaps an inescapable component of organizations in modern society, there are problems associated with bureaucracy such as the development of a *bureaucratic pathology*, whereby an individual loses sight of the purpose of the job or the needs of those being served and becomes excessively rigid in adhering to the rules of the organization. Such a bureaucratic virtuoso stresses the strict observance and narrow interpretation of a stated rule over the mission at hand or larger goals of the organization or society. This pathology can also become systematic, whereby "standard operating procedures" become institutionalized to an excessive degree throughout the organization. Because of the negative views toward bureaucracy and government prevalent in society, the

19

public sector also often suffers from a poor self-image, making it difficult to recruit, retain, and motivate employees. This competency crisis might also undermine an agency's ability to function, as the public distrusts government's intentions and basic ability to fulfill its mission. As such, the manager of a public agency or program is faced with the dual challenge of managing in a bureaucratic setting while mitigating the harmful effects of bureaucracy. On one hand, the manager must attempt to overcome the hurdles imposed by bureaucracy. On the other hand, public managers must know how to function within the bureaucratic system, as it is unrealistic to expect that the elements of bureaucracy would either not be present or would easily been reformed.

Types of Government Agencies

Popular views of bureaucracy often depict the public sector as if it were monolithic—that all governmental departments are the same. But, it is inaccurate to assume that there is a single type of governmental agency. Public agencies vary in composition, mission, and structure and exist in areas other than the executive branch of the federal government. Bureaucracies can also be found in state and local governments, in the private sector, and in the legislative branch of government. For instance, the U.S. Congress is comprised of more than representatives and senators; it includes numerous organizations such as the Congressional Budget Office (CBO), the Congressional Research Service (CRS), the General Accounting Office (GAO), the Library of Congress, and numerous other units. So too is the federal judiciary comprised of much more than the Supreme Court. There are courts of appeal, district courts, international trade courts, and courts of military appeals. The White House is home to a large bureaucracy with numerous offices and many employees who work directly for the president. The White House and the Executive Office of the President (EOP) contain such organizations as the Council of Economic Advisors, the Office of Management and Budget (OMB), the National Security Council (NSC), and the numerous ushers, cooks, secretaries, and other staffers that run the executive mansion. Likewise, a political bureaucracy of pollsters, fundraisers, and speechwriters exists to service campaigns, elections, the political parties, and the public figures pursuing elected office.

The primary unit of organization in the federal government is the *executive department*. This is what most individuals think of when they think of the federal government. The fourteen federal executive departments comprise roughly 65 percent of all federal employees, correspond to the major functional areas of the federal government, and, together, the heads of each department (known as *secretaries*) sit as the president's cabinet.[2] Even among the federal executive departments there is considerable difference between, for example, the largest department in terms of personnel (Defense) and the smallest (Education) as well as the largest in terms of budget (Health and Human Services) and the smallest (Commerce).[3] Some of the departments are referred to as clientele departments, as they exist to serve a specific interest or type of client as opposed to, in theory, the entire citizenry and nation. Examples of such departments include such older departments as Agriculture, established in 1862, Commerce, created in 1903, and Labor, organized in 1913, and newer departments including Education and Veterans affairs, established in 1979 and 1989 respectively.

Federal Executive Departments

- Agriculture
- Education
- Housing & Urban Development
- Labor
- Treasury

- Commerce
- Energy
- Interior
- State
- Veterans Affairs

- Defense
- Health & Human Services
- Justice
- Transportation

The executive department is the main organizational model for both federal and state government. But it is only one type of government agency. Other types of agencies include independent agencies that do not fall within the structure of one of the executive departments but rather report directly to the president or Congress. The rationale for establishing independent agencies has often been to avoid having them controlled or captured by the clientele they serve, to avoid the politics that accompanies traditional departments, or because the unique mission of the agency did not lend itself to the functions of any existing department or office. Some presidents, such as Franklin D. Roosevelt, also created such agencies out of frustration with the cumbersome executive departments, wanting more direct control of and efficiency from his agencies. These independent agencies include such small and relatively obscure bodies like the Federal Maritime Commission as well as the more high profile NASA (National Aeronautical and Space Administration) and the Farm Credit Administration, Peace Corps, United States Information Agency (USIA), and the National Science Foundation (NSF).

Often—but certainly not always—the independent agencies are regulatory agencies, another type of government organization. As the name implies, these agencies regulate industries, commerce, people, or other activities. Among the federal regulatory agencies are such well known acronyms as the NRC (Nuclear Regulatory Commission), the FTC (Federal Trade Commission), the ICC (Interstate Commerce Commission), the FDA (Food and Drug Administration), and the CPSC (Consumer Product Safety Commission). Another type of government organization is the government corporation. Such organizations are run like a business but are overseen by the federal government and include the Tennessee Valley Authority (TVA), the Postal Service, the Federal Deposit Insurance Corporation (FDIC), and the Export-Import Bank. There are also institutes and institutions such as the Smithsonian Institution and an abundance of advisory boards, commissions, and other bodies that are found in government. There are many models for government agencies. The diversity of tasks found in government necessitate this array of organizational models.

THE POLITICS OF MANAGEMENT AND ORGANIZATIONS

There are many ways to approach the study of organizations. For instance, one could consider the internal organization or the relationship of the organization to its external environment or organization-to-organization relations. Organizations vary in size, purpose, and objectives, so it is difficult but helpful to consider elements common to most organizations as well as models by which to study organizations. Among the elements of organizations are

(1) a social structure, comprised of relationships among members of the organization and others impacted by it; (2) actors, including members of the organization, customers or clients, and stakeholders in the organization, all of whom participate in the organization to different degrees; (3) goals; and (4) an external environment.

One popular method is to view organizations as systems, such as rational systems, natural systems, and open systems.[4] The *rational systems* model is a metaphor for a well-functioning machine. In this approach the organization exists as a means to achieve a specific goal and operates in a rational (purposive and deliberate) and formal manner to do so. The processes of the organization are established in a rational manner and assume a rational set of norms, actions, and consequences. The *natural systems* model sees organizations as self-maintaining organic systems. The organization is a complex array of relationships of those belonging to the organization and contains a distinct organizational culture. Not all behavior that occurs among the members of the organization is specified by the organization. Much of it is natural, as the formal, written rules of the organization cannot possibly cover all scenarios faced by the organization and its members. A third approach to studying organizations is the *open systems* model. An open system is defined by its exchanges and interactions with its environment, which come to define the organization. Organizations are in a perpetual state of change and influenced by an equally dynamic external environment. Relatedly, the internal organization is a collection of interdependent parts and systems.

Another way to study organizations is to consider the characteristics of organizations. One common structure of nearly all public organizations is the notion of a *pyramid*. Organizations have *hierarchies* or levels of management, with the highest levels, represented by the top of the pyramid, typically containing fewer managers with broader responsibilities. The number of managers and the amount of employees or units they manage, known as the manager's *span of control*, tends to increase as one moves down the organization pyramid. Here, a challenge is making sure that the number of units or employees reporting to a manager is neither too many nor too few. Within the pyramid, a *chain of command* exists. A manager serving at the top of the organization finds it difficult to oversee all units, employees, and transactions of the organization. As such, echelons or layers of command are necessary, each having its own jurisdictional area and responsibility. The managers and units on the lower levels of the organization report to those above them following the principle of *unity of command*.

Organizations are also divided into groups of employees based on their responsibility. One of the most basic divisions is between *line* and *staff* employees. Staff personnel are those members who do not actually implement the policies or services of the organization. Rather, they are specialists who offer the organization skills such as personnel administration, policy analysis, financial administration, and so forth. Line personnel are those employees who actually implement the policy or service. A final basic characteristic of organizations is the degree of *centralization* or *decentralization* found within the organizational structure. This age-old question pertains to how much authority and decision making should be vested in a central unit within the organization versus how much should be delegated among various units of the organization. For instance, political decentralization permits policies to be made at the state, local, or grass roots level. Administrative decentralization, then, permits the units responsible for actually implementing policies and services to have a degree of autonomy from the overall organization and authority to make decisions somewhat independent of the main body.

Decision-making Issues to Consider as You Read the Cases

The type of decisions made by managers is reflected in one's approach to management. There are numerous schools of thought regarding management theory, but two models in particular provide the conceptual basis for most management thought.

Classical Management

The dawn of the nineteenth century witnessed an effort to develop a science of management. One of the first scholars to study systematically the concept of management was Frederick Taylor (1856–1915). Taylor, an engineer, approached the issue much as someone of his profession might; he believed management, like disciplines in the sciences, had identifiable principles and rules.[5] Conducting his famous "time and motion" studies, Taylor sought to identify the "one best way" of managing or production. Studying the tasks of employees, Taylor noted which employees were able to perform their tasks in the most economical manner. He then advocated standardizing the most efficient process and training all employees to perform in the same manner. Taylor's work along with other early management theorists initiated what became known as *scientific management* or the *classical school of management*.

These approaches had the goal of efficiency and were characterized by the belief in scientific principles of management, the primacy of standardization and economy, and a top-down view of the organization from the perspective of management.

Human Relations Management

As opposed to classical approaches to management, the *human relations* school focuses attention on the psychological needs of employees and views organizations as social systems rather than rigid bureaucratic entities that fail to recognize the human element in organizations. The proponents of the classical school focused on bureaucracy, productivity, and efficiency, where individuals had to subordinate their interests to the organization. The human relations approach focuses attention on morale, motivation, and employee needs.

Management theorist, Chester I. Barnard, recognized that forces other than the actions of management influenced an employee's productivity and the nature of the organization. One of these Barnard identified was what he referred to as the *informal organization*.[6] Within a formal organizational structure there exists informal processes and an informal interpersonal dynamic that influences relationships, communication, and interactions. Barnard felt that informal and formal organizations co-existed, and a manager should be sure to make certain that such a co-existence benefits the goals of the formal organization. Another contribution to a new view of management came from Mary Parker Follet who pondered why employees follow orders.[7] Because orders are often taken as bossing and violations of self-respect, and some employees pit themselves against management, the manager must find a way to integrate the order-giver and order-receiver. Rationalizing that a manager cannot simply give orders and expect them to be followed and cannot assume that even reasoning and careful explanations will always result in an employee doing as told, Follet maintained that a manager should consider an employee's attitude. Here, it is best to appeal to their attitude and create or foster a disposition conducive to following orders. As such, orders are presented in a manner that is receptive to employees and based on the previous patterns of behavior and attitudes of employees. Another contribution to the study and discipline of management came courtesy of Henri Fayol, who recognized that it is beneficial to foster a sense of "esprit de corps" or sense of team and pride among the members of an organization.[8] Such a spirit helps the organization better achieve its goals and the promotion of it is a responsibility of management. All of these theorists and theories led to the development of the human relations school of management.

Perhaps the first to recognize and write about what became the human relations school, however, was Elton Mayo (1880–1949). Mayo, Frederick Roethlisberger, and other researchers from Harvard's business school, while engaged in a study to promote productivity at Western Electric's Hawthorne Factory in Chicago, discovered by chance a theory that would revolutionize management science.[9] In an effort to identify physical factors and workplace conditions that impacted employee performance, Mayo and his colleagues imposed different conditions such as increased and decreased amounts of lighting on a group of clerks. To their surprise, each time the lighting or other condition was altered, the productivity of the test subjects improved. It became clear that it was not the degree of lighting or any other stimuli that caused the response in employees, but rather the simple fact that the employee wanted to belong and felt that someone was paying attention to them. As such, it appeared that organizational problems did not always stem from task specialization or poor wages, but employee social and psychological factors associated with work. Workers do not always act logically and are not motivated simply by economic incentives. Social relations impact productivity, and the behavior of the worker cannot be separated from the feelings of the worker.

Another management theorist, Douglas McGregor, conceptualized two types of employees.[10] The first type—or Theory X employees—must be persuaded to perform through rewards and punishments, will work as little as possible if they can get away with it because they are lazy, and need to be led because they lack ambition and their self-centeredness precludes them from working for the betterment of others or the organization. McGregor's second type of employee—or Theory Y employee—is the opposite: a hard working, motivated, achiever. The significance of this model is that managers should recognize which type of employee they are managing and should tailor their approach to management to fit the particular type of employee. For instance, a manager faced with Theory X employees should direct and watch the employees, as the employees would fail to perform in the absence of strong managerial control. Theory Y employees are best managed when work conditions are arranged so as to permit employees ample flexibility and opportunities to achieve. This might be done by delegating authority and responsibility to them or involving them in decision making through participatory management.

This serves as a basis for theories of situational management whereby managers should tailor their approach to the circumstances present. Management and organization theory provide a basis for understanding the complex task of managing public organizations and inform how the manager sees (and thereby designs and reforms) public organizations and makes decisions. Keep these theories and approaches to the issue in mind as you consider the following four cases, which deal with an array of common but complex managerial dilemmas.

1

Working With Elected Officials: Managing Political Appointees

Cheryl M. Ramos

ABOUT THE ORGANIZATION

The ten-member *Carlton City Council Office of Research* serves the city council, which appoints the director of the Office of Research.

ABOUT THE CHARACTERS

Elena Torres has been the director of the Carlton City Council Office of Research for the past three years and is in the final year of her four-year term. She is the first woman and first Hispanic to serve as Director of the Office of Research. She has an MPA and worked previously for a major bank.

BACKGROUND

Carlton City is governed by the mayor, who is head of the executive branch of city government and the city council, which sits as the legislative branch of city government. The population of Carlton is approximately 150,000 and is ethnically diverse: 40 percent Asian (Filipino, Japanese, Chinese); 30 percent Hispanic (Mexican, Puerto Rican, Portuguese); 10 percent Pacific Islander (Hawaiian, Samoan, Tongan); 10 percent African American; and 10 percent European American. The Carlton city council consists of nine members, each elected from one of the city's nine council districts. The city council appoints three directors, each with day-to-day management responsibilities for one of the three offices: City Council Services; City Council Research; and City Elections.

The City Council Research Office is responsible for:

◆ Drafting legislation at the request of the city council
◆ Drafting reports of council committees and meetings
◆ Conducting program reviews and audits of city departments at the request of city council members, committees, or the full council

- ◆ Responding to requests for information as directed by city council members
- ◆ Assisting city council members in responding to complaints and requests for information from constituents in their respective city council districts
- ◆ Performing other duties as requested by their appointing city council member

Elena Torres is the director of the Office of Research for Carlton City. She supervises ten staff members. The staff of the office consists of nine researchers (seven positions are filled, two are vacant) and one secretary. Each researcher is appointed by a city council member and the secretary is appointed by the council chair. The researchers and secretary serve at the discretion of their appointing authority.

The following details the tenure and educational background of the seven researchers. Two researchers were appointed eight years ago, prior to Torres' appointment. They are college graduates (BA, Psychology and Sociology, MPA). Two researchers were appointed three years ago, one of whom is a college graduate (BA, Political Science) and the other one has a high school diploma. Three researchers were recently appointed. All are high school graduates but do not have college degrees.

CURRENT SITUATION

Torres is well respected and highly regarded by city council members and city government personnel. She was well credentialed and was "highly recommended" when she joined the city council staff. She prides herself on putting out very high quality work and has a "no-nonsense" style of management. Her professionalism is apparent and her formal working relationship with council members is defined by a "behind-the-scenes" approach and low public profile. She believes that her job is to "make city council members look good" by doing the best job she can.

In years past, the city council involved Torres in hiring the staff. However, during recent hirings and after the election of new city council members, the new city council felt that, as the appointing authority, it would hire staff that would best serve its individual needs. As such, the council did not consult Torres in the most recent selection process. Still, council members had assured Torres that she would have "full responsibility and authority" for researchers once they were hired. However, Torres believes that many of the newly appointed staff do not have the knowledge or skills necessary for their jobs. They were hired because of their family and/or political connections to their appointing city council member, not their abilities.

As such, Torres recently approached members of the city council individually. She expressed her concerns regarding staff attitudes and work performance. First, she made clear her concern regarding the staff's numerous typographical and grammatical errors in reports and legislation.

Second, she stated that she has received complaints from staff of city departments that researchers are making multiple requests for the same type of information. Department personnel have asked that the City Council Office Research better coordinate requests for information.

Third, Torres expressed frustration regarding her numerous attempts to train staff, schedule regular staff meetings, and establish clear timetables and guidelines for completing assignments. Some of the researchers have resisted these efforts, telling Torres that city council members repeatedly contact them directly to run errands, make field inspections in response to constituents' complaints, and work on assignments of an urgent or immediate nature. As a result, they are often unable to attend staff meetings or meet project deadlines. In addition, staff frequently attend social gatherings on weeknights and weekends on behalf of, or with, city council members. They thus complain that they put in long hours and find it difficult to attend early morning staff meetings.

Fourth, Torres criticized the attitudes of the newly hired researchers. Some researchers maintain that since the city council member is their appointing authority, they feel it is more important for them to take direction from their city council member than from Torres. Torres is also concerned about the tension that has surfaced between the new staff and the "old" staff. For instance, the four longer serving staffers are very loyal to Torres. In general, they work as a team, consult Torres frequently, and put out good work. The three newly hired researchers resist Torres' efforts to educate and train them. The "old" staff complains that the new staff is incompetent and disloyal to Torres. But the new staff complains that the previous hires are disrespectful to their appointing authority.

Torres asked for the city council's help in maintaining the integrity of the Office of Research and improving office morale. She asked that the city council members not give staff assignments directly but instead route all assignments through her, informing them that this approach would allow her to better manage her staff and provide city council members with higher quality research and supports.

City council members responded to this by reminding the head of the Office of Research that it is her responsibility to manage her office. The two eldest council members became rather irritated with Torres during the exchange. The council assured her that they would route assignments as she suggested and talk to the researchers about working more closely with Torres. But council members maintained their need to be able to work closely with their appointees in order to respond to the many constituent calls they receive each day. Good relationships with the people of their district, after all, are essential for their re-election.

Six months have passed since the meeting between Torres and city council members, and things have not changed. Researchers are still receiving assignments directly from their appointing city council member. Moreover, the city council has just informed Ms. Torres that they have appointed an assistant director—a position that was created fifteen years ago but never filled—to help Torres better manage the office and expedite work. They will also soon be hiring two researchers to fill the vacant positions. Torres has also found the two senior members of the council unwilling to work directly with her. She cannot put her finger on a specific example that would "hold up in a courtroom," but she suspects the poor relationship is partially in response to her sex and race. The two senior councilmen are Caucasian and have always "acted uncomfortable" around their younger administrator.

Torres did not think that the appointment of an assistant was necessary. However, city council members filled the assistant position in spite of her objections. As a result, she fears that the city council will once again hire incompetent staff that will create problems like some of the current staff. Torres feels pressured to make changes in her office, not only for the benefit of the city council, but in order to protect her reputation in the community. Good working relationships with city council members and the staff of city departments are necessary for her to be able to do her work. At this point she feels that both relationships are being threatened and she fears that she may not be reappointed when her term expires.

ROLE-PLAY ASSIGNMENT

You have been hired as the assistant director of the Office of Research. Torres has informed you of the current situation and has asked for your help in improving the management of the office and improving the quality and quantity of work. Specifically, she requests that you submit a "management plan" to the city council prior to them filling the two vacant researcher positions.

QUESTIONS FOR DISCUSSION

1. What problems exist in the Office of Research and city council? What are the sources of these problems?
2. What ideas do you have for the management plan to improve office operations and staff morale?
3. What are the implications of this plan on the relationship between you and your boss, the director? among the staff of the Office of Research? between city council members and their appointees?
4. What barriers do you anticipate regarding the implementation of your plan for change? What are your strategies for dealing with each of the barriers? What supports are necessary for the plan to be a success?
5. Torres has confided in you her suspicions about poor treatment of her owing to her race and sex. How do you respond to her request for advice? Are there any gender or cultural issues that may be impacting the dynamics of the Office of Research?

SOURCES FOR FURTHER READING

Berry, L. M., *Psychology at Work: An Introduction to Industrial and Organizational Psychology* (Boston: McGraw-Hill, 1998).

Yaffe, J. "Latina Managers in Public Employment: Perceptions of Organizational Discrimination." *Hispanic Journal of Behavioral Sciences* 17 (1995): 334–346.

Condrey, S., and S.B. Condrey. *Handbook of Human Resource Management in Government.* San Francisco: Jossey-Bass, 1998.

Fox, R. L., and R. A. Schuhmann, "Gender and the Role of the City Manager." *Social Science Quarterly* 81 (2000): 604–621.

Rubaii-Barrett, N., and A. C. Beck, "Minorities in the Majority: Implications for Managing Cultural Diversity." *Public Personnel Management* 22, (1993): 503–521.

Street-level Decision Making and Administrative Discretion: Assuring Public Safety at Heartland International Airport

Patrick Scott

ABOUT THE AGENCY

The *Federal Aviation Administration* (FAA) is an agency within the U.S. Department of Transportation. The FAA is responsible for the safety and certification of aircraft and pilots, the security of airports, and the around-the-clock operation of the nation's air traffic control system. The FAA strives to enhance safety, improve security, and increase the efficiency of air travel by modernizing the air traffic control system and expanding the capacity of the nation's airports.

ABOUT THE CHARACTERS

David Maxwell is a supervisory aircraft inspector who works for the FAA. Maxwell manages a team of fifteen federal aircraft inspectors/auditors at Heartland International Airport (HIA). He plays a key role in ensuring public safety through audits of inspections conducted by various aircraft maintenance crews.

INTRODUCTION

Bureaucratic discretion is a topic of central importance to the field of public administration. It is a phenomenon that occurs daily in thousands of different contexts throughout all levels of government. Whether public decisions involve deferring capital repairs on local roads or bridges, granting expedited approval for the marketing of drugs that show promise for combating disease, or providing vouchers for daycare services to assist clients in finding and maintaining employment, these decisions involve the exercise of bureaucratic discretion. Often, discretionary decisions seem insignificant, but collectively they determine the texture of the relationship between citizens and government, and the choices public officials make within the parameters of their discretionary authority can be especially critical. The airplane inspectors at HIA and their supervisor have ample discretion in their day-to-day jobs and decisions.

BUREAUCRATIC DISCRETION AND THE FAA

David Maxwell, a supervisory inspector for the FAA, manages a fifteen-member team of federal aircraft inspectors and auditors at Heartland International Airport. Maxwell's team is responsible for ensuring that maintenance checks are conducted on certain passenger and cargo aircraft based at HIA. The types of planes range from Cessna corporate jets to "dual-prop" passenger planes that fly into smaller and medium-sized metropolitan areas throughout the region. In all, there are about sixty airplanes assigned to Maxwell's team.

Maxwell and his team conduct inspection audits to provide assurance that maintenance performed by commercial crews is carried out in accordance with FAA regulations. Most airline and cargo companies, as well as private corporations, have their own maintenance crews, although some companies contract their maintenance work to outside companies. Over the years, Maxwell has seen vast differences in the quality of the work performed by the commercial maintenance crews. In fact, some have been suspended because random audits revealed serious deficiencies in their maintenance procedures. Fines have been levied against others, and indictments have been handed down against the owner of one company for falsifying inspection logs.

Even among his own team, Maxwell has seen a lot of changes. High turnover among younger recruits, coupled with a number of recent retirements, have heightened Maxwell's concern about the quality of his own staff of inspectors. While Maxwell is committed to making sure that nothing falls between the cracks, he knows that his technical coverage is spread very thin. Maxwell worries about how these changes have impacted the effectiveness of inspection audits conducted by his staff.

New Rules of the Game

The airline industry is always looking for new ways to reduce the high costs of doing business. That is why it was very pleased when the Vice President's Council on Competitiveness, as part of its efforts to reduce the regulatory burden on business, recently ordered the Department of Transportation to review its regulations concerning FAA inspection audits. The airline industry, which had been experiencing a considerable decline in profit margins, welcomed this news. Relaxing certain regulatory standards would undoubtedly provide much needed financial relief. Industry-wide, it was estimated that savings resulting from relaxed inspection standards would exceed $300 million annually.

Within six months, the FAA issued a new set of guidelines. Working in consultation with aircraft manufacturers, drafters of the new regulations developed provisions that continued to emphasize the importance of flight safety while relaxing certain types of maintenance requirements. While all of the changes were complex, overall, the regulations decreased the required frequency of inspections for newer aircraft and aircraft systems. In addition, they consolidated and streamlined the types of inspections required for certain types of aircraft systems between five and ten years old. These provisions thus reduced the amount of resources airline companies were having to allocate to maintenance and inspection activities, especially on newer aircraft and aircraft systems that had lower than average malfunction rates.

The Impact of the New Rules

What did these changes signify for Maxwell and his staff? Understanding the airlines' desire to cut costs wherever possible, Maxwell was concerned that some airlines might apply these new procedures on aircraft that did not fit within the prescribed limits, such as planes exceeding ten years of age. While he could shift more of his audit resources toward older aircraft, Maxwell knew this was not the optimal solution. It would still be necessary to ensure that maintenance crews were doing their work properly on all aircraft, both new and old.

But with the consolidated and streamlined inspection and maintenance procedures came pressure to reduce the size of Maxwell's staff. If the commercial crews were consolidating their operations, then it seemed that FAA audit procedures should be consolidated as well. After all, it is only logical that reduced regulatory burdens should lead to a reduced need for regulators. Thus, soon after the new rules were issued, FAA headquarters mandated personnel reductions for its entire field inspection staff. Most of the reductions would be achieved by instituting a hiring freeze and providing early retirement for eligible employees.

There were few visible changes immediately resulting from the implementation of the new regulations. Most of the commercial maintenance crews simply began scaling back the frequency of some types of inspections, while other types of inspection and maintenance procedures were consolidated. Overall, inspections became more perfunctory and involved fewer person hours, achieving considerable cost savings to the airline industry. However, some concern arose when Maxwell's staff began to uncover slipshod maintenance on a few of the smaller planes. Maxwell knew that consolidating and streamlining inspection procedures invited the potential for trouble, a maxim that applied equally to both commercial crews and his own audit staff. With these new procedures Maxwell began to wonder how many other potential problems were beginning to slip through the cracks.

THE DILEMMA

In an effort to provide "maximum flexibility and enhanced responsiveness" to local conditions, regulation writers in Washington saw the need to allow local FAA inspectors a good deal of discretion. One such area was in determining which aircraft, commercial maintenance crews, and inspection procedures would be audited within a given fiscal year. Maxwell was provided with discretionary authority to target limited resources to areas that were deemed most vulnerable, but he also understood that this was no fail-safe guarantee that all mishaps would be prevented.

One regulatory revision involved inspection and maintenance requirements for a type of engine assembly mount found on certain types of twin-engine propeller aircraft. Under the old standards, commercial maintenance crews were required to conduct inspections for structural integrity after every 500 hours of flight time. For planes having exceeded 5,000 hours, inspections were required after every 250 flight hours. Detection of any structural flaws required automatic replacement of the engine mount.

Under the new standards, however, the FAA did not require automatic replacement of the engine mount as long as structural flaws did not exceed certain tolerance thresholds. In addition, the frequency of tests for structural integrity were expanded to every 1,000 flight hours if the airplane had not logged over 7,000 flight hours. After 7,000 hours, the regulations required engine mount inspections following every 500 flight hours.

The technical standards embodied in these changes did not take into account the labor involved for this procedure. Testing the structural integrity of the engine mount required a major disassembly of engine components; accordingly, this procedure was one of the most labor-intensive for this category of aircraft. In addition, when the FAA conducts an audit of this procedure for a particular aircraft, the engine has to be disassembled twice—once as part of its normal maintenance and once again during the FAA audit. Because of the labor intensity, as well as the need to conduct other types of crucial audits, Maxwell was under pressure to conduct increasingly fewer audits of engine mounts. The costs were high, not only for his staff, but also for the companies that owned these planes.

Maxwell suspected, however, that this was one procedure where some of the commercial crews might try to cut corners. For example, commercial crews might be inclined to conduct tests on the engine mounts after every 1,000 flight hours and bypass the more restrictive 500-hour requirement for older planes. There was also the possibility that some crews might even tamper with the flight logs on some of the older planes in order to circumvent the more restrictive requirement. While engine mount failures are uncommon, once the structural integrity is compromised the probability of a mechanical failure increases significantly. Therefore, it would be necessary to continue audits of these inspections as much as Maxwell's limited resources would allow. While the new regulations permitted Maxwell much latitude in determining the frequency of this audit, how he exercised that discretion could have very definite implications on both flight safety and on his staff's ability to uncover small problems before they became big ones.

In weighing these decisions, Maxwell was faced with conflicting pressures: the need for public safety and the need for sensitivity to the economic realities that airline and air cargo companies faced. Maxwell realized that the manner in which he chose to exercise his discretionary authority was bound to have certain ramifications for himself, his staff, his superiors, the commercial maintenance crews, and the public.

ROLE-PLAY ASSIGNMENT

Acting as Maxwell, how do you approach the discretionary decisions before you?

QUESTIONS FOR DISCUSSION

1. Describe the various types of competing pressures that come into play. In your view, which of those pressures should be accorded the highest priority? What are the advantages and disadvantages accompanying your choice?
2. What course of action should Maxwell pursue regarding the issue before him? Is there a difference between "the right decision" from an ethical perspective, from an economic perspective, and from the perspective of the mandates handed down from one's superiors?

3. How do you approach the reality of working with less staff and resources due to FAA cuts? Would you fight the cuts?

4. What plan do you have for reallocating staff and inspectors? Do you target certain situations, aircraft (old or new, large or small), crews, or companies, or do you consolidate inspections?

5. Regarding the new regulations on twin-engine propeller aircraft, new procedures for inspecting structural integrity of the plane require replacing the engine mount, which is a time-consuming and costly process. How do you approach the dilemma, and what considerations do you have for the high costs, staff needed for the inspection, and safety concerns?

SOURCES FOR FURTHER READING

Bryner, G. C. *Bureaucratic Discretion: Law and Policy in Federal Regulatory Agencies* New York: Pergamon Press, 1987.

Burke, J. P., *Bureaucratic Responsibility*. Baltimore: Johns Hopkins University Press, 1986.

Gruber, J. E. *Controlling Bureaucracies: Dilemmas of Democratic Governance*. Los Angeles: University of California Press, 1987.

Lipsky, M. *Street-level Bureaucracy: Dilemmas of the Individual in Public Services*. New York: Russell Sage Foundation, 1980.

- economic - poss. endanger safety
- whistle blower - raise public consciousness - career stagnation
- use stricter scrutiney when inspecting
- reorganize FAA - new guidlines, new ways to perform job, develop strategy for inspections

3

Dealing With Bureaucracy and Intergovernmental Relations: The EPA and Hazardous Waste

Lisa Nelson

ABOUT THE ORGANIZATIONS

The *U.S. Environmental Protection Agency (EPA) regional office* is charged with overseeing the restoration of contaminated and hazardous waste sites in its region.

The *City of Bajada* is a mid-sized community in the southwestern United States in need of economic development and eager to move ahead with development plans.

The *Bajada Economic Development Partnership* is a community interest group that advocates developing under-utilized industrial parks and contaminated sites.

The *City of Hillview* is a wealthy college community neighboring Bajada.

Office of Congressmen Jim Fisher, the area's representative, is a booster of economic development projects in his district.

Sus Casas is a nonprofit, affordable housing advocacy group supporting a plan to build low-income housing on the site in question.

ABOUT THE CHARACTERS

Janet Lee, regional hazardous waste clean-up manager, is eager to clean up waste sites but is caught in the middle of bureaucratic red tape from her regional office and demands from a variety of agencies and interests.

Tom Valdez, regional water quality manager, is a politically savvy operator who opposes the development plan on grounds that it would develop a tract he has identified to be conserved as a wetland.

Chris Wilson is the EPA assistant regional administrator and Lee's boss.

INTRODUCTION TO THE PROBLEM

Chris Wilson, EPA's assistant regional manager, spoke with Janet Lee, the manager of hazardous waste cleanup for EPA's Region XV, to let her know she should expect a written request to speed up the approval of a treatment plan for a "brownfields" site. The site is located in Bajada. The reason for the request, according to Wilson, is that a local economic development board wants to include the property in a redevelopment plan but cannot proceed because of the unresolved liability and cleanup issues at the site.

The Bajada site is one of 160 brownfields sites in the region on which Lee is working. While not as severely threatening to public health as a Superfund site, the property is classified as a brownfields site since it has been vacant for a number of years due to suspected pollution problems. Developers tend to avoid such sites for fear of inheriting environmental liability should they assume ownership of the property. There are more than 400,000 brownfields sites across the nation, contributing to urban blight, sprawl, delinquent taxes, crime, and environmental problems. The EPA has been under considerable pressure to develop ways to reduce the liability threat so that the sites can be redeveloped for new uses.

Superfund

Congress passed the Comprehensive Environmental Response, Compensation, and Liability Act (Superfund) in 1980 in response to growing concern about the threat from hazardous materials. Almost 36,000 sites have been investigated since then and about 2,000 are on the National Priorities List (NPL), the list of worst sites that are eligible for federally funded clean-up. Superfund contains strict liability provisions that require cleanup costs to be shared by anyone having anything to do with the site—including new landowners, whether or not they were involved in the improper disposal of the hazardous waste in the first place. Because the cost of cleaning up the sites can be high, new businesses and developers avoid old industrial sites when looking for new locations. Therefore, the land often sits idle. The EPA has been under pressure to develop a speedier investigative process so that brownfields sites can be cleared for development. Lee thought it ironic to be in the role of the "bureaucrat in the way," especially after she had spent months dealing with delays while waiting for the EPA's central office in Washington, D.C. to approve procedures.

The Bajada Site

Lee took out the file on the Bajada site to remind herself of the details. The site is in the northern section of Bajada, a mid-sized (60,000), southwestern city in a larger metropolitan area. The property is near the east boundary of La Placa and the west boundary of Hillview, a wealthy college town. The file contained a two-year-old letter from the city manager in Hillview, requesting to be kept informed of decisions regarding the Bajada site.

The property was formerly a circuit-board plating factory owned by a major corporation. There is groundwater contamination in the underlying aquifer and soil contamination in some areas. The site did not qualify for the NPL because the groundwater contamination poses only a "moderate" health risk rather than the necessary "severe" risk to area drinking water wells. And the soil contamination posed no threats beyond the immediate property. Nevertheless, to be cleared for redevelopment, the soil would have to be treated or removed and a plan developed for remediation of the groundwater contamination.

THE REQUEST

The next day, Lee received an overnight mail package containing the proposal, a list of the project partners, and a map of the project site in question. The fifteen-acre brownfields property is across the street from an underutilized industrial park, the focus of the economic development proposal. On the west edge of the industrial park is property that includes a run-off ditch with the potential to be restored as a wetland. Lee knew from her previous conversation with Wilson that the economic development partnership originally targeted the ditch-wetland property as developable for low-income housing. However, state water quality officials have requested (with the support of Tom Valdez, the regional EPA water quality manager) that the former plating factory property (the brownfields site) be developed instead of the underutilized industrial park so as to leave the ditch for future restoration as a wetland. Valdez has a reputation in the agency for working hard behind the scenes to get political support for his pet projects. However, Valdez and foes of the planned development of the industrial park would have to contend with several powerful partners involved in the development project including the Cities of Bajada and La Placa, Sus Casas (a nonprofit, low-income housing advocacy group), the regional council of governments, the Bajada Chamber of Commerce, and the state Department of Economic Development. Another group, Ducks Unlimited, wanted the contaminated site cleaned and wetlands restored for waterfowl habitat.

An aide to Congressman Jim Fisher, the Bajada area's representative, called Lee to inquire about the status of the Bajada project. Lee said she was still looking at the project proposal and would return the call later in the afternoon. The aide assured Lee that Fisher was very interested in supporting the proposed project.

RULES AND SHARED POWERS

The office procedures that Lee had recently established for processing cleanup requests called for a preliminary prioritization of the sites according to severity of threat, ease of cleanup, and length of time the property had been underutilized or vacant, with longer periods of time ranked higher. Lee now wished she had factored in community needs; that would have allowed her to move the Bajada site to the top priority list and satisfy the array of interests now weighing on the development.

However, Lee also wondered if placing low-income housing on this site rather than the one originally planned would raise concerns about environmental justice. This was a relatively new impact that EPA was required to consider, and the image presented of building low-income housing on a contaminated site invited criticism. She also wondered if the housing advocacy group knew of the alternative proposal to build the housing units on a site other than the one targeted for wetlands renewal. Lee also noticed that the City of Hillview was not a partner listed on the project. A wealthy college community, Hillview would most likely support cleaning up the contaminated site for development and reclaiming the ditch area as a wetland.

To sign off on the project would also require quick approval of a cleanup plan and approval of contractors designated for soil removal and groundwater remediation. Lee wondered if any of the companies on the approved contractor list would be available on such short notice to assess the site and write a proposal. Such environmental projects would need approval from the state Department of Environmental Quality, even though the state's Economic Development Department was a project partner. Sorting out that potential conflict would probably require guidance from the governor's office.

Lee could see that her decision about what to do on the Bajada site would have an important effect on the project. A "no" to the cleanup of the brownfields would probably put pressure on developing the wetlands area for low-income housing. A "yes" to the planned clean up would mean that she would need to secure an array of bureaucratic approvals from a number of agencies and interests. A "yes" might also backfire if Hillview or the state Department of Environmental Quality did not like the idea. Clearly, economic development was a legitimate priority for the Bajada area, and the proposal cited studies showing a need for additional affordable housing.

Lee had been a field agent prior to her promotion to the regional office. Her practice had been to visit the actual waste sites and their surroundings, but as an administrator in an office, she was 350 miles away from the site. She liked Wilson, the young regional administrator, but was not sure she trusted Valdez, the water quality expert, who was away from the office most of the time. The office atmosphere was friendly and casual, but hardworking, and there were often small celebrations when projects were completed. Lee was eager to tackle the large backlog of cases remaining from her predecessor, but had felt it necessary to establish fair and impartial procedures for deciding which cases should receive attention first. Her boss, Wilson, encouraged her in this activity but she was concerned that she would so quickly need to ask him to approve making an exception in order to process the Bajada paperwork as soon as possible. On the phone, Wilson had assured her that he would support her decision, but he was now unable to further discuss the situation, as he was away at a senior executive training workshop and unavailable. She would have to decide for herself.

ROLE-PLAY ASSIGNMENT

You are Lee and must decide how to handle the plans for developing and cleaning up the brownfields site and/or developing the adjacent industrial park.

QUESTIONS FOR DISCUSSION

1. What interests or interest groups are involved in the outcome of this decision and on which side of the decision? How should Lee prioritize the conflicting issues at stake in the Bajada proposal?

2. How important is it for someone in Lee's position to develop effective working relationships with people in other government agencies as well as state and local agencies? What relationships should she try to build? How? What groups and inter governmental organizations need to be brought to the case?

3. Are there ethical trade-offs present in this case? If so, what are they? And how should Lee approach the rules for prioritizing cleanup sites?

4. Lee found a note in her in-box from Valdez that said, "This is a case where rules are made to be broken!" Is he right? How should Lee respond?

5. What is your decision? Should you clean up and develop the brownfields site or the adjacent old industrial park? What is your decision regarding the wetlands renewal and affordable housing plan?

SOURCES FOR FURTHER READING

Hird, J. *Superfund: The Political Economy of Environmental Risk* Baltimore: Johns Hopkins Press, 1994.

Luke, J. *Catalytic Leadership: Strategies for an Interconnected World* San Francisco: Jossey-Bass Publishers, 1998.

Mazmanian, D.A., and M. E. Kraft. *Toward Sustainable Communities: Transitions and Transformations in Environmental Policy.* Cambridge, MA: MIT Press, 1999.

O'Leary, R., R. F. Durant, D. J. Fiorino, and P. S. Weiland. *Managing for the Environment: Understanding the Legal, Organizational, and Policy Changes.* San Francisco: Jossey-Bass, 1999.

Stranger in a Strange Land: A Non-Indian Administrator Working on an Indian Reservation

Peter T. Suzuki

ABOUT THE AGENCY

The tribal *Environmental Protection Department* (EPD), like the EPA, tries to see to it that the reservation environment is kept safe and clean. EPD is part of the tribe's administrative structure and reports directly to the tribal council or its representative, the tribal executive officer (TEO).

ABOUT THE CHARACTERS

Terry Green, a non-Indian administrator (director of EPD) is employed by the Niauxal Tribe of Nebraska. Those agencies reporting to Green include: geographic information system (GIS) coordinator; chief of pesticides control; four field workers; and one clerical employee.

The *Tribal Council* is comprised of seven members of the Niauxal Tribe.

Richard Tallgrass is a tribal court judge.

Eric Thomas, a non-Indian farmer living on reservation lands, has been accused of dumping illegal toxic substances on his property.

GOVERNANCE OF INDIAN RESERVATIONS

The 1990 census counted 1,945 tribal members living on the Niauxal Reservation, which is 185,000 acres in size and shares a common boundary with another Indian tribe. Through the Allotment Act of 1887, approximately 70 percent of the Niauxal Nation's original land was lost. The land-use pattern on the reservation, like that found on many other reservations, is termed "checkerboard" because many non-Indians (mainly Whites) own land on the reservation. This same Act established four non-Indian towns on the reservation. One of these towns, Fowler, is the county seat, although the reservation occupies the entire county. Each of the four towns, while small in population (ranging from 230 to 510), has its own law enforcement agency. The county sheriff's office is located in Fowler.

The tribe is governed by a tribal council, a group of seven individuals who are elected in at-large seats and serve three-year terms. As there are no staggered elections, an entirely new team of tribal council members may be elected in any election year. The tribal council is all powerful because there is no system of checks and balances built into the political structure. The tribal council is the executive branch and administers largely through a tribal executive officer (TEO). The council also legislates and controls the judicial branch by hiring/firing those affiliated with the tribal court (a judge, prosecutor, and public defender), as well as those affiliated with the tribal police department.

Like many tribes, the Niauxal Tribe has not escaped factionalism within the tribe. Extended families, who have taken on important roles have replaced the original eight clans that were the prominent kinship units many generations ago. Factionalism among these families is especially intense during tribal elections. Under President Richard Nixon, a policy of self-determination was promulgated regarding the right of Indian tribes to be less dependent on the federal government. The Bureau of Indian Affairs (BIA), in part, accomplished the policy that President Ronald Reagan reinforced by recognizing tribes as nations.

ILLEGAL DUMPING OF HAZARDOUS SUBSTANCES?

Because she is the director of the EPD, several tribal members have met with Terry Green to complain about what they consider to be an illegal dump site near their homes. Green sent two field workers to the site, which is approximately four miles away from Green's office. With a camera in hand, the two workers documented the site in question and brought back a plastic bag containing some of the materials in the dump site for testing. The photos provided evidence that the complainants' allegations were true. Lab tests that the EPD's pesticide specialist conducted indicated that toxic wastes are present in the dump site. As such, Green asked the geographic information system coordinator to pinpoint the exact location of the site. The analysis reveals that the site, while very close to the complainants' residences, is on private property owned by a non-Indian farmer, Eric Thomas.

Armed with the photos, lab report, and the official rules and regulations of the EPD in hand, Green, accompanied by the GIS coordinator, a pesticide specialist, and a field worker, decided to visit the property and its owner, Thomas, to inform him of the findings. Green told Thomas that he has illegally created not only a dump site, but one that he has been using to dump toxic materials. Thomas was told that he must cease his operations and that, according to the EPD, he must have the dump site cleaned up at his own cost. The cleanup must be done within five working days or else Thomas must pay a heavy fine. While Thomas was cordial to Green, he showed little concern over the news because, he claimed, the dump site is on property he owns that is some four miles away from his actual place of residence—another piece of land he owns.

After the deadline given to Thomas passed and nothing was done, Green decided to go to the tribal court and see the judge to get a court injunction against Thomas that would legally force him to follow the EDP regulations and the cleanup. Judge Richard Tallgrass was sympathetic to Green's argument and immediately drew up a document decreeing the dumping improper and ordering its cleanup. Once again, Green visited Thomas with the same entourage but this time accompanied also by Donald Stevens, chief of the tribal police department and a tribe member. Green handed Thomas the court order and a compliance deadline of five working days. Stevens agreed with Green that the Thomas case was a

serious one, but he doubted whether his department would be of much help, except to ac-
company Green as a "show of force."

Once again, Thomas was very cordial, even smiling as he read the court order. The
farmer said he would think about it. However, the court order had no impact on Thomas.
The dump site was not cleaned up. In fact, five days following Green's last visit, the contamination appears to have even grown a little larger.

Plan B

Even though Fowler is the county seat, it is too small to have a counterpart to the EPD.
Therefore, Green decided to go to Lincoln, Nebraska's state capital, to discuss the matter
with the EPD's state director. Like the tribal police chief and tribal judge, the director listened sympathetically to Green's case. However, Green came away discouraged. She
learned that "given the fact that the Niauxal Tribe is a sovereign nation, the state of Nebraska has little power over what takes place on Nebraska's three reservations."

The state director's reaction surprised and angered Green. After all, the people on the
reservation, irrespective of their race, live in the state of Nebraska, and environmental issues should be the concern of everyone. After Green asked whether the state should have
the welfare of all its people as its main consideration, the state official produced a copy of
the rules and regulations of Nebraska's EPD. Several sections dealing with the reservations
point out the limited power of the state to intervene.

As Green departed the state office, the official recommended consulting the regional
EPA office and the Bureau of Indian Affairs (BIA), whose office is on the reservation. However, Green later learned the BIA no longer deals with environmental issues, except for such
things as measuring the water table and ground solidity when federal housing is going to be
constructed on a reservation. And to make matters worse, Green returned from the unsuccessful trip to Lincoln to find another complaint. The Carlins, a tribal family living in Bluffs
View—the largest town on the reservation—filed a complaint that their fellow tribe member neighbors, the Crestfeathers, have been dumping gasoline from their lawnmower and
snowblower and oil from their car into their back yard, which borders the Carlin home.

Plan C

With this added problem, Green decided to go to Kansas City, where the EPA's regional office is headquartered. However, EPA officials told Green that their hands were tied because
the tribe is a sovereign nation. Green began to worry that the EPD office had no jurisdictional power in the Thomas case nor in Bluffs View. Upon returning to the reservation,
Green called a staff meeting to inform the office of the results of the visits to Lincoln and
Kansas City. When the staff offered no advice, Green suggested that because the parties in
question in the latter case were members of the tribe, the EPD office might have authority
to act. Accordingly, perhaps a warning letter to the Crestfeathers would be in order. However, the staff, all of whom were tribal members, advised Green against doing anything.
They were adamant. Puzzled by this reaction, Green questioned the wisdom of a "do nothing" policy concerning the Crestfeather family. It was then revealed that the tribal council
chair, is related to the Crestfeathers through marriage, as are several other members of the
tribal council. The Crestfeathers are one of the most powerful families on the reservation.

Green's staff then advised that, should the issue with the Crestfeathers of Bluffs View be pursued, the entire EPD staff would be in jeopardy of losing their jobs.

Green is frustrated, angry, and feeling uncertain about the complicated situation.

ROLE-PLAY ASSIGNMENT

Acting as Green, director of the environmental Protection Department on the Niauxal Reservation, come up with a plan of action.

QUESTIONS FOR DISCUSSION

1. Public administration and political science textbooks generally assume that students understand the concept of sovereignty. Discuss its parameters and then examine the sovereignty issue with regard to Indian nations and this case. What considerations must an administrator have when working in an intergovernmental situation?

2. There is an ethical dimension regarding the politics involved with the Crestfeathers of Bluffs View. Why do you feel Green's job would be jeopardized by pursuing the Crestfeather family? How and why do you feel such a political situation came to exist on the reservation? What course of action—if any—should Green take regarding the political ramifications of working with powerful political families? How should this issue be handled?

3. What is the main ethical issue confronting Green, and what would you do about it? What can be done in the larger sense so that such problems do not plague administrators?

4. As a non-Indian working for a tribe on the reservation, discuss how you would feel as an administrator with a racial minority status. What issues would require your sensitivity?

5. What should be done in the Thomas case? What would be your course of action?

SOURCES FOR FURTHER READING

Castelle, G. P., and R. L. Bee. *States and Reservations: New Perspectives on Federal Indian Policy.* Tucson, AZ: University of Arizona Press, 1992.

Deloria, V., and C. Lytle. *The Nations Within: The Past and Future of American Indian Sovereignty.* New York: Pantheon, 1984.

Suzuki, P. T. "Pan-Indianism, Ethnicity, and Omaha Tribe of Nebraska." *Contemporary Society: Tribal Studies* 1 (1994): 103–114.

———. "The Rebirth of a Nation: The Winnebago Tribe of Nebraska," *Contemporary Society: Tribal Studies* 4 (1999): 71–83.

Wilkins, D. E. "Tribal-State Affairs: American States as 'Disclaiming' Sovereigns." *Journal of Federalism,* 28 (1998): 55–81.

Note: "Indian" is not a pejorative. In the author's research, it was found that, more often than not, it is Whites who use the term "Native American."

Part II

Managing Human Resources

THE HUMAN RESOURCE CHALLENGE FOR MANAGERS

Organizations are made up of people and many organizational problems ultimately end up being people problems. As such, managerial tasks like recruitment, selection, and training are vitally important for the health of the organization. These tasks come under the purview of human resources or personnel administration.

Human Resource Functions

There are essentially five functions a human resources manager must perform: (1) staffing; (2) classification and compensation; (3) training and development; (4) employee advancement and promotion; and (5) handling grievances and disciplinary action.

Staffing is the process by which organizations recruit, screen, and select employees. In the public sector, such actions must be performed under a strict set of rules and regulations and must adhere to the principle of *merit*, where employees are judged solely on the basis of their abilities. The staffing function involves everything from examining resource needs to posting job announcements to developing examinations that serve as one of the criteria for selection. In screening and selecting employees, human resource managers utilize written tests, performance tests, experience, ratings of pertinent qualifications and training, and other methods to evaluate the employability of prospective hires. Once a prospective employee completes the examination(s) and written application for a position, human resource managers and civil service commissions rate and rank all candidates and certify employees to the appointing official as eligible for selection. The hiring official then selects the employee from a short list of roughly three certified and qualified applicants.

The second major function of human resources is classification and compensation. One of the tenets of the civil service system is *job classification*. Human resource managers classify each position according to the duties and responsibilities of the position. Such classification systems help the organization determine employees' pay and the hiring needs of the organization. Pay is then tied to the position in the classification system. The rigid job classification system in the public sector has come under much criticism, although the system has succeeded in minimizing unequal treatment of employees and hiring or promoting unqualified employees.

To ensure that government employees are able to perform their jobs at an adequate level and remain able to do so regardless of changes in technology, operating practices, and society, managers rely on training and development, the third function of personnel. *Training* not only improves the delivery of public services and programs, but it helps employees improve themselves, provides opportunities for advancement, and might increase employee morale and motivation. Many jobs within the government are unique and require special skills—skills that are often difficult to obtain through simply a traditional education or employment outside of government. Some training is performed in-house through the agency or government while other training might involve continuing education, attendance at workshops, or participation in assessment centers.

Most public sector jobs involve a period of probation to permit the new employee adequate instruction and training and a general adjustment to the job, during which time the organization assesses the fitness of the employee. It is usually after this point in time that the employee becomes eligible for advancement, the fourth personnel function. *Advancement*, is a key ingredient to ensuring employee morale and a viable career service. The final core task for human resource managers is managing *grievances and discipline*. Many grievance and disciplinary problems can be avoided by monitoring employee performance and attitudes on a continual basis and making clear to everyone in the organization what is expected of them. If disciplinary action is necessary, managers usually try to avoid serious consequences to the employee by first attempting to correct the problem and improve employee performance. If, however, disciplinary action is required, it should be based on careful analysis of the situation, must be documented in writing, and usually reviewed by an impartial board.

THE POLITICS OF HUMAN RESOURCE MANAGEMENT

Development of a Civil Service System

Historically, there was no coherent or systematic approach to staffing governmental agencies.[1] Perhaps the most common employment practice was rewarding political loyalty by offering jobs to friends, family members, and political allies. Known as the *spoils system*, this approach was widespread and undermined the continuity of public service—as employees were often replaced after each election by the winner of the election. Moreover, the autonomy of administrators to function in a manner free from politics and often even the ability of the public service to function at all, as many of those employed lacked the requisite skills required for the position, were byproducts of such political *patronage*. So extensive was the practice and associated abuses that many cities were governed by political "bosses" and "machines" who functioned largely on their ability to reward loyalty and punish opposition through employment.[2]

The spoils dilemma came into focus in 1881 when a dillusioned job seeker assassinated President James Garfield. Moreover, the advent of the Industrial Revolution witnessed the rise of an increasingly industrialized, urbanized, and complex society, replete with an array of new and difficult challenges. It became apparent that for government to respond adequately to these new demands, a competent, professional, and politically neutral corps of employees would be needed. Thus, in 1883 the Civil Service Reform Act, known as the *Pendleton Act,* was passed. Pendleton created a new approach to staffing government, one based on competence and the concept of *merit.* It established a bipartisan Civil Service Commission charged with setting and implementing federal personnel policies, offering employees the protection of tenure, and enacting a selection process based on examinations, merit, and job requirements. The selection process attempted to staff the public service with individuals from all across the country in an effort to achieve a *representative bureaucracy.* Over time, most states and local governments adopted similar civil service and merit systems.

The majority of public employees are covered by a civil service system. There are still, however, *political appointees* who are not afforded the benefits of civil service protection. As the name implies, political appointees are picked by an elected official and such selections need not be based on examination or qualification. For instance, at the federal level, the president makes several hundred of such appointments, as do, to a lesser degree, governors and mayors. These appointees usually serve as heads of major departments. The justification for making political appointments is that these individuals can be fired with little or no recourse, perform largely political rather than administrative functions, and directly serve the chief executive.

For much of the country's history, one of the main abuses experienced by public employees was being forced to campaign or vote for certain politicians or being fired for failure to do so.[3] In an effort to remedy this problem, the 1939 Political Activities Act, known as the *Hatch Act,* for its sponsor, Senator Carl Hatch of New Mexico, sought to eliminate such practices and protect civil servants from political pressures and retribution by forbidding politicians from forcing employees to engage in partisan political activities. On the other hand, it also limited public employees by restricting the extent of campaign activities in which they could participate on behalf of an elected official or political campaign. Since its inception, the Hatch Act has been adopted in one form or another by many states and localities. With the Pendleton and Hatch Acts, the public personnel system had achieved the goal of *neutral competence,* or staffing government with professional, able employees while promoting professionalism and independence from the pressures of politics.

Reforming the Civil Service

A key reform in the development of the contemporary civil service system came in 1978 with the Civil Service Reform Act. Led by President Jimmy Carter, these reforms sought to improve the personnel practices of the federal government and make public service more effective and more attractive to potential employees.[4] A core part of the reforms involved merit-based pay raises to make public service more competitive with the private sector. The federal pay scale (the General Schedule) begins at the G.S. 1 level and involves "steps" at each level up to the Executive Schedule level. These are listed in Tables 2.1 and 2.2.

In an effort to retain senior civil servants and improve their effectiveness, the Hatch Act established the Senior Executive Service (SES), a group of top public employees who received attractive pay options and whose expertise was better utilized. The 1978 reforms also encouraged the practice of *whistle-blowing,* or making public any unethical or

General Schedule Rates of Pay (2000)

Grade					Steps					
	1	2	3	4	5	6	7	8	9	10
1	13,870	14,332	14,794	15,252	15,715	15,986	16,440	16,900	16,918	17,351
2	15,594	15,964	16,481	16,918	17,107	17,610	18,113	18,616	19,119	19,622
3	17,015	17,582	18,481	18,716	19,283	19,850	20,417	20,984	21,551	22,118
4	19,100	19,737	20,374	21,011	21,648	22,285	22,922	23,559	24,196	24,833
5	21,370	22,082	22,794	23,506	24,218	24,930	25,642	26,354	27,066	27,778
6	23,820	24,614	25,408	26,202	26,996	27,790	28,584	29,378	30,172	30,966
7	26,470	27,352	28,234	29,116	29,996	30,880	31,762	32,644	33,526	34,408
8	29,315	30,292	31,269	32,246	33,223	34,200	35,177	36,154	37,131	38,108
9	32,380	33,459	34,538	35,617	36,696	37,775	38,854	39,933	41,012	42,091
10	35,658	36,847	38,036	39,225	40,414	41,603	42,792	43,981	45,170	46,359
11	39,178	40,484	41,790	43,096	44,402	45,708	47,014	48,320	49,626	50,932
12	46,955	48,520	50,085	51,650	53,215	54,780	56,345	57,910	59,475	61,040
13	55,837	57,698	59,559	61,420	63,281	65,142	67,003	68,864	70,725	72,586
14	65,983	68,182	70,381	72,580	74,779	76,978	79,177	81,376	83,575	85,774
15	77,614	80,201	82,788	85,375	87,962	90,549	93,136	95,723	98,310	100,897

Executive Schedule Rates of Pay (2000)

Level	Rate
I	$157,000
II	$141,300
III	$130,200
IV	$122,400
V	$114,500

inefficient governmental practices, by protecting the person making the allegation. Lastly, the old Civil Service Commission (CSC) was divided into two agencies to reduce an inherent conflict of interest in CSC practices. The Office of Personnel Management (OPM) was responsible for personnel policies such as pay, recruitment, and selection while the Merit Systems Protection Board (MSPB) dealt with employee grievances.

DECISION-MAKING ISSUES TO CONSIDER AS YOU READ THE CASES

Equal Opportunity

Historically, fair and open employment opportunities have not been accessible to all people. The legacy of "separate but equal"[5] lasted well into the twentieth century. Among the early efforts to integrate the workforce included Executive Order 8587 signed by

President Franklin D. Roosevelt in 1940 prohibiting discrimination by government agencies or by organizations under contract with the government. Roosevelt's successor, Harry S. Truman, issued Executive Order 9981 in 1948, which integrated the U.S. armed forces. A successful challenge to "separate but equal" occurred in 1954 with a landmark ruling in *Brown v. The Board of Education* that ended legal separatism in public facilities and changed the way equality would be defined.

The concept of *equal employment opportunity* is based on the premise that all people should have an equal opportunity to gain employment and be free from discrimination based on race, color, religion, sex, national origin, or physical disability. Regardless of the gains made by the country in extending equal opportunities to all citizens, by the 1960s it had become increasingly clear that additional legislative mandates would be needed in order to realize this goal and basic right. The 1964 Civil Rights Act, signed into law by President Lyndon Johnson, marked the cornerstone of the civil rights-equal employment movement. The legislation prohibited discrimination in the workplace in a comprehensive manner that included hiring, firing, promotion, assignment, and other aspects of employment.

Affirmative Action

In 1965 President Johnson signed Executive Order 11246, requiring all contractors performing work for the federal government to prohibit discrimination and use *affirmative action* to ensure equal employment opportunities. The 1972 Equal Employment Opportunity Act reiterated the government's commitment to equal opportunity in the workplace by extending the reach of the Civil Rights Act to government agencies, political organizations, and state and local governments. Such bodies as the Equal Employment Opportunity Commission (EEOC), a commission appointed by the president and the Civil Service Commission (now OPM), have been charged with administering equal employment policies.

The advent of affirmative action also brought a conceptual difference between equal employment and affirmative action. Equal employment is a passive strategy for achieving employment goals in that it implies only nondiscrimination. Affirmative action, on the other hand, is an active strategy that promotes hiring and employment for certain classes of people. As such, equal employment mandates that employers simply do not discriminate to be in compliance with the goals and faith of the law, whereas affirmative action mandates that employers do more and aggressively pursue a variety of employment goals and objectives. Examples of affirmative action include developing aggressive recruitment plans, training programs, selective certification for specific positions, and job-related, culturally unbiased evaluations for minority candidates. The EEOC offers basic approaches to achieving an effective affirmative action program including; (1) developing a written policy stating the organizations' commitment to equal opportunity and affirmative action, (2) designating an individual in the organization to manage the program and goal, (3) publicizing the commitment to the goal internally and externally, (4) assessing current employment conditions for minorities, (5) developing goals, timetables, and plans to include underutilized segments of the population, and (6) establishing an audit or evaluation process for monitoring the program.

One of the criticisms of affirmative action is that it has the potential to produce *reverse discrimination*. Critics allege that affirmative action practices weaken merit-based decision making and stigmatize the beneficiaries it otherwise intends to help, possibly resulting in less-qualified applicants from the "protected class" being hired over, for example, white male candidates.[6] If this occurs, the policy has produced reverse discrimination. The key court case in defining reverse discrimination is the 1978 ruling in *Regents of the University of California v. Allan Bakke.* Bakke, a white male attempting to gain admission to the medical school at the University of California at Davis, sued the university claiming his application had been rejected, and a less-qualified minority student had been admitted in his place. Even though Bakke twice applied for admission and had higher scores based on admissions criteria than several minority applicants admitted to the school, he was twice denied. Bakke argued that in a merit-based, objective assessment he was more qualified for admission than several of the minority students admitted to the UC-Davis Medical School. Even though the university maintained that diversity was a goal of the school and a practice that benefited not only its students but society, the U.S. Supreme Court ruled in a 5–4 decision in favor of Bakke citing several concerns. First, UC-Davis had never adequately defined what constituted a "disadvantaged" person or group and had not adequately identified the nature of the problem or the proposed remedy. As such, the Court ruled that race, as the sole criterion, was a violation of the 1964 Civil Rights Act and constituted reverse discrimination. But, the Court upheld the concept of equal opportunity and permitted quota- and affirmative action-based decisions, yet not if the quota was inflexible and if the goals were unclearly defined. The Court also distinguished between the permissibility of affirmative action when used to remedy past racial wrongs versus affirmative action programs enacted without specific incident or grounds, which amount to reverse discrimination. And, lastly, they distinguished between private and public institutions, noting that the university was a public sector organization.

Disabilities

The Americans with Disabilities Act (ADA), signed into law in 1990, recognized the struggle of individuals with disabilities in achieving equal opportunities in the workplace. Equal opportunity also came to be seen as equal physical access to the place of employment. The ADA required the removal of any physical barriers to access in public and private facilities and in the workplace. Employers must provide "reasonable accommodations" for both clients and employees, and employers cannot discriminate against qualified individuals who happen to have a disability. Yet, in accommodating individuals with disabilities, employers need not experience "undue hardships" that might, for instance, jeopardize the financial health of the organization. Here, such factors as the number of individuals employed, the financial resources of the organization, and cost of accommodation are considered by government in rendering a decision.

Sexual Harassment

Even though legislation has been enacted and court verdicts rendered that precluded discrimination against classes of individuals, female employees still encounter difficulties and challenges unique to their sex. Measures such as the Equal Pay Act of 1963 protect women from discriminatory compensation practices. Regardless of equal pay laws, some occupations dominated by women (known as "pink collar" jobs) such as librarians or child care workers tend to receive pay scales far below those found in predominately male occupations. Also, a female employee working in one job (such as a secretary) in an organization might make less than a male employee working in another job (such as a technician), yet both positions have comparable importance to the organization and comparable demands on the employee. This concept is known as *comparable worth.* Although the courts and Congress have generally not forwarded viable measures for testing and enforcing comparable worth, some litigation and collective bargaining decisions have sought to remedy the practice.

Sexual harassment entails a variety of harmful acts but can generally be defined as "unwelcome sexual advance or conduct or language that is sexually abusive or intimidating"[7] The EEOC conceptualizes two fundamental types of sexual harassment. The first type is *quid pro quo*, which involves job-related rewards or punishments tied to sexual behavior or intimidation. This was recognized in the 1986 Supreme Court case *Meritor Savings Bank v. Mechelle Vinson*, where the court ruled that making employment conditional on sexual favors or acts was illegal, even if the sexual relations were voluntary. The second type of sexual harassment is the creation of a *hostile environment*. In *Price Waterhouse v. Hopkins*, Ann Hopkins was denied a promotion at the prestigious accounting firm even though she appeared to be the most qualified applicant among a pool of male employees. Ruling in favor of the plaintiff, the Supreme Court noted that an array of inappropriate and sexist comments had been made about Hopkins' appearance and demeanor by her employer. Such comments created an environment hostile for women to be taken seriously as employees.

Employers are liable for the behavior of their agents and are responsible for having appeals or grievance plans developed to mitigate sexual harassment problems and charges. Ironically, even though the most discussed type of sexual harassment is the quid pro quo sexual advance, the second type of sexual harassment is the more common. But it is also the more difficult manifestation of harassment to prove in a court of law.

Such issues as discrimination and sexual harassment, along with the core personnel tasks of hiring, training, and promoting employees highlight the central importance of human resources management. So too do numerous problems remain with the civil service system. Critics allege that the meritocracy is in fact not based on merit; that the extensive protections offered to employees, the prevalence of seniority as a criterion for advancement, and the relatively new priority of equal employment opportunity all act to undermine merit as the basis for employment, pay, and promotion in government. It is also difficult to define adequate means for merit-based assessments. In the public sector, after all, performance-based measures and outcomes are not always readily apparent. Job security as a personnel goal has been achieved, yet critics maintain that it has been achieved at the cost of productivity, as many employees that are unresponsive to their clients or their managers still retain their positions. Indeed, many organizational problems end up being problems with people in the organization.

The following four cases examine a variety of typical and frustrating personnel issues. As you consider these cases, keep in mind the primary personnel administration functions and laws as well as the many internal and external forces acting to influence employee relations and behavior.

Managing Conflict Among a Hospital Staff

J. Gary Linn

J. Gary Linn

ABOUT THE AGENCY

The *Sewanee State Mental Hospital* was established more than ninety years ago as the major inpatient psychiatric facility and teaching hospital for the region. Over the past three years, the new managed care system has changed the hospital's treatment approach. There was a shift from long-term to short-term care with the new goal of stabilization only. Required patient documentation increased two-fold, yet the facility continued to train scores of residents and medical students annually from Tidewater University, a prestigious private school.

ABOUT THE CHARACTERS

Stephen Renfro III, M.D. is the attending psychiatrist in an acute care, inpatient psychiatric unit. He graduated from a prestigious southeastern medical school in the 1960s, and he has completed more than thirty years of service as a physician in a large state mental health institution.

Constance (Connie) Thoroughgood, RN is the acting head nurse in the same acute, inpatient psychiatric unit and has been the nurse in charge for six years, working actively with Renfro. She is completing her master's in nursing at nearby Metropolitan State University.

MANAGING CONFLICT

Conflict can happen in any setting and is a healthy part of decision making. When issues are confronted promptly, many conflicts are preventable. However, unresolved conflict results in a breakdown in communication and team building and undermines organizational growth and progress toward mutual goals.

Research has shown that the greatest source of workplace stress in hospitals is nurse-supervisor and nurse-physician interpersonal conflict. The issue in this case is the latter form of conflict. The perceptions of physician and nurse differ in a number of respects, including the degree to which collaboration and joint decision making are valued, the definition of what is adequate and appropriate inter-professional communication, the quality of nurse-physician interactions, and understanding of respective spheres of responsibility as well as patient goals. These differences have been explained by gender, the historical origins of the two professions, and disparities between physicians and nurses with regard to socioeconomic status, education, and professional socialization. Male-female communication problems can be attributed to cultural and professional socialization. Given that most physicians are men and that 96 percent of nurses are women, the influence of gender on conflict and communication is one to consider.

The Joint Commission of Health Care Organizations emphasizes the growing importance of collaborative practice, which, although beneficial for service delivery, poses the risk of further nurse-physician interpersonal conflict. Yet, studies demonstrate that positive professional relationships have a beneficial influence on patient outcomes. The actions of the nurses and physicians in the clinic have a significant influence on each other and on the patient. Clinical settings marred by nurse-physician conflict are counterproductive to patients. Many factors promote a climate of nurse-physician conflict. Some of these are: divergent values; distinct goals; differing methods; need for control; lack of role definitions; and need for self-protection.

Also, because the delivery of comprehensive nursing care has become more difficult in the managed care environment, nurse-physician alliances are critical to attaining the efficiency standards mandated by managed care.

THE WORKPLACE RELATIONSHIP

Connie Thoroughgood, RN is the acting head nurse of the acute care psychiatric unit. She has been the nurse in charge for six years, working actively with Dr. Stephen Renfro. Thoroughgood and Renfro had a professional relationship that resulted in a high level of clinical proficiency.

At the beginning of their working relationship, Renfro served as Thoroughgood's mentor, helping her develop her knowledge of mental illness while studying nursing at Metropolitan State University. Thoroughgood has described this period of her life as an exciting time marked by personal and professional growth. At the hospital she enjoyed practicing what she had been learning at school. She was inquiring, enthusiastic, and considered her clinical expertise to be her strength. Renfro was impressed with the new nurse and her ability to meet their patients' medical needs.

It was also during this period that Renfro developed cardiac symptoms related to coronary artery disease. He was having difficulty stabilizing his condition with his medications. Thoroughgood did considerable "patient teaching" with her mentor to define his symptoms and explain how his medications would work. He often expressed great comfort in her presence because he was confident that she could care for him in the event he should have a heart attack.

THE WORKING RELATIONSHIP CHANGES

Several years ago, managed care changed the treatment approach to behavioral health. There was a major change from long-term care to short-term care with the objective of stabilization only, not treatment. Behavioral health organizations were responsible for setting a patient's length of stay and did so in a bureaucratic manner. Mandatory documentation of every detail of the delivery of care expanded two-fold for all disciplines that comprised the treatment team. Both Thoroughgood and Renfro opposed the changes and worked together to ensure that the necessary documentation was completed in order to obtain as many hospital days as they could to provide for the patients' assessed needs. All of the staff worked toward this aim. At this point, the relationship between doctor and nurse was still one of teacher/student, but Thoroughgood had become more confident in her psychiatric nursing skills and more independent in her clinical work with patients and thus began to exercise more decision-making autonomy.

Under Renfro's direction, the medical students and residents showed nurses respect and courtesy. The nursing staff participated in their education and training. It was also at this time that Renfro was given more responsibility for the Tidewater University medical students and resident program. Up to this time, the supervision of the medical students and residents was shared between Renfro and a senior resident.

Throughout the previous year, the professional relationship between nurse and doctor changed. Both were experiencing significant life changes. Moreover, managed care documentation requirements took time away from clinical responsibilities and changed the nature of their jobs. Documentation became a major focus for the physician. Medical students and residents were no longer oriented to the outpatient milieu, and they became less courteous and less respectful to the nursing staff. Renfro and Thoroughgood had frequent discussions and arguments about the "inadequate" way the hospital was providing for patients' care. She felt she no longer needed a mentor and wanted a partner to work with in managing and assuring the delivery of effective treatment.

As such, the relationship became distant, and they began to avoid each other on the ward. They also found that they no longer shared goals, and Thoroughgood was disillusioned with his leadership. She felt she lacked power to make any significant changes without Renfro's approval and support. She was also intolerant of the residents' disrespectful behavior towards the nursing staff and saw their failure to follow procedure as increasing the nurses' workloads. Renfro, in her opinion, was no longer stressing the need to treat nurses with respect so she asked him to orient the med students to the unit treatment protocols.

The interpersonal conflicts experienced by the nurse and physician escalated into a major disagreement. The psychiatric ward had been very volatile on one particular day, and in Thoroughgood's assessment, was at risk for violence. The treatment team met in the conference room to discuss the matter. At this point, Thoroughgood requested assistance to decrease the level of patient agitation. According to her, she had made the request for additional staff assistance in very clear and concise terms, including the urgent reason for asking for their help. Her reasoning: In a crisis of this type, the more known staff present in the unit, the quicker the patient will regain control. Groups of angry patients can be more easily separated. It gives the ward a sense of safety and patients have authority figures to address their concerns. Timing in a critical situation of this type is crucial.

Following the request, Thoroughgood returned to the acute ward with the rest of her nursing staff, expecting Renfro and the medical staff to follow. They did not. After further discussion with her nursing staff, she immediately returned to the conference room. Renfro and the medical staff were still there. Thoroughgood was visibly upset and demanded immediate help. In a very condescending tone of voice, Renfro said, "Well, what would you have me do, Constance?" She restated the demand for staff assistance. Renfro and the other medical staff came onto the acute ward and, within a short time, calmed a potentially dangerous situation.

Subsequently, instead of having the useful debriefing, Renfro and Thoroughgood had an angry verbal exchange in front of most of the medical and nursing staff. Thoroughgood was uncompromising and was prepared to carry the dispute as far as Renfro would take it. The argument concluded with each of them leaving the room in different directions.

ROLE-PLAY ASSIGNMENT

Because you are the hospital's human resources administrator, Thoroughgood and Renfro come to see you about their conflict, both asking you to address the matter.

QUESTIONS FOR DISCUSSION

1. When organizations go through major changes—like the new "managed care" approach to health care facing hospitals—what human resource issues are impacted? What organizational changes at Sewanee State Mental Hospital were introduced by managed care? How were Thoroughgood's professional ethics regarding patient care challenged by the implementation of managed care? How do you think this factored into the growing conflict between the two characters? What should human resource departments do to assist employees before and during such dramatic changes?

2. What other factors contributed to the deteriorating relationship? What impact did the changing nature of the two characters' roles have in contributing to the conflict? And did their previous relationship contribute to the problem between them?

3. How do you feel Thoroughgood should have made her request for staff assistance? How should Renfro have responded? What system would you put in place to prevent such future problems?

4. What is the appropriate model of nurse-physician professional relationships that you would adopt at Sewanee State Mental Hospital? What policies would you advocate to institute professional relationships? How would you handle dispute resolution?

5. What is the role of administrators or the human resources department in such inter-personal problems? At what point should administrators become involved in such matters and how?

SOURCES FOR FURTHER READING

Anderson, A. "Nurse-Physician Interaction and Job Satisfaction." *Nursing Management* 27 (1996): 33.

Forte, P. "The High Cost of Conflict." *Nursing Economics* 15 (1997): 119.

Larson, E. "The Impact of Physician-Nurse Interaction on Patient Care." *Holistic Nursing Practice* 13 (1999): 38.

Martin, G. E., and T. Bergman. "The Dynamics of Behavioral Response to Conflict in the Workplace." *Journal of Occupational and Organizational Psychology* 69 (1996).

Woodard E., and B. House. "Nurse Physician Communication: Women and Men at Work." *Orthopedic Nursing* 16 (1977): 39.

Sexual Harassment: Innocent Initiation or Hostile Work Environment?

Sharon J. Ridgeway

ABOUT THE ORGANIZATION

Yellow Bluff is a 120-year-old town in the West with a population of just under 50,000 people. It is a typical small town that has changed little in the last hundred years. Phones, televisions, and computers have been showing up in town, but many of the ideas about how the world should work have not changed. The typical job for women is still teacher, waitress, or secretary. The town is now in for a shock, as the city government has just mandated the implementation of a comparable worth plan for all public agencies and employees.

ABOUT THE CHARACTERS

Barbara Balance is the new personnel director for Yellow Bluff. She has a masters in public administration and is just beginning her career.

Colleen Keenan has been the receptionist in the city's main office for five years. She has an English degree from the local community college.

NEW JOB, NEW CHALLENGE

A fundamental trait for a successful career in the field of human resources is the ability to be a good judge of people. The "rule of three" (recommending three candidates for positions) and other guidelines of civil service employment assure that merit is the guiding principle of public sector employment, but within these criteria there is always room to apply other skills of judgment. A good personnel manager has to be able to find the right fit between the worker and the job description, as well as getting a feel for how the worker might fit into the informal culture of the work area. It is always these intangibles that make a position in personnel more challenging.

So far, Barbara Balance has shown exceptional political skills in her new career as personnel director for the small town. Political skills are always critical for a bureaucrat, but it was even more necessary for Balance to tread lightly because there were many within the city administration who felt a full-time staff position for personnel was unnecessary. This, of course, was exacerbated by the inherent tension within any bureaucracy that exists between line and staff positions in the city. Yet, it was also clear that the growing number of regulations governing public sector employment necessitated a separate, full-time staff office to implement them. A primary new area of the personnel function was implementation of equity legislation, including a new comparable worth program and a formal policy on sexual harassment.

EQUALITY IN THE WORKPLACE

While these new equity polices had made her position more secure, they had also caused Balance headaches. Until the 1990s, the American workforce was still somewhat divided into gendered occupations. Within this division of labor, typical "male jobs" had higher pay than typical "female jobs." The argument often was that men had to support a family on their wages, while women were working for "extra" money. This remained the trend in spite of the Equal Pay Act of 1963 (an amendment to the Fair Labor Standards Act of 1938), which prohibited discrimination in wages based on sex. Thus, employees should receive the same pay for equal work, unless higher pay is a result of seniority or part of a system based on the quality and quantity of worker production. However, this did not address levels of pay across typically gendered positions. For instance, virtually all positions in the city's street department were higher paying than the office jobs regardless of levels of education, training, or skill required. In a classic case for comparable worth, all of the positions in the street department were held by men and all the office positions were occupied by women.

Balance's first major challenge had been to implement the new comparable worth program. All jobs within the city were subjected to a job analysis. Factors such as level of supervision, education and/or training, and risk level were calculated for each position. As was expected, the positions occupied by women were found to be underpaid according to the new job analysis. The problem for the city was then what to do about the pay inequities? As with most cities, budgets are planned out years in advance, and the largest portion of the budget is for payroll. In response to the findings, the city devised a five-year plan to help raise the pay to meet the new criteria of the revised job descriptions for the underpaid jobs, which were primarily office jobs held by women.

While the comparable worth analysis had completely strained Balance's small staff, she was confident that things would settle down. She would soon realize, however, that her problems were just beginning. During the year-long job analysis, an increased awareness of the pay inequity began to become evident among the women working in city offices. Once or twice in the past, a woman had tried to apply for a position in the street department or another male-dominated department within the city, but none had ever been hired. A few months into the analysis, a position opened in the street department for an entry-level job. Colleen Keenan, with five years of experience as a city receptionist, was tired of being inside all day, stuck in a dead-end position. The salary was higher for the posted position, but even more importantly, she would have a chance for promotion in the street department. So she applied for the job.

A job with the city was considered a good opportunity, and there were many applicants. The civil service exam and other minimal requirements narrowed the candidates to three: two men, who had never worked for the city, and Keenan. Aside from Keenan's experience with the city, in all other aspects the applicants were equally qualified. The position itself and all positions within the career track did not require physical skills beyond the capacity of the three applicants. A harder criterion was how each applicant would "fit" within the culture of the all-male street department. Balance suspected that Keenan might have some extra hurdles to overcome to "fit in with the guys," but she was impressed with Keenan's personal interview and her determination to succeed. Keenan seemed confident and very able to take care of herself. The final decision then came down to a judgment call for Balance and the managers of the street department. Following a policy in the city that favored promoting from within, Keenan was awarded the job.

THE FALLOUT

Sexual Harassment

Six months later Balance was somewhat surprised when she received a message saying that Keenan needed to speak to her about the city's sexual harassment policy. This new policy followed state guidelines that were based on the Equal Employment Opportunity Commission's (EEOC) definition of sexual harassment. Under these standards there are two types of conduct that violate federal law. One is commonly referred to as "quid pro quo" and the other as "hostile work environment."

EEOC guidelines define quid pro quo harassment as unwelcome or sex-based conduct that impacts employment. For instance, quid pro quo harassment would be when a supervisor demanded sexual favors in return for continued employment. If the claimant can prove that the conduct happened, and it was "unwelcomed," the organization is liable. The problem with the unwelcome standard is that the harassed person must generally confront the supervisor actively and on the record. This is often a very high hurdle for the harassed individual to verify, given that they are often in a subordinate position within the hierarchy and are probably traumatized by the experience.

The second type of conduct—the so-called hostile environment—includes conduct by anyone, including co-workers. Under EEOC guidelines, the purpose or effect of this conduct has to be judged unreasonable, interfering with the individual's work performance, or "creating an intimidating, hostile, or offensive working environment." With this type of harassment, the courts have generally looked to see the severity and/or pervasiveness of the unwelcomed conduct. Thus, unlike the quid pro quo that may be only one incident, hostile work environment persists over time and interferes with the ability to perform one's job.

Employers are strictly liable for the quid pro quo harassment perpetrated by supervisors and also liable for hostile environment sexual harassment, if it can be proven that the employer knew or should have known about the conduct and did nothing to prevent it.

The Complaint

Balance used these EEOC guidelines and the Supreme Court rulings in 1998 to establish the grounds for what is called an affirmative defense. The core of this approach is a formal written policy on sexual harassment, which is then communicated to every employee. The final step in this approach is to actively follow up on each complaint. Balance had disseminated the policy to all the supervisors and had tried to impress upon them the importance of communicating this policy to all people working in their departments. Until Keenan's call, there had been no reaction to the policy.

As soon as Keenan walked in the door, Balance could tell something was wrong. Their conversation follows:

Balance: Colleen, come in. Have a seat. So, how is it going in the street department?

Keenan: I'm not really sure. Most of the work I do is not difficult, but some things are starting to happen that make me feel weird.

Balance: Weird?

Keenan: Yeah, I don't think some of the men want a woman working in *their* department.

Balance: What do you mean? Has something happened?

Keenan: At first I thought everything was going to be great and then I started to notice different things show up in the area we eat in. It is kind of a lounge where we can relax during breaks and lunch. The first thing was a couple of *Playboy* magazines that were left open on the table to the pictures. I didn't think too much of it until a couple of days later when I found one of the centerfolds taped inside my locker. It was just there. No one ever said anything to me about it.

Balance: Did you tell your supervisor about it?

Keenan: No, I didn't know what to say, and I didn't want to be seen as a trouble maker.

Balance: Did anything else happen?

Keenan: Mostly it would be things that the guys say. They tell a lot of sex jokes around me. I'm not sure what to do. They aren't funny to me, but I'm afraid that the guys won't accept me. If I don't laugh, they tell me to lighten up and stop acting like a prude. I've known a lot of these guys for years and this is just kind of how they act. They have always been sort of rowdy. For instance, there is a poster of a nearly nude woman on a motorcycle hanging on the wall in the shop. That's why I wanted to talk to you. No one has tried anything really serious with me, but they do ask me personal questions like, "How is your sex life going Keenan?" Sometimes a couple of the guys pinch me on the butt, and last week I found a jockstrap in my locker. I'm beginning to have trouble sleeping, and I am getting to where I don't even want to go into work. Is this sexual harassment or am I just too sensitive? I want to know what is going on before I make a big deal of this. Maybe there is just something wrong with me.

ROLE-PLAY ASSIGNMENT

Acting as Balance, what course of action, if any, do you pursue regarding Keenan's statements?

QUESTIONS FOR DISCUSSION

1. What should be your first course of action? Should either you or Keenan talk to anyone else or consult with anyone else?

2. Under the new policy of affirmative defense every complaint must be taken seriously, but is this really a complaint or is Keenan just being too sensitive? How do you know if this is really a complaint? What does it mean to "take something seriously"? Are words enough if they carry no direct proposition, and does the pinch make it more serious?

3. Should you try to comfort Keenan? Is it possible that the guys in the street department are just trying to give Keenan a kind of initiation into their culture? Aren't departments allowed to have informal cultures and does everyone have to be politically correct all the time?

4. The hostile work environment standard requires the complainant to show that the conduct is harmful to her ability to perform her job. How do you determine if the incidents are true? How do you determine if the incidents were harmful to Keenan's job performance?

5. How might you make sure that the sexual harassment policies are taken seriously by all city employees and departments? How do you prevent future such incidents from happening?

SOURCES FOR FURTHER READING

Barrier, M. "Sexual Harassment: The Supreme Court's Message." *Nation's Business* December (1998): 1–20.

Kelly, R. M., and P. M. Stambaugh. "Sexual Harassment in the States." In *Current Issues in Public Administration*. Frederick S. Lane ed. New York: St. Martin's Press, 1994.

Merit Systems Protection Board home page. http://www.mspb.gov

Lemoncheck, L., and M. Hajdin. *Sexual Harassment: A Debate* New York: Roman and Littlefield, 1997.

U.S. Equal Employment Opportunity Commission home page. http://www.eeoc.gov

- "informal- solve it yourself
- disciplinary action against males who harass
- training program - educate about harassment
- combine all

V

7

Picking Up the Pieces: Grievances in the Hiring Process

Saundra J. Reinke

ABOUT THE AGENCY

Boone Air Force Base (AFB) is a large education and training facility, supporting more than 3,000 military and 1,200 civilian service personnel. Like most military installations, Boone AFB has a child development center that provides federally subsidized childcare for military personnel.

ABOUT THE CHARACTERS

Marilyn James, chief of the staffing section in civilian personnel, is ultimately responsible for making sure the more than 1,200 civil service positions on Boone AFB are filled with qualified people.

Claudia Tyson, director of the child development center at Boone AFB, is an aggressive, competent manager who has worked hard to ensure the new center will be ready to open when construction is finished in about thirty days.

Sheri Delgado and Dawn Jackson are the two non-appropriated fund employees who filed the grievance in this case.

John Brown is the union representative for Delgado and Jackson. He is currently running for president of the union.

Jim Smith is the staffing specialist working with the child development center.

BACKGROUND ON THE GRIEVANCE

Marilyn James, the new chief of staffing at Boone AFB has been on the job for less than a week, and she is already facing her first serious crisis. This morning, she received a call from John Brown, a representative of the union. He asked for an appointment to discuss a grievance involving the selection process for two positions at the child development center. To get the facts, James held a long meeting with George Jones, the base labor relations specialist, and Jim Smith, the staffing specialist serving the child development center. They provided James with the following background information.

The child development center will provide federally subsidized childcare for military personnel. The subsidy is not paid directly to users. Instead, the Air Force pays for construction, repairs, utilities, food and other supplies, and a portion of the staff for the center. The manager, the training specialist for the center, and one-third of the childcare providers are civil service employees; the remaining employees are paid through fees charged to users. This latter group of employees, referred to as "non-appropriated fund employees," is paid the same as the civil service employees. However, they are governed by a different personnel system, closely modeled on private practice. As a consequence, they have fewer benefits and protections than their civil service co-workers; hence, non-appropriated fund employees have a strong desire to move to civil service positions when they become available.

The new child development center, currently nearing completion and scheduled to open in thirty days, will almost double current capacity. As a consequence, the Air Force approved the addition of two new, full-time, civil service positions for childcare providers. The manager, Claudia Tyson, had heard from a peer at another base that she could split the full-time positions into part-time positions and gain flexibility in staffing patterns while still being able to work the part-time employees up to a maximum of thirty-five hours per week. Tyson called Smith, and he advised that this would be OK. Tyson split one of the new positions into two part-time positions and worked with the staffing specialist to advertise and fill those positions. Two new employees hired in this process have been on the job for about a month now, and Tyson is very happy with their performance. She kept the other position open, intending to fill it when the new center was closer to completion.

IMPROPER PERSONNEL PROCEDURES

The day after the two new employees had been hired, Smith discovered, during a routine conversation with the payroll office, that he had given Tyson bad advice. While she could indeed split the two positions, by law she could not work the part-time employees for more than twenty hours per week. When informed of the mistake, Tyson was furious and told Smith that if that was the case, she was not interested in having part-time employees. When asked what he would do to fix this problem, Smith advised her to simply convert the one split position back into a full-time position, and he would place one of the new employees in the reconverted full-time position; the other employee could be placed in the still vacant full-time position. He assured her there was no need to re-advertise the positions. Satisfied, Tyson agreed to this solution and the two of them completed the appropriate paperwork to make the changes. Smith admitted he had not reviewed either regulations or the local union contract before advising Tyson to take this action.

Two weeks later, an individual working in another unit at Boone AFB who wanted to apply for one of the two full-time positions as a childcare provider confronted Tyson with an informal grievance. In it the individual alleged that Boone AFB and Tyson had violated Air Force regulations and the union contract by not properly opening and advertising the two new full-time civil service positions at the child development center. Tyson told the individual that there was "nothing she could do" and that she was "only following civilian personnel's instructions."

[Handwritten margin notes:]
- *adopt new proper procedures*
- *re advertize*
- *move the part times to full then adopt new.*

As a consequence, John Brown, the union representative, asked for a meeting with James, chief of the staffing section; Tyson, the director of the center; Sheri Delgado and Dawn Jackson (the two employees placed into the positions) and the aggrieved employee to try and work out a fair solution at the informal level of the grievance process. The aggrieved individual has demanded that the two positions be re-opened and properly advertised.

The AFB labor relations specialist advised James that, while the contract does not cover this specific situation, the intent of its provisions on selection is to ensure that all employees are afforded the opportunity to apply for all vacancies. He is deeply concerned about the possible impact and adverse publicity, since Brown, the union rep, is running for president of the union. He recommends the positions be re-opened and advertised.

Smith, on the other hand, is adamant that he advised the only fair solution since, if the positions were re-opened and advertised, the two incumbents (Delgado and Jackson) might lose their jobs. Further, he is convinced that the personnel office will lose all credibility with management if the positions are re-opened and advertised, and that the child development center could lose two good employees.

ROLE-PLAY ASSIGNMENT

As the newest member of the civilian personnel management team and personal assistant to James, your credibility is on the line, as is your relationship with management and the union. What will you advise James to do?

QUESTIONS FOR DISCUSSION

1. Who do you think is right—Jones, the labor relations specialist, or Smith, the staffing officer?
2. Who should take the responsibility for redressing the grievance—your office or management? What advice do you have to redress the informal grievance?
3. If you do decide it is best to re-open and advertise the positions, how will you convince management to accept this decision? What should you do with those already in the positions?
4. If you think Smith provided management with bad advice, do you think he should be disciplined?
5. What will you do to rebuild relations with the union and with management? How can such problems be prevented in the future, and what process would you recommend be put in place regarding such personnel decisions?

SOURCES FOR FURTHER READING

EEOC Regulation. *Uniform Guidelines on Employee Selection Procedures*. 1607. 1978. http://www.eeoc.gov/regs/index.html

Hays, S.W. "Staffing the Bureaucracy: Employee Recruitment and Selection," *Handbook of Human Resource Management in Government*. Stephen Condrey ed. San Francisco: Jossey-Bass, 1999.

Witt, S. L., and W. D. Patton. "Recruiting for a High-performance Workforce." In *Human Resource Management in Local Government: An Essential Guide*. Siegrun Fox Freyss ed. Washington, D.C.: International City/County Management Association, 1999.

Cherry County Blues: A Problem of Low Morale and High Turnover

Jeffrey S. Ashley & Kimberly Bejcek

ABOUT THE AGENCY

Cherry County Human Services Department (CCHS) is a state agency responsible for a wide range of social intervention services. The Children's Services Program handles caseloads of protective services, foster care, delinquency, and prevention. This program is noted for its high caseloads, overwhelming paperwork, and stressful, sometimes dangerous, field work.

ABOUT THE CHARACTERS

David Klenk is the Cherry County Human Services Department (CCHS) director.

Nancy Jones is the CCHS program manager who was recently hired to fill the vacancy left for several months. She has supervisory experience in children's services but is not a native of Cherry County. She oversees the Children's Services supervisors. Klenk is her boss.

Bob Strong, a supervisor in the Children's Services Program, was recently turned down for promotion to CCHS program manager.

Ann Smith, a supervisor in the Children's Services Program, is so overwhelmed that she is asking to be transferred to a position in another department.

Mary Carter is a caseworker within CCHS who appears to be able to write her own rules. She has a reputation for handling tough cases and has developed a high profile in the community.

Judge Kathleen Owen, the family court judge of Cherry County, finds herself having to rely on evidence and information that CCHS provides workers and is frustrated with their lack of professionalism and inability to work together.

OVERVIEW OF THE PROBLEM

The Cherry County Human Services agency (CCHS) employs sixteen child welfare social workers. They handle children's protective services, foster care, delinquency services, and child abuse prevention cases. Two supervisors—Bob Strong and Ann Smith—supervise these workers. The supervisors report to a program manager, who in turn reports to David Klenk, the CCHS director.

CCHS has had a great deal of staff turnover in the past ten years, and the staff who have remained have a reputation for being burned out. They are perceived by their peers and the community as unwilling to pursue legal and social work intervention on child abuse and neglect referrals, unless the allegations are so obvious that they cannot avoid taking action or unless law enforcement has intervened. Three of the five protective services workers have more than fifteen years in protective services, but each has been reprimanded numerous times for failure to complete paperwork in a timely manner. Aside from these reprimands, there have been other instances of misconduct throughout the organization. One worker was fired six months ago for gross negligence of duty. Several workers are known for their tendency to leave work early. And many employees conduct non-work-related activities on county time. The agency has responded to these problems by creating more stringent reporting requirements for the caseworkers in the field. The responsible workers find these new requirements more time consuming and a demonstration of management's lack of confidence and trust in them. Low morale has resulted. Those employees trying their best find the stringent reporting requirements to be added paperwork that takes away from their client contact time.

As with most social service agencies, stress levels are high. This can be partly attributed to a change in public attitudes toward the cost of assisting others and the negativity in general toward welfare programs. Those who enter the field with the hope of helping people who are less fortunate often find themselves overworked, underpaid, and the object of public scorn.

A TROUBLED AGENCY, TROUBLED WORKERS

There are currently four foster care workers. There has been a 100 percent turnover in this position several times in recent years. The average foster care worker remains on the job about two years. Yet, it takes approximately one year for a new foster care worker to learn all the policies and legal procedures needed to do the job well. New foster care and protective services workers are required to attend eight weeks of training before getting their own caseloads. Currently, there is one foster care worker on mental health disability leave, with no anticipated date for returning to work. CCHS is not able to fill this position until more definite information is received regarding the employee's condition. Foster parents in Cherry County even joke about how many new foster care workers they "have broken in and trained." Paperwork, policy mandates, high caseloads, and demanding court requirements create a stressful atmosphere, resulting in burnout in this position.

The nature of the work requires teamwork among staff and cooperative working relationships. This is all but non-existent at CCHS. In fact, many of the workers display open contempt for one another. One protective services worker, Mary Carter, has had a long standing feud with her co-worker. This has been allowed to fester to the point that Carter often calls her colleague derogatory names in public and in meetings. Despite supervisor attempts to curb this behavior, Carter's outspoken personality and reputation for handling some of the worst child molestation and abuse cases seem to grant her immunity from discipline. Additionally, she has developed alliances with important community leaders. Others in the office are aware of the situation and hope they never get on Carter's bad side. In fact, most employees avoid her.

Most workers prefer to go about their business without conferring with other workers, even though they might have important contacts on a case. In some instances, this causes significant lapses in key information and time for court hearings regarding child custody and protection matters. The situation at CCHS is so bad that community members have lost respect for the agency and are reluctant to make child abuse referrals unless there is no other alternative. This frustration with CCHS is universal throughout the community. Workers with poor reputations are also unlikely to be hired by another agency or county, should they want to transfer.

Cherry County Family Court judge, Kathleen Owen, has met with Klenk, expressing her concerns regarding the problems at CCHS, particularly as it relates to her courtroom. Although she understands the problems workers have with overwhelming paperwork requirements and policy mandates, Owen is asking CCHS to remedy the situation as soon as possible. Professional relationships between many CCHS workers and the court have been strained. CCHS workers who believe they are doing a good job presenting evidence to the court are feeling slighted and maligned during court proceedings.

Several months have passed since the previous program manager retired. CCHS has finally been given approval to hire Nancy Jones, a former protective services worker and current supervisor of children's services in a neighboring county. Bob Strong, a supervisor in CCHS, interviewed for the position and felt he had a good chance of being promoted, because he had handled many of the program manager duties while the position was vacant. He has interviewed on a number of occasions for upper management positions but has not been promoted. His disappointment is evident. Strong rarely does anything beyond his immediate duties now. Ann Smith, the other supervisor, did not interview for the program manager position. She has been a supervisor in Cherry County for three years and has spent so much time dealing with disciplinary problems of employees and constant staff bickering that she is feeling overwhelmed and wants to transfer to another agency.

THE CHARGE

Jones began her new job with a meeting between herself, the judge, and Klenk, the head of CCHS. During this meeting the basic problems with the staff were discussed. As a result of the meeting, Klenk has given Jones three months to put a plan together to improve relationships among the staff, repair strained relationships with the community, and increase worker effectiveness in the courtroom. Jones understood the difficulty of the charge, as there were other issues facing the agency. For instance, CCHS workers are supported by a strong union and any attempt to fire a burned out worker or even move them unwillingly into another position would result in a union grievance. Protective services workers are the highest paid children's services workers, so a move to another position within the agency would likely result in a pay cut.

Jones was also contemplating another problem that was brought to her attention before the meeting. It seems the budget had again been cut for the next fiscal year. This had become a common occurrence, especially during election years. More and more, the agency was asked to do more with less. Child abuse, neglect, and abandonment were at an all-time high, while funding to tackle the problems was insufficient. CCHS might even lose a position (most likely one of the caseworkers) that, under personnel policies, would be the least senior worker, who happened to be one of the few, hard working, enthusiastic employees in the agency. Jones realized that the agency director had little commitment to the child welfare program, mainly because he viewed the staff as incompetent and lazy. Klenk had little experience in children's services throughout his career and did not understand the complexity of the job. His focus was largely on raising his level of prominence within the community, and he had little time or patience to concern himself with staffing problems. Jones worried that Klenk would try to eliminate the child worker position in favor of a computer technology position.

ROLE-PLAY ASSIGNMENT

You are Nancy Jones, the new program manager. You must develop a plan for David Klenk, CCHS director.

QUESTIONS FOR DISCUSSION

[handwritten margin notes: "market" leader pay + pay higher wages • pay per performance • motivation theories ↳ McClelland Need for Achievement ↳ Maslow's Needs • McGregor's Theory X↔Y]

1. There are a number of serious problems with the organization. Identify some of the most serious of them. How did the atmosphere of the agency get to be so negative and problematic?

2. What do you do first? Identify the barriers to any plan of action. What interests and pressures will be facing Jones? What other resources could be utilized to improve the overall atmosphere of CCHS?

3. What plan should be developed regarding low morale among the staff?

4. It seems the agency has a PR problem. How would you improve the agency's relations with the community and court?

5. A new manager dealing with long-time employees always faces the challenge of gaining their support and respect. This is especially true for Jones, who is not from Cherry County and who must contend with Strong, who had applied for her job. What problems can Jones expect to have in working with the employees, and what should be done to facilitate positive relations with the staff?

[handwritten: • establish a multi-disciplinary team]

SOURCES FOR FURTHER READING

Harrison, M. T. *Occupational Culture in the Workplace*. Ithica, NY: ILR Press, 1995.

Harrison, M. T., and J. M. Beyer. *The Cultures of Work Organizations*. Englewood Cliffs, NJ: Prentice-Hall, 1993.

Herzberg, F. *Work and the Nature of Man*. Cleveland, OH: World Publishing, 1966.

Vroom, V. *Work and Motivation*. New York: John Wiley & Sons, 1964.

Part III

Managing Budgets, Financial Resources, and Technology

THE BUDGETING CHALLENGE FOR MANAGERS

There are several ways to study budgets and budgets serve many functions. In general, the budget serves as the basis for action taken by an organization.[1] Budgets specify the funding amounts, resource needs, and duties to be undertaken by the agency and its employees. At the macro level, a budget considers the amount and type of resources needed by agencies in order to fulfill their mission. At this level, the budget reflects government's role in society, the state of the economy and macroeconomic impacts of government spending on employment and other economic forces, and broad goals of the agency. At the micro level, budgets focus on such questions as which program within an agency receives funds and how much. In such instances, budgets tend to itemize expenses in *line items* with funds being listed and appropriated in categories such as supplies or travel. In between such macro and micro levels is a mid-range whereby the budget of each agency is determined.

Most government budgets are annual documents, even though reformers have been encouraging a more long-term focus for budgeting.[2] The federal government functions on a fiscal year running from October 1 to September 30, as mandated by the Congressional Budget Act of 1974. Many state and local governments operate on a July 1 to June 30 fiscal year. Still, the effects of budgets are rarely restricted to only one year. In reality, the budget also shapes the organization for more than the year covered in the document, as it often serves as a planning document, establishing a course of action for the future.[3] Relatedly, the budgeting process tends to be *incremental*, which means that previous budgets serve as the basis for future budgets, so there is often continuity from budget to budget. In an effort to increase long-term planning, many agencies at different levels of government submit five-year budget forecasts. This positions the budget to be a planning document and promotes a long-term focus for public services and programs.

The budget is also something of a legal document in that it is an agreement between the executive and legislative branches of government that states publically the nature of public services offered for the upcoming fiscal year. Even though the legislative branch is charged with approving the amounts contained within the budget, budgets are very much administrative and executive documents. Article I of the Constitution grants the legislature primacy in taxing and spending, but it is the executive branch that initiates and develops the budget. Moreover, the executive branch must implement the programs contained in the budget with the resources allocated through the budget.

Because of the role government plays in economic affairs, as well as the sheer size of government budgets, budgets are economic documents. In many communities the public sector is among the largest employers. The simple existence of the number of citizens employed by government stabilizes or drives the economies of many small communities. Pay day brings with it an injection of income and spending in the community's economy. Likewise, public spending has far reaching effects. Money invested in one program or sector of the economy might have multiple intended or unintended effects. Beginning in the 1930s with Franklin Roosevelt's New Deal, which used government spending and an assortment of public programs from *public works* projects to banking regulations, government assumed a key role in the state of the U.S. economy. This *Keynesian* revolution, named for John Maynard Keynes' theories of the benefits of public spending in promoting economic growth, positioned government as manager of the economy.[4] Ever since the administration of FDR, government budgets have used taxing and spending to achieve a full range of economic goals. The expansion of public programs in the ensuing years has resulted in ever-increasing budgets.

THE POLITICS OF BUDGETING

As discussed above, budgets serve many functions, but chief among them is that they are political documents. In his classic book *The Politics of the Budgetary Process*, Aaron Wildavsky stated that the budget is the "heart of the political process."[5] It is through the political process that budgets are developed and public programs funded. The dollar amounts devoted to each program reflect political values and the give and take of the political process. This remains the case even though part of the federal budget, for instance, is beyond the control of those crafting the budget. For example, the rise of entitlement programs such as social security, unemployment insurance, and medicare are programs that are funded according to how many individuals qualify for their eligibility requirements. As such, there are legal obligations to fund such programs and the level of funding is to a degree decided by a formula, thus taking some control out of the hands of elected officials. So too at the state and local level are some programs beyond the full discretion of managers or elected officials while other programs share funding between several governmental units.

Historically, the budgetary process was haphazard and inadequate. In part because of the debts resulting from World War I, the 1921 Budget and Accounting Act sought to institute a more formalized budgeting process. Departments within the executive branch were required to forward their budget requests to the president through the old Bureau of the Budget (now known as the Office of Management and Budget or OMB). This approach remains to the present day. With the assistance of OMB, the president then proposes the annual budget, sets priorities, and submits the document to Congress, which debates and often alters the budget before approving it. The process has been described as "incrementalism" because most budgets are increased gradually and predictably based on the previous year's budget amount.[6] There are a variety of reasons why the base budget of the previous year is used to formulate the following year's budget. For instance, because of the limited time and expertise of those making decisions on the budget, the safest and most politically expedient approach is often one defined by small, incremental variations on the past.

In recent years, the U.S. Congress has not always completed all work on the budget before the period marking the start of the new fiscal year, as disagreements between the executive and legislative branch, between the House and Senate, and among members of the Congress are common. Likewise, the Congress does not always approve all appropriation bills, and agencies do not always get the resources they want or need to operate. When Congress fails to complete work on the budget in a timely manner, agencies are often appropriated what is known as a *continuing resolution*, a measure that permits agencies to continue functioning at the spending level of the previous year until action can be completed on the new budget. Sometimes agencies also receive *supplemental funds* in addition to the initial amount appropriated. Agencies can borrow from the Treasury if funds are needed but unavailable through the traditional legislative appropriation process. However, mechanisms are in place to limit and regulate their borrowing authority. If the administrative agency fails to spend all the money allocated to it by the legislature, the remaining funds, known as the *overhang*, must be returned to the Treasury at the end of the fiscal year. In certain circumstances, arrangements are made to retain these unspent funds for future spending. Yet, because of the way the budget is derived, agencies have a vested interest in spending all the money they are given, as unspent money might often result in lower appropriations in future years.

The agencies of the executive branch spend their funds, and often the funding is made available to agency managers on a quarterly basis. Federal managers are informed of how much money is available by the Treasury Department and the General Accounting Office (GAO), which is an agency of the Congress. The GAO also monitors spending to make sure it is spent as intended and as stated. Because of the nature of the budgetary process as a highly politicized task, managers face uncertainty about the amount of funds they will have available. This makes it difficult to plan for the future and, ironically, offers an argument for the predictability of incremental budgeting.

Other challenges to managers include dealing with cycles and varying amounts of funds needed. For instance, if an event threatening the nation's security arises, the armed forces will require an amount of funds perhaps unforeseen when the budget was developed in order to respond to the crisis. The U.S. Park Service typically requires more resources in the summer months, when visitors to the national parks increase dramatically. The same phenomenon is experienced by the U.S. Postal Service during holidays, when the volume of mail increases.

DECISION-MAKING ISSUES TO CONSIDER AS YOU READ THE CASES

It is difficult to find many champions of the budgetary process as it has been practiced and, not surprisingly, numerous attempts at reform have been undertaken.[7] Some reforms have focused on how budgets are developed while other reforms have sought to overcome the degree to which plain old politics shapes budgets.

PPBS

One approach to budgeting, credited to the administration of President Lyndon B. Johnson, is known as Planning Programing Budget Systems. PPBS was also adopted by several state and local governments. Conventional approaches to developing a budget designated items such as the costs of travel, equipment, and supplies to organizational units. But PPBS allocates resources to the various activities and services of the agency. Emphasis is also placed on analyzing expenditures and thereby attempting to use the most economical approach to providing the service.

The primary characteristic of PPBS includes replacing organizations as the unit of analysis with the program and the program's goals. Nor are programs and goals limited to a particular agency or unit. Rather, they could cross the boundaries of organizational units. Likewise, resources are allocated according to goals and program units as opposed to organizations. Goals also drive the development of programs and budgets and each goal is subject to analysis. This analysis includes efforts to identify alternative approaches to goal attainment, and each agency must justify its requests in light of the analysis of alternative methods. In the PPBS approach, conventional line items remain how costs are listed, however the budget document lists the aggregate costs necessary to attain goals.

Unfortunately, PPBS encountered opposition by legislative bodies who often favored traditional budgeting processes and existing relationships with agencies. These legislators had mastered the old system and had built networks within the agencies and interests to obtain preferred items for their constituencies. As such, they were reluctant to limit their political advantages. Similarly, some managers and agencies also opposed PPBS, as the power of agencies was threatened by the new approach. In the previous system, it was easy to identify how agencies were spending money because the organization was the unit of analysis.

ZBB

With a reliance on analysis of data as the basis of budgetary decision making, Zero-Based Budgeting (ZBB) hoped to replace the traditional reliance on previous budgets and incrementalism as bases for budget development. This reform, initiated by President Jimmy Carter, used both agencies and programs as the decision unit. Under ZBB every expenditure was subject to comprehensive analysis, and this analysis would occur from the foundation without a base. As such, in theory the entire budget would be evaluated, and for any program to be continued it would have to be justified each year. The result of ZBB would be the elimination of unnecessary programs and expenditures.

Managers were instructed to prepare multiple approaches and programs and rank each one. This not only permitted comparison but forced the various approaches to compete with one another. Managers also considered various possible cost options for each activity based on the bare minimum amount needed to achieve the intended result to optimal budgetary amounts. All budget options would then be ranked and assessed by street-level managers on up to OMB.

The problem with ZBB was that it failed to consider the political realities of the budgetary process. Managers were hesitant to rank programs and thus reveal honest "base" amounts of funding for fear they would lose funds or even entire programs or agencies. It also proved to be too time consuming. Evaluating every facet of the budget on an annual basis takes too long, requires considerable information, and itself costs too much money.

Recent Reforms

One of the problems with reforming how budgets are developed is finding a way to neutralize the natural political practice of padding one's own pockets. It is easy to cut someone else's program but difficult to cut your own. Members of Congress find it necessary to bring special favors and programs back home to their constituents, but such practices inflate the budget. Recent reforms have attempted to deal with run-away spending and the prevalence of such *pork barrel* politics.

One such effort was undertaken by Senators Phil Gramm, Warren Rudman, and Ernest Hollings in the 1980s. In an effort to force cuts in the budget, the 1985 Balanced Budget and Emergency Deficit Control Act initiated automatic cuts in the event the Congress failed to reduce the size of the budget deficit. To tame the huge deficits of the '80s, targeted amounts for the deficit were identified. The goal was to gradually cut the amount of the deficit each year until a balanced budget was realized in 1991. The mechanism for achieving this was an automatic cut that took effect if Congress failed to shrink the deficit to the targeted amount. A *sequestration* would then cut half from defense and half from non-defense programs in the amount needed to reach the targeted deficit goal. The effort was challenged in the Supreme Court and, because of legal-Constitutional questions and the ever-present politics of the budgetary process, was never put into practice.

Another failed reform was the *balanced budget amendment*. Proponents of spending cuts attempted to push a Constitutional amendment that would force Congress to pass a balanced budget each year. The exception to this was in the event of an extreme crisis such as war. In such instances, a clause such as a two-thirds vote in the Congress would override the mandatory balanced budget. Theoretically, this reform was, like the previous effort, intended to force legislators to make the tough decision and live within balanced budgets. Most critics felt that in addition to being politically unrealistic, the measure was shortsighted because it ignored the fact that budgets are prepared over one year prior to their effective date. It would therefore be impossible to forecast such a crisis and incorporate such contingencies into the budget. Advocates of Keynesian economics also believed that the amendment would undermine government's ability to spend money aimed at boosting economic growth.

A popular reform for controlling spending in the states is the *line-item veto*. The majority of governors have at their disposal the line-item veto, which enables them to veto—or eliminate—a particular line item from a larger bill without having to veto the entire bill in a pass-all or veto-all approach. Chief executives are thus theoretically able to weed out unnecessary spending items while passing necessary bills. Many members of Congress have been opposed to extending this practice to the president, as it might limit their ability to include favored projects or pork barrel spending in bills. After briefly being passed into law during the Clinton administration, the high court overturned the line-item veto on grounds that it violated the system of checks and balances by granting the president lawmaking powers.

Administrators must abide by the budget, and part of the managerial task is influenced by budgetary matters. Managers try to expand their budgets and attempt to justify budget requests to elected officials. Skilled managers learn to operate within their budgets or find ways of increasing their budgets. For instance, interest groups and clients served by agency programs might be employed in the fight to increase budgets.

The politics of the budgetary process remains as a defining characteristic. A lasting impact of PPBS, ZBB, and some of the more recent reforms, however, has been an emphasis on making explicit the goals of budgets and programs as well as conducting budget analysis has been institutionalized in many of the performance-based budgeting and management initiatives of the 1990s. Additionally, management information systems (MIS), computer technologies, and other technology-driven initiatives are aiding managers in developing and analyzing their financial resources and needs.

The Politics of County Budgeting: Piecing Together the Budget Puzzle

Clinton P. Taffe

ABOUT THE ORGANIZATION

South County, with a population of roughly 270,000, is a medium-sized jurisdiction. There are three incorporated cities within South County, with the majority of the population living within these cities. The county has enjoyed a healthy fiscal condition, but that has changed.

ABOUT THE CHARACTERS

Board of County Commissioners each has his/her own agenda on issues, but as far as budgeting is concerned, they firmly want their projects funded without having to raise the millage rate. In the past they have been hesitant to raise revenues to help fund programs like libraries, parks, and rural fire protection. All three of these county functions are major expenses (multi-million dollar programs). In part, because of this, the county is now facing budget problems.

George Wiley is the county administrator and has been with the county for nearly twenty years. He enjoys much support from the county commission and is known for attacking personnel issues like a surgeon. He goes in quick, takes out the problem, and deals with any fallout issues as they come up. During his tenure there have been five different directors of the Office of Management and Budget (OMB). Three have left because of the long hours and weekend work the job requires, and two were given the option of resigning. The administrator is employed through a contractual relationship with the board.

Mike Ketchem, the OMB director, controls a small staff whose responsibility is to develop a balanced budget for the board's approval annually and to produce a professional budget document that citizens can understand. The director "serves at the pleasure" of the administrator and board.

SOUTH COUNTY

South County is a non-charter county which, as such, operates under state law that, in terms of governance, has not changed since statehood in the early 1800s. The South County Board of County Commissioners is composed of seven commissioners, five elected by district and two elected at-large to ensure representation of the county's very diverse population. The board itself is comprised of four White males, two African-American males, and the chairperson is a White female. With seven members, it takes at least four votes to win any decision that comes before the board.

As the OMB director for South County, Mike Ketchem has, for his six-year tenure, managed to balance the accounting books by finding a dollar here and a dollar there. He has also managed to win five consecutive national budgeting awards. The commission, along with Ketchem's direct supervisor, the county administrator, have come to depend on Ketchem's "expertise" to pull the county out of its yearly revenue dilemma at the last minute. But this year is different. The county faces a budget shortfall.

BUDGET SHORTFALL

Many years ago South County limited the type of industrial development that could be sited within its boundaries in order to protect a pristine water aquifer that flows within the limestone beneath the county. Although the act assured protection of the natural environment, the building limitations have drastically reduced the county's ability to attract businesses to the area, which would help boost Ad Valorem (property tax) revenues. Raising revenues is further hindered by the fact that three quarters of the property within the county encompasses a federal forest, junior college, state correctional facility, or public facilities owned by cities, the county, and school boards, all of which are exempt from Ad Valorem taxation. In short, this means that the property owners living or conducting private business—on what amounts to only one quarter of county lands— cover the entire cost for improvements and basic operating expenses for the county.

South County has been experiencing an Ad Valorem revenue shortfall for the past five years. Each year, in order to fund unplanned and unbudgeted projects approved by the board, the General Fund Contingency (Ad Valorem rainy day fund) has been tapped and thus reduced. This General Fund Contingency has dropped from a healthy $16 million— exceeding the county's policy of 10 percent of Ad Valorem revenues—down to $9 million, the bare minimum amount permitted by county policy. Similarly, the General Fund Unappropriated Fund Balance (a mouthful that includes the funds needed to run the county's operations in case of an emergency, without the need to incur debt) has fallen drastically to cover the revenue shortfalls needed to close the financial books at the end of each year. The county commissioners themselves have further restricted the revenue base by holding steady or reducing slightly the annual Ad Valorem millage rate over the same five year period. Also, with reserve funds so low, South County's bond rating is in jeopardy of being lowered. Yet, the commission has opposed various revenue programs like the creation of special tax districts, such as Municipal Services Taxing Unit (MSTUs). The commission has always seen MSTUs as a tax and thus worried that voters would not support its adoption, except if the funds were to go for something the public really wanted.

COURSE OF ACTION

Even though county officials hope that Ketchem will come up with a miracle remedy for their budget woes, Ketchem fears that there is no rabbit to pull out of the hat this year. The commission has not heeded Ketchem's pleas and concerns over the years about the dwindling General Fund Contingency and Fund Balance. All the little over-budgeted programs in the county have been tapped and now Ketchem must inform the county administrator and the board of the situation at a public budget meeting.

To Ketchem's credit he has always unveiled at this annual meeting all the possible revenue options open to the county. Ketchem sees a possible ally in the daunting task before him in George Wiley, the county administrator, who has always admired Ketchem's work and has also seen the fiscal "writing-on-the-wall" coming over the past few years. However, in the past, the board has refused Ketchem's recommendations to adopt special taxing districts, like MSTUs, or raise millage rates. MSTUs are an option, although they are politically unstable because they are adopted annually, through highly debated public hearings, and can be withdrawn with a majority vote.

Ketchem has called a meeting with his staff to plot the strategy for this annual pre-budget meeting. He informs the staff that two other large issues loom in the county. First, the current two cent sales tax—which has three more years to run, based on its passage by the voters some years back—drastically needs to be extended now. With this being an election year, the option to extend the sales tax for another fifteen years would provide funding for road projects, planned construction of stormwater facilities, popular parks, and other projects. A positive vote now by the public would also firm up the county's bond rating and would allow the county to fund projects in advance. This would reduce the need for Ad Valorem revenues for these projects, thus allowing them to be put back into the General Fund Contingency or to firm up the General Fund's Fund Balance. The board has consistently worked hard for the passage of taxes like the sales tax because in the end everyone pays including persons just passing through the area, visitors to the county's museums and natural attractions, and residents. The commissioners see the sales tax as a fairer tax than the Ad Valorem tax, which comes from only those owning property.

The second big issue is the fact that the unionized police forces of the three incorporated cities are threatening to go on strike if they cannot reach agreement on a new contract. Under the non-charter form of governance, the county is responsible for the budgets of numerous agencies and offices such as the sheriff's department. The sheriff, as with other county elected "Constitutional Officers," is responsible for law enforcement within the entire county and is a non-unionized department. The three cities' Board and the Commissions within the county have squabbled over the fact that the sheriff's patrol within the jurisdictions of the three cities is a duplication of services.

ROLE-PLAY ASSIGNMENT

You are Ketchem's assistant and he has asked you to develop a plan to present to the county commissioners for addressing the budget dilemma and to offer some advice on a strategy for gaining approval of the plan.

QUESTIONS FOR DISCUSSION

1. Identify the major problems facing the county. How did the county's financial situation become a problem? What could be done to assure that this does not happen again in the future?

2. What are the problems you face in developing the plan? There are sensitive political issues at hand, among them is the fact that Ketchem has informed you of the past voting record of the board, which has opposed alternative revenue sources. He also feels that his job could be on the line, depending on how the plan is presented.

3. Which options do you favor? MSTUs? raising the millage rate? extending the sales tax?

4. What data would you request from OMB to assist you in developing the plan and making decisions?

5. What considerations should be made to build political and public support for your plan?

SOURCES FOR FURTHER READING

Meyers, R. T. *Handbook of Government Budgeting*. San Francisco: Jossey-Bass, 1998.

Mikesell, J. L. *Fiscal Administration*, New York: Wadsworth Publishing, 1995.

Rachlin, R. *Handbook of Budgeting*. New York: John Wiley & Sons, 1998.

Scott, D., J. D. Martin, and A. J. Keown. *Basic Financial Management*. Englewood Cliffs, NJ: Prentice-Hall, 1999.

Wildavsky, A. *Budgeting: A Comparative Theory of Budgetary Processes*. New York: Transaction Books, 1986.

Coping with Revenue Shortfalls: The Experience of a Rural Southern County

Alex Sekwat

ABOUT THE ORGANIZATION

Kimu County, a rural county with a population of 75,000 inhabitants, is located in the southeastern United States. The county's economy is in decline, suffering from business failures and rising unemployment. As a result, budget analysts are predicting serious revenue shortfalls.

ABOUT THE CHARACTERS

Tom Liki, county administrator, is a fiscal "hawk" who values balanced financial practices. He is prone to selecting safe, conservative approaches to budgeting, yet takes a short-term view of budgets.

Rachel Timons, county budget director, is less hawkish than Liki and willing to experiment with creative and controversial budgeting practices, while taking a long-term focus of budgeting.

A COUNTY IN CRISIS   *Budget Shortfall*

In the past decade, Kimu County experienced a series of revenue shortfalls caused mainly by cutbacks in federal and state grants, unfavorable court decisions that mandated increased spending on county correctional facilities, and, most recently, the closure of two medium-sized apparel factories that employed a total of 500 workers. According to researchers at a nearby university, the closure of the apparel factories reduced the county's tax base by approximately 5 percent during the past six months. Moreover, there is speculation that the largest remaining apparel factory in the county, which employees 800 workers, will relocate to Mexico early next year.

Nationally, the apparel industry experienced a downturn spiral over the past decade, in spite of a robust U.S. economy. Apparel plant closings increased after the U.S. Congress passed and the president signed into law the North American Free Trade Agreement (NAFTA). NAFTA removed most trade barriers between the United States and its neighbors, Canada and Mexico. Before NAFTA, the apparel industry provided one in every three manufacturing jobs in Kimu County and local union leaders now blame NAFTA for the county's unemployment woes. They contend that low wages in Mexico—which average about $2 per hour compared to the current $7.50 per hour rate in the United States—enticed companies to move their business south of the U.S. border. County officials estimate a net loss in revenues of approximately $850,000 within the next twelve months as a result of a decline in property and sales revenues caused by the rising unemployment in the county due to recent business closings.

The Revenue Question

These problems spell impending financial shortfalls for the county government in the next fiscal year. According to experts, Kimu County is heading towards serious fiscal crisis unless it takes draconian measures to address the looming shortages. In the past three years, the county barely balanced its operating budget by tapping into its budget stabilization accounts ("rainy day" funds). Although the budget stabilization accounts provided a cushion against expenditure cuts in the past, the current fund balance will not cover projected budget deficits during the next fiscal year.

And the revenue base is shrinking. Squeezed by a shrinking revenue base, county officials face a major dilemma next fiscal year—whether or not to: (1) reduce current levels of service provision by cutting spending; or (2) increase taxes in order to balance the operating budget. To avoid serious political fallout, county officials must quickly resolve the approaching fiscal crisis. State law mandates that all local governments must balance their operating budgets. The Kimu County charter vests the responsibility for spending cuts and tax hikes in the hands of the elected governing body—the board of commissioners. The board of commissioners is composed of five members serving four-year staggered terms with each member representing one of the county's five districts. The charter further stipulates that the chief administrative officer of the county—the appointed administrator—shall recommend to the board of commissioners new revenue sources and both budgetary and expenditure control measures necessary to balance the operating budget. Other formal responsibilities of the appointed administrator include: preparing of the annual operating budget proposal and submitting it to the commissioners for consideration and approval; making administrative appointments to county offices; and advising the board of commissioners on policy matters.

To assess the gravity of the county's revenue shortfalls, the board of commissioners convened an executive session to hear an update on the revenue forecasts for the next fiscal year from Tom Liki, county administrator, and Rachel Timons, the budget director.

In her presentation, Timons, who is also the chair of the budget committee, noted that her office projected a deficit of $1.5 million for the next fiscal year if no additional revenues were raised. In light of the grim revenue estimates, the board of commissioners directed Liki to make recommendations for how to resolve the impending imbalance in the next fiscal year's operating budget. The board of commissioners may accept or reject such recommendations or it may issue directives about what specific taxes to raise and/or what services to cut. In good economic times, the budget committee meets twice a year to study departmental budget requests and recommend the budget to the county administrator for final review prior to its transmission to the board of commissioners for perusal and consideration for approval. The county charter, however, states that the county administrator may call upon the budget committee to work on emergency situations such as the current projected revenue shortfalls.

The Budget Committee's Proposal

In response to the commissioners' request, Liki called on the budget committee to analyze, review, and propose new revenue sources and expenditure cuts for next fiscal year's operating budget and report its proposal to him within the next two months.

After forty five days of hard work, the budget committee, under the direction of Timons, proposed five options to the county administrator. The following are the Budget Committee's recommended options.

Option 1: *Make across the board cuts.* The budget committee proposed a 5 percent across-the-board cut in all of the county's spending units or departments. This strategy, according to the budget committee, would generate an estimated savings of up to $990,000. The budget committee, however, noted that across-the-board cuts do not provide safeguards for high priority programs. For example, to realize the estimated savings, a pay raise freeze for all county employees must be implemented to avoid a direct reduction of compensation benefits. Such a scenario, however, would most likely trigger opposition from organized labor, including workers in the sheriff's department who gave up pay raises and cost of living adjustments in the past two years with the understanding that they would be given pay raises of up to 5 percent spread-out over the following three years.

Option 2: *Impose new taxes on "outsiders."* Taxing outsiders, or non-constituents (those without voting rights), is attractive and a far less controversial approach to generating new revenues among local governments. Knowing that the burden of proposed new taxes is not borne by local taxpayers, policy makers do not have to worry about voters' wrath at the ballot box in future elections. The budget committee identified hotels, motels, local theme parks, and shopping centers as potential sources for generating additional revenues from politically weak outsiders. It was noted, however, that there are sobering implications of taxing tourism and travel in the long run if the proposed new taxes are perceived by would-be visitors to be excessive. For instance, levying new hotel room taxes, which the average customers consider excessive, can reduce tax revenues if tourists shift their dollars to nearby communities without such taxes.

Option 3: *Downsize the county workforce.* The budget committee identified temporary hiring freezes for all vacant and proposed new positions as an option that, coupled with a reduction in force of the Corrections Department, would reduce the county's workforce. Citing some positive results in spending reductions in neighboring counties realized through prison privatization, the budget committee recommended that Kimu County privatize its main correctional facility—the county prison. It estimated that prison privatization would generate an annual cost saving of approximately $500,000 per year—an equivalent of 15 percent in annual reduction of the cost of incarcerating prisoners. Most importantly, by privatizing the main county prison, the county government would not have to meet the previous additional spending costs mandated by the courts. It was noted, however, that this option would likely be challenged by various groups including the corrections department, the American Federation of State, County, and Municipal Employees (AFSCME), and the American Civil Liberties Union (ACLU). Based on what happened in other counties, these groups might argue that prison privatization not only threatens the jobs of public employees, but puts profits ahead of inmate rights, jeopardizes public security, and diffuses responsibility and accountability of the county government.

Option 4: *Temporarily increase sales and sin taxes.* The budget committee proposed this strategy with the knowledge that temporary taxes are usually easier to pass, as taxpayers are more willing to accept them than permanent taxes. It was noted, however, that this strategy stands a greater chance of success if the funds are earmarked for a specific and important issue such as public safety. The estimate is that a half-percent increase in local sales taxes would generate up to $1.4 million. However, mindful of voters' tendency to resist tax hikes, the committee understands that proposing a sales tax increase in the midst of rising unemployment can be politically exploited by anti-tax interest groups and politicians. Yet, the budget committee deems sin taxes (adult entertainment services, tobacco, and alcohol) easier to pass because society generally feels that there is something immoral about them. It is estimated that $250,000 can be generated through this approach.

Option 5: *Postpone spending on capital improvements.* The budget committee recommended shifting funds from the capital budget to the operating budget in order to balance the latter. This proposal is attractive because it would not involve major cuts in the operating budget or layoffs. The downside is that delaying construction and repair of infrastructure facilities would increase future capital improvement costs.

ROLE-PLAY ASSIGNMENT

As the assistant budget director, both Liki, county administrator, and Ketchem, budget director, approach you about your ideas and proposal.

QUESTIONS FOR DISCUSSION

1. What are the political risks of each option? What interests would support/oppose each option? How would you propose building public and political support for your actions/plan?
2. What option or mix of options do you recommend? What other options would you propose to Liki and Timons in addition to those identified by the budget committee to balance the budget? For instance, the long-term issue might be to expand and diversify the county's revenue and economic base. How would you recommend this be achieved? Evaluate the strengths and weaknesses of each of your options.
3. What are the ethical implications of generating revenues by privatizing the county prison and taxing newcomers, tourists, and the politically weak?
4. What criteria should the board of commissioners use to make their final decision?
5. Should county residents be informed of the impending budget imbalance? If so, when, how, and who should communicate the information?

SOURCES FOR FURTHER READING

Banovetz, J. M. *Managing Local Government: Cases in Decision Making*. Washington, D.C.: International City/County Management Association, 1998.

Bland, R. L., and I. S. Rubin. *Budgeting: A Guide for Local Governments*. Washington, D.C.: International City/County Management Association, 1997.

Garvey, G. *Public Administration: The Profession and Practice, A Case Study Approach*. New York: St. Martin's, 1997.

Rubin, I. S. *The Politics of Public Budgeting: Getting and Spending, Borrowing and Balancing*. New York: Chatham House, 2000.

- 5% across the board cut
- imposing new taxes on "outsiders"
- downsizing the workforce
- postponing spending on capital investments/improvements
- temporarily increase sales/sin taxes

Getting Control
of the Greenfield City Budget

Nicholas C. Peroff & Mark Funkhouser

ABOUT THE ORGANIZATION

Greenfield is a Midwestern city with a population of about 400,000 people set in a metropolitan area of 1.5 million people. The city has a council-manager form of government with about 7,000 employees and a budget of nearly $1 billion. There has been some talk of changing the form of government to a mayor/council or "strong mayor" form. Greenfield has a mayor and twelve council members who serve terms of four years and are limited to two terms in office. The mayor and half the council are elected at-large, the remaining council members are elected by district. The city manager appoints all department heads and prepares the budget for the mayor and council to consider. The mayor and council appoint the city manager and city auditor. The city auditor's office does performance auditing and is overseen by the city council's finance committee. A commercial accounting firm conducts the annual financial audit of the city.

ABOUT THE CHARACTERS

Herb Campbell is the mayor. He campaigned on a pledge to improve basic city services and is completing his first term in office.

John Scott, the city manager, is a home-town boy who came up through the ranks of the city bureaucracy, serving as a department head, assistant city manager, and finally, for the last four years, city manager.

Susan Cheong has served as budget officer for many years under several city managers and is widely regarded as a solid, professional number-cruncher.

Lori Valdez is the city auditor and has been for ten years, during which time her office has earned a reputation for turning out careful, but aggressive, audits and evaluations.

THE PROBLEM diminishing confidence & inadequate gov't executions

Mayor Campbell is feeling a little desperate. It is not a feeling he experiences often and certainly not one he enjoys. He is a success. He is a smart guy with a reputation for coming up with the right ideas at the right time. He moved back and forth between business and politics and did well in both, especially business. But people were surprised when he announced early as a candidate for mayor and most discounted his chances. The big money and the "boys downtown" initially leaned toward the other guy. But Campbell staked out a strong position for basic services—bridges and roads, curbs, and sidewalks, more cops, and better maintenance of parks and community centers. The race evolved into a debate between a pro-businesses agenda focused on revitalizing downtown on the one hand and basic services for neighborhoods on the other. Once again, Campbell had the right idea at the right time and won an overwhelming victory at the polls.

Lately, however, it feels like things are turning south in a big way. For the last several months, every week seems to reveal a new problem in city government. The mayor, riding through the early morning streets in the back of a Lincoln Town Car, sunk lower in his seat thinking about a recent string of small disasters.

The first was a citizen survey issued by city auditor, Lori Valdez. It asked a random sample of citizens about their satisfaction with a wide variety of city services and then compared the results to similar surveys in other cities within the metropolitan area. The results painted a grim picture. Out of more the than thirty services compared, Greenfield's citizen ratings were above the twenty-fifth percentile in only four instances. For many services, the percent of citizens checking "satisfied" or "very satisfied" was dead last among the fourteen cities included in the report.

Some people felt that it was unfair to compare a diverse urban city like Greenfield to smaller suburban towns and cities, and the Mayor had to admit that, at first, he was angered by the report. Valdez, however, stoutly defended her work when she was called into his office. She said that Greenfield competes with other cities in the area for residents and for businesses, making accurate comparisons with its competitors imperative if services are to be honestly evaluated and improved. The Mayor finally decided that, rather than "shoot the messenger," he would publicly declare his dissatisfaction with the results of the survey and challenge the city manager and his staff to improve the situation before the next survey was done.

Shortly thereafter, in November, the newspaper printed a devastating series of articles about restaurant inspections. Restaurants are to be inspected by the city for cleanliness and overall food safety at least twice a year. The newspaper found, however, that most were not inspected as often as required and some had gone more than two years without an inspection. The whole situation was very embarrassing and the Mayor heard plenty of jokes about whether it was safe to eat or even drink the water in Greenfield. When the Mayor and city council called the city manager on the carpet about the issue, they heard what seemed to be a lot of excuses about insufficient funds, staff turnover, difficulties in filling vacant positions and the need to work out the details of new food safety regulations.

Then, in mid-December, it snowed. After three years of mild winters, Greenfield got one of the worst snowstorms anyone could remember. It began on a Monday afternoon at rush hour with a layer of ice, followed by snow on and off until Tuesday morning. The total accumulation was about seventeen inches of snow (and many aggravated citizens). The weather remained very cold throughout the week. Some residential streets became virtually impassable, as snow and ice were packed hard and even some arterial streets remained hazardous. Residents made thousands of calls to the public works department complaining about the streets and asking for service. The newspaper and television stations ran stories making unfavorable comparisons of the condition of streets in Greenfield to other cities in the area. The consensus in Greenfield was that the city did a poor job getting the snow cleared. Later it became evident that, while some errors in judgment were made on timing when contractors had been called out to plow streets, the dominant factor was that resources devoted to snow removal were inadequate.

BUDGET PROBLEMS

These events were unfolding at the same time that the mayor and council were deliberating over the budget for the coming fiscal year. Budget discussions provided a forum for the Mayor's critics on the council to focus attention on the problems and to imply that he should be doing more to solve them. And to make matters worse, Nancy Schmidt, a newspaper writer, was hammering away at him. Schmidt was hired nearly fifteen years earlier by the local paper to increase readers' interest in the editorial page, and she met that objective by skewering public officials with facts and sarcasm. She demanded that more money be focused on basic services, that performance be improved in city hall, and that "bureaucratic foot dragging" cease. And she wanted the Mayor to show some leadership.

Under Greenfield's council-manager form of government, the budget is submitted by the city manager. The Mayor can make suggestions for changes, but if the city manager does not include them, the only way the Mayor can get changes included is to get the council to amend the budget. During the budget deliberations, the Mayor talked to the city manager, at first privately and, later, more publicly. More funding was needed to address the areas rated most poorly by citizens in the survey and to fix other problems that had come to light.

Always it seemed that John Scott gave him endless platitudes about how complex the city budget was and how great the needs were. Then Scott would turn to his budget officer, Susan Cheong, who would earnestly launch into an absolutely mind-numbing series of spreadsheets. It often seemed to the Mayor that every suggestion he made for changes in funding was simply buried under those spreadsheets. When Cheong finally finished, he was sure of two things: no one knew as much as she did about the Greenfield city budget, and as long as she was budget officer, no one would.

TIME TO SHAPE THINGS UP

Mayor Campbell had lunch with David Jamieson at the exclusive River Club in downtown Greenfield. Jamieson is a well-regarded civic leader, who has been prominent in the affairs of the city for many years and who recently retired as CEO of a large local company to take a position as head of the largest charitable foundation in Greenfield. Jamieson supported the Mayor early in his campaign when it was not at all clear who would win. The Mayor values his opinion and wants to retain his support. Jamieson told him point blank that people were wondering why all the Mayor's talk about basic services did not seem to generate any action. The changes he made in the first year were steps in the right direction but now things were not going far enough or fast enough. People wondered whether the newspaper reporter was not right when she stated that bureaucrats, not the Mayor, made the real decisions in city hall.

The finance committee prepared to hold its last public hearing on the budget. The process has ground along since mid-summer and will end next week when the full council votes to adopt the city budget. Then the Mayor will testify to the committee. As Campbell searches for a way out of his problems, he reminds himself that he has usually succeeded in the past. So what now? Then inspiration struck. He would not simply request a reallocation of a few dollars. No, he would show some leadership and shake things up! He would completely revise the budget process and, at the same time, strengthen his role. He did not, however, know exactly how to do that. He needed some help—technically and politically. He started to think about how some of the principal players in the process would react to his emerging idea.

He probably could not get help from the city manager. Scott has a vested interest in the way things are and, even if he wanted to help, he is too close to the process to see a way to make serious changes. Besides, the mayor was sure that Scott would see his idea as an attempt to "micro-manage." Cheong did have enormous technical expertise with regard to the Greenfield City Budget. But even holding aside the fact that she worked for Scott, could he really benefit from her expertise? Asking her questions about the budget always makes him feel claustrophobic. With her, a straight question never gets a straight answer. The problem is that she seems to see complications in every issue and every new idea is met with "yes, but. . ." Campbell wants to present the idea in a positive way so that the chair of the finance committee, will not see it as a criticism of her or her handling of the legislative side of the budget process. The chair, now in her second term on the council, is a friend and supporter and has tried her best to get the Mayor's fiscal agenda adopted.

Some in the community feel the Mayor's push for basic services could reduce services to the low-income, minority community in the urban core of the city. Greenfield provides a lot of social services like daycare for needy children, prenatal care for at-risk mothers, and support for indigent care at health clinics. Others worry that the Mayor has a hidden agenda in mind, like using the budget issue as a way to get more power into the hands of the Mayor.

As the Mayor's Lincoln pulls into the city hall garage, he is smiling ever so slightly. He has an idea that might work. He will call the finance chair and Lori Valdez, the auditor, into his office and tell them he is going to ask the finance committee to study the budget process and recommend ways to strengthen the role of elected officials. The finance committee will then turn to Valdez to provide them with a study. That will provide the technical input he needs. But the charge will be to the finance committee to come up with the final recommendations. That will do two important things. It will give the finance chair a role in working through the problem, and it will ensure that political as well as technical considerations go into whatever suggestions are made. And that will make it more likely to be supported by the entire community. By focusing on the role of elected officials, instead of just the role of the mayor, he will hopefully lessen the fears of folks who believe that it is simply a power grab on his part. Involving the city auditor will help on that front, too. She is well respected for technical expertise but also for fairness and credibility. Most knowledgeable observers will see her involvement as a signal that this is a legitimate effort to improve the process and not a political power grab. As he gets out of the car, he is sure this is a good idea.

EXHIBIT 1. THE EMERGING AUDIT FUNCTION

In this case study, the City of Greenfield is one of the growing number of cities in the United States that has a strong audit function as part of the structure of municipal government. A strong audit function is one that is:

◆ Established in the charter or other basic legal document
◆ Organizationally independent of management
◆ Conducted with complete access to employees, property and records, usually accompanied by subpoena power for the auditors
◆ Sufficiently funded
◆ Performed by auditors that can conduct all types of audits, especially those related to performance

In cities where a strong audit function exists, the auditor often wields significant influence within the policy making process. This influence results from the credibility accorded to the audit function because of its ability to provide the public, elected officials and management with rigorous, fair, objective and reliable analyses of local government performance. Auditors usually have substantial expertise and training in accounting and financial management.

ROLE-PLAY ASSIGNMENT

As Mayor Campbell's aide, assist him in dealing with this issue.

QUESTIONS FOR DISCUSSION

1. What are the problems facing the City of Greenfield?
2. What do you think of the Mayor's plan for changing the budget process? Will it solve the problems he sees himself facing? Besides asking the finance chair to develop a reform proposal, what other recommendations do you have for approaching the issue of reforming the budget process, and what other groups might be considered in doing so?
3. How do you think Scott, the city manager, will react when he learns about the Mayor's plan?
4. What do you think of Cheong's performance as budget officer? What advice do you have for the Mayor regarding Cheong's work?
5. Is there a conflict of interest if the mayor tries to strengthen his institutional role in the budget process? Can this be done without interfering with the important task fulfilled by the city auditor? Is there a trade-off in power between the two entities and a "lesser of two evils" scenario existing?

SOURCES FOR FURTHER READING

Bland, R. L., and I. S. Rubin. *Budgeting: A Guide for Local Governments*. Washington, D.C.: International City/County Management Association, 1997.

Ebon, C. "The Relationship between Citizen Involvement in the Budget Process and City Structure and Culture." *Public Productivity & Management Review* 23 (2000): 383–393.

Hendrick, R. "Comprehensive Management and Budgeting Reform in Local Government: The Case of Milwaukee." *Public Productivity & Management Review* 23 (2000): 312–235.

National Advisory Council on State and Local Budgeting. *Recommended Budget Practices: A Framework for Improved State and Local Government Budgeting*. Chicago: Government Finance Officers Association, 1998.

Wheat, E. M. "The Activist Auditor: A New Player in State and Local Politics." *Public Administration Review* 51 (1991): 385–392.

- Citizen dissatisfaction, improper inspections, inadequate action by ~~clearance~~ ~~clearance~~ Snow Removal, dismissal citizen complaints, lack of funding for specific programs, lost trust in city gov't, lack of understanding among citizens

- Management by Objective
  ↳ share power
    - Clear goals

Revenue Forecasting
in the City of Envy

John D. Wong & W. Bartley Hildreth

ABOUT THE ORGANIZATION

Envy City is the largest city in the state. The state cities and counties may impose a retailer's sales tax in addition to the state-imposed sales tax. These local sales taxes are collected by merchants in the normal course of business and are remitted to the Department of Tax Tracking and Yields (DoTTY) with the state sales tax return. The returns are reviewed and the appropriate share of the moneys is returned to the cities or counties in which the taxes were collected. As such, local governments must be able to accurately forecast sales tax revenues in order to establish and control the local budget.

ABOUT THE CHARACTERS

Ian Crowe is the director of the Department of Tax Tracking and Yields (DoTTY), the state agency responsible for tax collections.

Tim Mann is the director of The Office of Tax Oversight (TOTO), the state legislative audit agency responsible for overseeing tax collections. In response to concerns expressed by several state legislators and local government officials, the legislature has asked TOTO to determine whether local sales tax collections have been accurately distributed to local governments.

Ima Lyon, the finance director for Envy City, is concerned because local sales tax distributions seem to be falling.

OVERVIEW OF LOCAL SALES TAX COLLECTIONS
IN THE CITY OF ENVY

In many states, local governments have the authority to impose local retail sales taxes to diversify their revenue base and reduce reliance on the ad valorem property tax levy. In some states, local governments are allowed to establish their own collection systems, while in other states local governments must rely on the collection system of the state.

State Retail Sales Tax

Generally, the tax base for the state retail sales tax has been gross receipts from retail sales of personal property and certain services. Since 1994, the tax rate has been 4.9 percent on most taxable transactions. Prior to this time, the tax rate was 4 percent for four years and 4.25 percent for three years. Certain services and utilities associated with construction were subjected to a special 2.5 percent tax in 1993. However, this was repealed in 1999, so now there is no tax on such services. The state also imposes a "use tax" on retail purchases made outside the state. State officials are concerned about the potential impact of the increasing number of remote sales made over the Internet, which are typically beyond the ability of the state to capture.

Local Sales Tax

State law also allows local governments to enact local sales taxes. Generally, the tax base for the local sales tax is the same as for the state sales tax, with the exception of most residential utility services, which are subject to local taxes but exempt from the state tax. Revenue from a countywide sales tax is apportioned among the county and cities.

The State's Sales Tax Collection System

Although local governments enact local sales taxes, local businesses collect them (together with state taxes) and have an obligation to send these collected taxes to the state, which the state then distributes back to the local governments that imposed the tax. As a result of that process, local governments mainly rely on the state to ensure that they receive the proper amount of tax revenue on a timely basis. There is no local "use tax" on most items except "big ticket" items such as automobiles. Local officials are concerned that sales over the Internet are hard to tax and are thus harming the local sales tax base.

When remitting taxes, each business must indicate where taxes were collected. That allows DoTTY to identify the local governments that should receive those taxes. As part of its processing, DoTTY compares the current information provided by retailers to information provided in the past. Any significant deviations noted (for example, locations added or dropped) help keep business locations current and identify data entry errors. For countywide taxes, proper distribution involves allocating amounts collected among the county and all the cities within that county. The allocations are based on property and taxes levied.

Retailers send taxes collected to DoTTY either monthly, quarterly, or annually. The frequency required depends on the amounts collected. Establishments collecting larger amounts must send in those amounts more frequently; establishments collecting smaller amounts must send in those amounts less frequently. Regardless of which schedule a business is on, taxes are due by the twenty-fifth of the month following the end of the collection period. For example, if a business is on a quarterly schedule, it must send in taxes collected during January, February, and March by the twenty-fifth of April. One exception to this basic process is that the largest retailers must deposit sales taxes on an "accelerated schedule." That schedule calls for depositing an estimated amount for taxes collected during the first two weeks of the month in which the deposit is made, instead of waiting until the next month to make that deposit.

PROBLEM: DISTRIBUTING LOCAL SALES TAXES

State law requires the state to distribute local sales taxes to the appropriate local governments at least quarterly. DoTTY distributes sales taxes monthly—more often than required. Rather than waiting until all taxes for a collection period have been processed before making the distribution, DoTTY distributes all amounts that have been processed by the end of each month. (This practice results in distribution of about 90 percent of taxes collected for each month, with the remaining 10 percent distributed the following month). Along with the sales tax returns, retailers file information DoTTY needs to determine how much in local sales tax receipts should go to which cities and counties. The sales tax returns are recorded in one part of DoTTY's system and the payments in another. The payment and corresponding return are eventually matched as processing continues. DoTTY does not know what portion of these sales tax payments should go to cities and counties and what portion goes to the state until it processes the sales tax returns that accompanied them.

Money is distributed once a month (around the twenty-fifth), even though state law only requires them to be made on a quarterly basis. DoTTY officials say this practice helps ensure that local governments have adequate cash flow to finance their operations.

The New Automated System

DoTTY began using its new computer system to process sales tax returns in the year 2000. DoTTY wanted to check this system out for a few months before relying on the information it generated about how local sales taxes should be distributed. Thus, for the first three months the amounts distributed to localities were based on estimates of the local sales taxes owed to them (given their previous year's actual distribution for those same three months plus or minus a growth factor). After distributing estimated payments in November, December, and January, DoTTY used the new computer-generated data to determine how much it actually should have paid each city and county during those three months. It made corresponding corrections in the sales tax distributions sent out the following year.

Problems Converting Old Technology to New Technology

In late 2000 and early 2001, DoTTY converted business sales tax accounts from the old computer system to the new one. During the conversion process, DoTTY took small groups of returns and processed them through the system, manually checking each for accuracy— a time consuming method. To ensure uninterrupted cash flows to local entities, during the transition period DoTTY distributed local sales taxes to cities and counties based on estimates of amounts owed to them.

If this was not the correct amount, payments to reconcile the difference were made at a later date.

However, in the months since the conversion took place, DoTTY has heard repeated concerns from local officials who think they have not received the correct amount of sales taxes. Because of the decline in revenue experienced by the City of Envy in 2001, Ima Lyon, the city's finance director, has been especially vociferous, charging that DoTTY is either "consciously or incompetently" withholding local sales tax collections due to the city. Ian Crowe, director of DoTTY, has vehemently denied these accusations and rigorously defends his department and the procedure, stating that DoTTY's distributions to local governments are "competent, consistent, and correct."

The Audit

During the initial three-month conversion period to the new system, DoTTY sampled several communities and found that most of them eventually received the correct sales tax distribution. But there were some problems. DoTTY initially calculated the adjustments incorrectly and exacerbated the problem by not explaining things well to the localities. Further, auditors found at least one city that appeared to have gotten a substantial overpayment. In general, if all the information is in order and communities and businesses file the correct date on sales taxes, the automated system performs perfectly. However, the system was not catching those cases deviating from the normal filing process.

In April of 2001, DoTTY sent a letter to localities noting any additional amounts owed to them relating to the conversion period with the February and March sales tax distributions. DoTTY had computed that, statewide, it had underpaid localities almost $2 million for this period. But, DoTTY later discovered it had made an error in its calculation—it had mistakenly included payments it received during the transition period that had not been processed until later. When it corrected this error, the department realized it actually had overpaid localities about $13.4 million for the period. To remedy the overpayment, the department reduced the amount of local sales taxes it distributed to them in April by about $6.7 million, or half the amount overpaid. This was done without notifying the local governments in advance. The local sales tax distribution during the following payment cycle was also cut by about half (to cover the remaining $6.7 million overpaid). After that cycle, DoTTY sent a letter to the localities explaining the $13.4 million overpayment and the agency's subsequent actions to correct the error.

The confusion these letters caused contributed to local officials' concerns about whether they were receiving the correct amounts or would receive the full amount owed to them during the conversion period. In all, roughly 90 percent of the localities ultimately were paid the correct amount of sales taxes owed to them during the three-month conversion period.

In response to growing criticism of the system and "mistakes" made by DoTTY, the state had another audit performed. To determine whether payments were being accurately distributed, auditors reviewed a random sample of 249 of the 48,000 retail sales tax payments DoTTY received from vendors in October of 2001. Auditors traced these payments through DoTTY's system, calculated the amount of tax due to the localities, and compared this figure to the amount of local sales tax actually distributed. The results of the audit are summarized below:

◆ Roughly 98 percent of sales tax payments that included all the information DoTTY needed to process and distribute them were accurately distributed. Four mistakes were made. DoTTY distributed three payments totaling less than $8 twice because of computer processing errors. (Department officials told auditors that the "bug" that caused these duplicate payments was fixed.) The fourth error was distributed incorrectly because the taxpayer reported having negative net sales in some jurisdictions and DoTTY staff entered these negative figures as positive numbers in the computer, causing the distribution to be off.

◆ Roughly 11 percent of payments could not be distributed because the information DoTTY received from retailers was incomplete or wrong. Most of these cases involved retailers that did not return sales tax information or were supposed to submit their returns electronically. Also, one retailer wrote the wrong account number on the payment voucher, and another did not provide information about net sales or the tax jurisdiction.

In general, auditors found that DoTTY staff researched and resolved most sales tax returns in a systematic and quick manner. However, they found problems with the way the agency handled sales tax payments that came in without a return or complete data. The auditors reported that two other states have policies of distributing sales tax payments even if they had not received a corresponding return. In such cases these states distributed payments based on an estimate that considers prior filing history. Adjustments are then made after the fact as needed. Officials from these two states told auditors that they implemented these procedures to avoid creating a backlog of unprocessed checks and felt that an estimated distribution was better than no distribution at all.

To protect the integrity of the sales tax data being processed, the auditors recommended that the computer system have automatic "edits" built in to check the data at different points. For example, after the data are entered the computer software could automatically check such things as whether the account number matches an existing account, or whether the math on the sales tax return is correct. The computer software also could be programmed to check that numbers do not inadvertently change when data go from one process to another. As part of this audit, auditors reviewed DoTTY's sales tax computer system and found it to have some "editing" capacity.

However, DoTTY does not have an automatic check built-in to ensure that the correct amounts went to the correct local entity. Thus, if the computer processed a sales tax return and allocated a tax payment to the wrong cities or counties, DoTTY would have no way of knowing a mistake had been made. Currently, the only way DoTTY could identify such a mistake is if one of the local entities complained they were not getting enough money. To address this potential problem, periodically DoTTY was advised to track a sample of payments through the system.

ROLE-PLAY ASSIGNMENT

You are the assistant to Tim Mann, the state audit agency responsible for overseeing tax collections. Mann has asked you to work with local communities to alleviate their concerns about the tax collection and reimbursement system.

QUESTIONS FOR DISCUSSION

1. In response to concerns about the new technology and the system of basing sales tax funds to local governments on estimates, the state legislature has asked Mann, director of TOTO, and his staff to answer the following questions: *Has DoTTY accurately distributed local sales tax revenues to counties and cities? Is DoTTY using an appropriate system/process for doing so?* Mann, your boss, has asked you to initially determine if there is any evidence to support the finance director allegations that the state has erred and the system is problematic, or whether DoTTY Director Ian Crowe's assertion that local sales tax distributions are "competent, consistent, and correct" is accurate.

2. Do you feel the problems DoTTY encountered with the new computerized system are acceptable? For the state? For the local governments? How could DoTTY have better handled the conversion to the new system and new approach to collection and reimbursement?

3. Officials from the county and Envy City have asked you to look into the share they contribute and receive. The current tax rates are 4.9 percent state and 1 percent local. Based on the tax rates in effect for each given year, the table below presents annual collections for the state retail sales tax in the county, the county retail sales tax, the county's share of the county retail sales tax, and Envy City's share of the county retail sales tax. Note that the difference between the county total and the county share and the city share is the amount distributed to smaller jurisdictions in the county. Estimate revenues for each of the jurisdictions for years 16 and 17 using any method that is appropriate. What did you find?

Annual Sales Tax Collections in the County

Year	State	County Total	County Share	City Share
1987	$91,559,841	$22,327,240	$9,959,471	$22,710,686
1988	$119,091,013	$36,951,283	$10,491,740	$23,685,829
1989	$126,432,841	$38,771,457	$12,012,747	$24,920,636
1990	$133,774,668	$40,591,631	$12,529,542	$25,227,035
1991	$146,766,113	$42,143,664	$13,831,022	$26,304,536
1992	$151,665,708	$44,432,753	$14,173,409	$26,742,910
1993	$161,705,948	$46,766,184	$14,999,622	$24,978,593
1994	$214,192,348	$50,851,852	$16,652,206	$31,627,266
1995	$208,850,276	$53,731,178	$17,501,364	$33,065,939
1996	$205,977,958	$56,555,442	$18,097,026	$32,477,282
1997	$212,062,264	$55,903,696	$18,450,964	$34,266,021
1998	$226,953,301	$59,219,913	$19,677,473	$36,237,219
1999	$241,115,267	$64,649,274	$22,773,689	$38,344,037
2000	$249,473,032	$66,525,507	$22,265,831	$38,008,578
2001	$243,460,732	$65,194,997	$21,501,227	$38,541,342

4. The table below presents monthly sales tax collections for the county and Envy City for years 9 through 15. Do sales tax collections appear to be seasonal? Which months have unusually high collections? Which months have unusually low collections? Explain what accounts for any seasonality you identify.

Monthly Sales Tax Collections

County Share	1995	1996	1997	1998	1999	2000	2001
January	$1,535,539	$1,473,807	$1,473,436	$1,836,770	$2,092,420	$2,004,720	$1,663,286
February	$1,610,318	$2,004,591	$1,628,633	$1,745,913	$2,083,798	$1,800,457	$1,966,817
March	$1,215,167	$1,181,342	$1,581,712	$1,449,730	$1,750,970	$1,450,901	$1,704,749
April	$1,275,175	$1,587,875	$1,418,764	$1,581,205	$1,994,380	$2,218,170	$1,758,316
May	$1,431,119	$1,374,570	$1,425,082	$1,549,505	$1,473,900	$1,906,092	$1,965,211
June	$1,554,953	$1,595,752	$1,651,159	$1,840,881	$1,849,206	$1,565,801	$1,880,072
July	$1,400,283	$1,522,382	$1,527,767	$1,571,702	$2,102,013	$1,980,968	$1,494,095
August	$1,541,303	$1,515,647	$1,673,214	$1,695,506	$2,050,914	$2,017,210	$1,901,469
September	$1,451,909	$1,451,858	$1,658,338	$1,888,178	$1,637,352	$1,855,436	$1,718,113
October	$1,352,218	$1,519,026	$1,457,259	$1,394,396	$2,271,689	$1,898,417	$1,867,708
November	$1,792,188	$1,401,629	$1,563,497	$1,979,272	$1,850,081	$1,912,600	$1,906,527
December	$1,341,193	$1,468,547	$1,392,104	$1,144,415	$1,616,966	$1,655,059	$1,674,864
Annual	$17,501,364	$18,097,026	$18,450,964	$19,677,473	$22,773,689	$22,265,831	$21,501,227

City Share	1995	1996	1997	1998	1999	2000	2001
January	$2,287,793	$2,166,166	$2,884,520	$2,604,396	$2,995,123	$2,505,904	$3,001,460
February	$2,400,768	$2,911,606	$2,587,357	$2,840,588	$3,411,490	$3,831,081	$3,096,592
March	$2,694,365	$2,520,478	$2,598,878	$2,783,640	$2,521,182	$3,292,080	$3,460,954
April	$2,927,506	$2,926,049	$3,011,197	$3,307,086	$3,163,162	$2,704,351	$3,311,015
May	$2,636,309	$2,791,513	$2,786,141	$2,823,516	$3,595,601	$3,421,402	$2,631,268
June	$2,831,881	$2,779,164	$3,014,460	$3,045,926	$3,506,991	$3,444,225	$3,348,698
July	$2,667,634	$2,662,198	$2,987,660	$3,392,054	$2,799,815	$3,170,008	$3,025,787
August	$2,484,470	$2,785,360	$2,625,396	$2,504,990	$3,884,509	$3,241,395	$3,289,241
September	$3,292,839	$2,570,096	$2,816,795	$3,555,703	$3,163,573	$3,265,612	$3,357,605
October	$2,464,214	$2,692,799	$2,508,014	$2,055,906	$2,764,955	$2,825,880	$2,949,622
November	$2,702,444	$2,701,765	$3,309,125	$3,758,970	$3,428,002	$2,839,927	$3,309,069
December	$3,675,716	$2,970,088	$3,136,479	$3,564,444	$3,109,635	$3,466,713	$3,760,032
Annual	$33,065,939	$32,477,282	$34,266,021	$36,237,219	$38,344,037	$38,008,578	$38,541,342

5. The table on the next two pages presents an economic profile for the metropolitan statistical area (MSA) that includes the county and Envy City for the years 1 through 13. Do sales tax collections in the respective jurisdictions appear to be consistent with economic factors? Explain why or why not.

Metropolitan Statistical Area Economic Profile

	1987	1988	1989	1990	1991	1992	1993
Personal income ($,000)	7,415,162	7,780,932	8,314,005	8,785,337	9,350,228	9,942,928	10,621,274
Nonfarm personal income	7,384,832	7,744,921	8,280,311	8,758,944	9,321,694	9,912,934	10,574,524
Farm income	30,330	36,011	33,694	26,393	28,534	29,994	46,750
Net earnings ($)	5,283,398	5,574,124	5,922,774	6,194,565	6,553,207	6,858,726	7,448,210
Transfer payments ($)	788,767	824,281	886,058	975,051	1,057,855	1,176,966	1,307,107
Income maintenance	62,929	63,743	69,894	77,140	83,875	93,224	110,406
Unemployment insurance benefit payments	27,744	26,167	29,667	31,373	29,302	36,058	56,254
Retirement and other	698,094	734,371	786,497	866,538	944,678	1,047,684	1,140,447
Dividends, interest, and rent ($)	1,342,997	1,382,527	1,505,173	1,615,721	1,739,166	1,907,236	1,865,957
Population (number of persons)	464,698	470,191	475,565	482,130	486,419	494,182	504,754
Earnings by place of work ($,000)	5,829,985	6,145,547	6,543,853	6,853,628	7,255,753	7,608,584	8,254,445
Wage and salary disbursements	4,623,230	4,835,765	5,107,207	5,389,580	5,760,138	6,027,773	6,509,407
Other labor income	603,576	645,776	663,552	722,400	789,626	878,838	969,238
Proprietors' income	603,179	664,006	773,094	741,648	705,989	701,973	775,800
Nonfarm proprietors' income	579,510	634,545	746,231	721,925	684,527	678,228	734,903
Farm proprietors' income	23,669	29,461	26,863	19,723	21,462	23,745	40,897
Total full-time and part-time employment	279,086	288,877	294,743	301,607	307,764	312,912	315,047
Wage and salary jobs	231,108	237,947	244,690	252,385	259,505	261,929	266,314
Number of proprietors	47,978	50,930	50,053	49,222	48,259	50,983	48,733
Number of nonfarm proprietors	43,996	46,980	46,199	45,313	44,335	47,074	44,914
Number of farm proprietors	3,982	3,950	3,854	3,909	3,924	3,909	3,819
Average earnings per job ($)	20,890	21,274	22,202	22,724	23,576	24,315	26,201
Average wage and salary disbursements	20,005	20,323	20,872	21,355	22,197	23,013	24,443
Average nonfarm proprietors' income	13,172	13,507	16,153	15,932	15,440	14,408	16,362

(continued)

Metropolitan Statistical Area Economic Profile (continued)

	1994	1995	1996	1997	1998	1999
Personal income ($,000)	10,904,135	11,183,467	11,786,613	12,618,101	13,477,098	14,254,965
Nonfarm personal income	10,862,120	11,140,040	11,769,136	12,563,147	13,420,999	14,232,860
Farm income	42,015	43,427	17,477	54,954	56,099	22,105
Net earnings ($)	7,563,479	7,728,695	8,085,286	8,687,604	9,383,975	10,046,018
Transfer payments ($)	1,386,464	1,459,205	1,504,286	1,545,822	1,628,404	1,654,000
Income maintenance	120,242	129,151	134,913	136,292	134,328	126,196
Unemployment insurance benefit payments	63,833	46,904	33,034	30,066	26,238	23,843
Retirement and other	1,202,389	1,283,150	1,336,339	1,379,464	1,467,838	1,503,961
Dividends, interest, and rent ($)	1,954,192	1,995,567	2,197,041	2,384,675	2,464,719	2,554,947
Population (number of persons)	511,740	515,840	520,024	526,111	533,970	543,850
Earnings by place of work ($,000)	8,376,571	8,570,323	8,966,910	9,645,279	10,428,527	11,175,545
Wage and salary disbursements	6,541,331	6,663,237	7,067,003	7,644,395	8,318,647	8,993,022
Other labor income	992,891	1,012,977	997,826	1,030,124	1,059,717	1,106,006
Proprietors' income	842,349	894,109	902,081	970,760	1,050,163	1,076,517
Nonfarm proprietors' income	806,856	858,601	892,963	925,527	1,004,518	1,066,426
Farm proprietors' income	35,493	35,508	9,118	45,233	45,645	10,091
Total full-time and part-time employment	316,956	320,533	327,303	336,482	347,539	358,741
Wage and salary jobs	267,776	270,442	274,314	283,326	293,118	303,167
Number of proprietors	49,180	50,091	52,989	53,156	54,421	55,574
Number of nonfarm proprietors	45,429	46,362	49,257	49,511	50,755	51,846
Number of farm proprietors	3,751	3,729	3,732	3,645	3,666	3,728
Average earnings per job ($)	26,428	26,738	27,396	28,665	30,007	31,152
Average wage and salary disbursements	24,428	24,638	25,762	26,981	28,380	29,664
Average nonfarm proprietors' income	17,761	18,519	18,129	18,693	19,792	20,569

Mikesell, J. L. *Fiscal Administration*. New York: Wadsworth Publishing, 1995.

Frank, H. A. *Budgetary Forecasting in Local Government: New Tools and Techniques* Westport, CT: Quorum Books, 1993.

Holcombe, R. G., and R. S. Sobel. *Growth and Variability in State Tax Revenue: An Anatomy of State Fiscal Crisis*. Westport, CT: Greenwood Press, 1997.

- Streamlined Sales Tax Plan
- California Auditing Plan
- Online Tax Collection
- Hybrid

Part IV

Managing Ethics

THE ETHICAL CHALLENGE FOR MANAGERS

The act of managing is not value free. Decisions made by both policy makers and public administrators involve moral choices and have the potential to impact many people. Moreover, the environment within which public administrators function regularly presents complex ethical situations and dilemmas. Because the *right* choice is rarely clear or simple, and because government serves a pluralistic populace, any act or decision by managers is subject to questioning. It is also subject to public oversight. Managers must consider what values are appropriate for the situation, and which of society's values should be reflected through their decisions and behavior.

The diverse nature of the United States means that a wide array of values are present at all times. So how is a manager to decide what course of action is the ethical course of action? One place to start is to identify widely agreed upon values or the dominant values in society. For instance, most Americans would agree that honesty, tolerance, and compassion are important values. This can be extended to include administrative values and public sector values. Although some critics suggest that the very existence of bureaucracy is incompatible with ethical behavior, a core set of administrative values in the public sector includes such concepts as responsiveness, lawfulness, accountability, fairness, openness, and participation.[1] But ethical management is more than simply the process of perpetuating these characteristics.

THE POLITICS OF ETHICS

The headlines repeatedly feature high-profile, political scandals. From President Richard Nixon's Watergate to President Ronald Reagan's Iran-Contra scandal to President Bill Clinton's affair with a White House intern, there have been numerous, serious ethical shortcomings in government at the highest level. But ethical lapses are not limited to the financial and sexual peccadillos of politicians. The bureaucracy has had its share of problems from widespread fraud, embezzlement, and conflict of interest improprieties of defense contractors to individual cases of corruption, collusion, and coercion in localities around the country. Indeed, ethics is a major concern of the public service, and improving the ethical conduct of public employees and agencies must be a priority for public managers.

The nature of public service places in the hands of public servants the trust and confidence of the citizenry. As guardians of the public interest, it is especially important for government—even more so than the private sector—to devote attention to ethics and to adhere to a "higher" ethical standard.[2] When one is charged with enforcing laws and acting on behalf of the public there are ample opportunities for unethical behavior. Temptations to accept bribes and gifts, to lie, and to misrepresent the truth are readily available as are, of course, the occasional inadvertent mistake and lapse of sound judgement. Ethical problems cost the taxpayers large sums of money in court costs, require time and resources for investigations and disciplinary actions, and undermine the public's confidence in their government. As such, ethical management should be a goal of all public agencies and managers. Ethical considerations should also inform decision making as a primary criterion in the decision-making process.

DECISION-MAKING ISSUES TO CONSIDER AS YOU READ THE CASES

Public Service as an Administrative Value

A commitment to ethics should be a core value of administration. Government service means one accepts working in an environment replete with rules and regulations. But one also accepts working for the public interest and an implicit higher ethical standard. Having rules to govern proper and improper behavior in public organizations is, however, only part of the solution to instilling a commitment to ethics as a core administrative value. Institutional checks and balances can only go so far in promoting ethical behavior. In addition to institutional controls on behavior there must be an ethical basis or moral compass that guides behavior. This suggests that there might be two conceptual approaches to promoting ethics: (1) regulations controlling behavior and (2) an inner dedication to ethics.

This latter notion of ethics is what is known as *outcome-centered obligations*, where employees are encouraged to contemplate the consequences to the public or their clients of their behavior.[3] All public employees have a task to perform and a duty to the public to fulfill that obligation. On the other hand, the idea of employing formal rules and restrictions to govern ethical behavior is deemed *action-centered restrictions*, whereby legal codes place parameters on activities so as to assure ethical actions. This latter notion falls within a larger school of what can be seen as *rule-driven ethics*, when behavior is seen as ethical simply because it adheres to a stated rule. Yet, just because someone follows rules does not solve the problem of situations where stated rules are inadequate, vague, or when those rules themselves are wrong. Segregation and discrimination by race, religion, or sex were once permitted by law. That did not make it right morally and ethically.

The alternative to rule-driven ethics is an individual commitment to ethics or altruism. Thinking of others and the consequences of one's behavior on others is a guideline for determining ethical codes dating to the ancient Greeks and beyond. Here one might consider the justness of one's action to others. This implies an obligation to others. The notions of an individual commitment to ethics or a rule-driven approach to promoting ethical behavior both depend to a degree on the basis for motivation of the employee. Most people tend to be motivated both intrinsically and extrinsically. Extrinsic motivation means one draws inspiration from external or material rewards such as pay, job perks, awards, and other forms of tangible recognition for one's work. Given the standardized pay scales and formal rules governing promotions and conduct that exist in the public sector when compared to the private sector, it is often difficult to offer employees extrinsic rewards for proper behavior. Fortunately, most employees in the public sector do not accept the job to get rich. They are motivated by something else. Intrinsically-minded individuals find satisfaction and motivation in their commitment to the service of others. They value making a difference, civic mindedness, and participatory democracy. Such values are important for public managers, given the nature of public service, the limited extrinsic rewards available, and, because laws and rules cannot possibly cover every potential ethical situation and dilemma, public managers must have a sense of right and wrong and maintain a commitment to ethical management.

Accountability as an Administrative Value

Public managers must be accountable to the public for their actions. A challenge of this concept is that managers in the public sector have numerous obligations, (1) to the organization, (2) to the department, (3) to their clients, (4) to any stakeholders in the agency or program, (5) to the general public, (6) to the Constitution, (7) as well as obligations to their own personal values, and (8) the principles of public service.[4] Instances might arise where managers must contend with inconsistencies between their personal ethical beliefs and standards espoused by the agency. When an individual's personal perspectives are blended with her or his job, it is known as *role absorption*. It is not only common for this blending to occur in the public sector, but it is difficult to separate individual views from the demands of the job at hand. Some feel this is a problem and managers must be more impartial when acting as agents of the organization, while others favor the infusion of personal codes of ethics into job performance.[5] Clearly, there are multiple dimensions of accountability, yet at the same time, bureaucrats must be free from the politically-driven whims of elected officials.

The notion of accountability is complex and is one of the central administrative values and a basic principle of democracy. To be accountable, public managers must be responsible. Public administration scholar, Grover Starling, sees administrative accountability and responsibility among the core issues of public administrators administrative accountability and responsibility.[6] He defines them as consisting of six basic characteristics.

1. *Responsiveness*. Responsiveness requires prompt action by an agency to the demands of its clients. Government is usually perceived as being slow to respond and burdened by cumbersome practices and policies. When the public has difficulty making inquiries, requests, and complaints to government, there is a problem of responsiveness. But responsiveness is more than accommodating requests from the public. It involves taking a genuine interest in one's clientele and serving them to the best of one's ability.

2. *Flexibility*. Most principles of management state that in order to be fair one must treat others the same and not discriminate against or show preference to any one individual or issue. Rules and standardized processes are one way to assure this, and they also help government to be accountable, efficient, and effective. Yet, in spite of these imperatives, managers need to design operations so as to be flexible. In some situations, flexibility may promote responsiveness, especially if the clientele served varies by geographic, cultural, demographic, and other factors.

3. *Competence*. Managers must be capable of performing their assigned task.

4. *Due process*. As guaranteed in the fifth amendment of the Constitution, citizens should not be "deprived of life, liberty, or property without due process of law." This means government will function in accordance to laws and not according to the whims of people, and the actions of public servants will not be arbitrary or deny people a public hearing. The Administrative Procedures Act of 1946 (APA) established this legal notion as a core administrative practice. The APA limits administrative discretion, ties agencies to their jurisdictional area, and gives fair process or hearings regarding administrative rules and processes in an effort to promote due process.

5. *Accountability*. Managers must be held responsible for their actions and answerable to others.

6. *Honesty*. Public scrutiny is enhanced by openness, truthfulness, and candor by public employees.

Organizational Humanism as an Administrative Value

Humanistic organizations have as a goal the practice of treating all members of the organization humanely. It is believed that this goal is compatible with such objectives as effectiveness and productivity. Organizational humanism achieves the latter goals by making the employee feel a part of the organization and incorporating the concept of ethics into all organizational practices and policies. This might prove to be especially helpful in public agencies, where the organization strives to promote such values as service to others and where individuals are often prone to losing their sense of identity or self in the larger bureaucracy. The problems of impersonality, unresponsiveness, and other dysfunctions of the bureaucratic persona can be minimized by the practice of organizational humanism. In the end, such practices may result in better service to clients and the establishment of a moral organizational culture.

Codes of Ethics

So how does one determine what constitutes ethical behavior? Government has attempted to answer this question by establishing codes of ethics. Congress passed one of the first such legislative efforts to establish a standard or code of ethics for federal employees in 1958. Two decades later the Office of Government Ethics was created in 1978 with the passage of the Ethics in Government Act. This office monitors the ethical climate of the public service and establishes standards for ethical behavior. It was not until 1992, however, that the Office of Government Ethics established a comprehensive code of ethics for all federal employees, as prior to this each agency tended to develop their own codes and standards.

Codes of ethics have become commonplace in spite of concerns that the establishment of strict rules of conduct will create a climate of distrust and excessive rules will simply add more red tape to both the organization and the work of employees. There are also questions as to whether codes of ethics amount to excessive legalism, or if they succeed in altering an individual's behavior. Codes must thus be designed to promote truly ethical behavior above and beyond mere rule compliance.

Efforts to manage ethics include both measures within the organization and external measures that attempt to establish the parameters of acceptable behavior. External controls on ethical behavior include laws and court decisions as well as oversight by the media, other agencies, and the public. There are principles such as public openness and checks and balances in the design of the U.S. political system that assist in promoting ethical behavior. Additionally, the APA permits formal hearings and adjudication regarding administrative actions. These formal hearings, along with the increasingly litigious nature of society, provide controls against improper activity by government. Internal controls on ethics are present within the organization and include financial disclosure requirements, workshops and training on ethics, encouragement of whistle-blowing, the establishment of a representative bureaucracy, and written codes of ethics.

The Hippocratic Oath of antiquity guided the behavior and commitment of practitioners of medicine. So too do codes of ethics seek to instill in practitioners a commitment to the principles contained in the code. An obstacle to ethical codes is that the tasks of management are too complex to be codified and covered in a comprehensive manner by a single document. Questions will inevitably arise that are not covered in the code. In attempting to answer such concerns, managers often design the code to be widely applicable but not so general as to be of no use. Another potential problem is that codes of ethics seek to reflect a certain set of values, but the values stated might be in conflict with managers' or clients' values.

A written code can be used to train employees, represent or communicate the organization's ethical norms and goals to its members and clients, and provide some parameters on which to base behaviors. Even if a comprehensive code of ethics is developed, it is still not enough to simply ask employees to follow the letter of the code. Corresponding to the code must be something deeper than obedience to authority.

American Society for Public Administration Code of Ethics

I. Serve the Public Interest
   1. Exercise discretionary authority to promote the public interest.
   2. Oppose all forms of discrimination and harassment, and promote affirmative action.
   3. Recognize and support the public's right to know the public's business.
   4. Involve citizens in policy decision making.
   5. Exercise compassion, benevolence, fairness, and optimism.
   6. Respond to the public in ways that are complete, clear, and easy to understand.
   7. Assist citizens in their dealings with government.
   8. Be prepared to make decisions that may not be popular.
II. Respect the Constitution and the Law
   1. Understand and apply legislation and regulations relevant to their professional role.
   2. Work to improve and change laws and policies that are counterproductive or obsolete.
   3. Eliminate unlawful discrimination.
   4. Prevent all forms of mismanagement of public funds by establishing and maintaining strong fiscal and management controls and by supporting audits and investigative activities.
   5. Respect and protect privileged information.

(continued)

American Society for Public Administration Code of Ethics (continued)

6. Encourage and facilitate legitimate dissent activities in government, and protect the whistle-blowing rights of public employees.
7. Promote constitutional principles of equality, fairness, representativeness, responsiveness, and due process in protecting citizens' rights.

III. Demonstrate Personal Integrity
1. Maintain truthfulness and honesty, and to not compromise them for advancement, honor, or personal gain.
2. Ensure that others receive credit for their work and contributions.
3. Zealously guard against conflict of interest or its appearance.
4. Respect superiors, subordinates, colleagues, and the public.
5. Take responsibility for one's own errors.
6. Conduct official acts without partisanship.

IV. Promote Ethical Organizations
1. Enhance organizational capacity for open communication, creativity, and dedication.
2. Subordinate institutional loyalties to the public good.
3. Establish procedures that promote ethical behavior, and hold individuals and organizations accountable for their conduct.
4. Provide organization members with an administrative means for dissent, assurance of due process and safe guards against reprisal.
5. Promote merit principles that protect against arbitrary and capricious actions.
6. Promote organizational accountability through appropriate controls and procedures.
7. Encourage organizations to adopt, distribute, and periodically review a code of ethics as a living document.

V. Strive for Professional Excellence
1. Provide support and encouragement to upgrade competence.
2. Accept as a personal duty the responsibility to keep up to date on emerging issues and potential problems.
3. Encourage others, throughout their careers, to participate in professional activities and associations.

13 Supervising with Sharks: A Project Manager Deals with an Exploitative Boss

Pamela Tarquinio Brannon

ABOUT THE AGENCY

Community Organization (CO) is a county-wide fund-raising entity, affiliated with a national organization. CO provides in-kind services and raises funds for distribution to nonprofit service agencies and is the official sponsor of the Senior Volunteer Project (SVP).

The *Volunteer Center* is an adjunct service of the CO. There are seven projects within the center, one of which is SVP. The Volunteer Center's staff includes four employees.

The *Senior Volunteer Project* (SVP) is a program for adults age fifty-five and over that provides volunteers to both nonprofit and governmental agencies. A federal grant provides the majority of funding. Additional non-federal funds are supplied by the CO, the county, and donations. Total funding is about $250,000.

ABOUT THE CHARACTERS

Julia Masterson, newly hired director of the SVP, has a background in nonprofits and elderly services.

Denise Hunter is Masterson's immediate supervisor and director of the Volunteer Center, which includes the SVP.

Angela Dixon is the statewide monitor of SVPs.

Ethan Washington is the statewide coordinator of SVP.

A NEW JOB

Julia Masterson was excited and happy when she landed the director's position at the Senior Volunteer Project (SVP). She had worked in the senior nonprofit field before she returned to the local state university to earn her MPA, and she was anxious to get back to it. However, six months into the position she was wondering if she had made the right career decision.

Masterson remembered that her interview went well, although it was a panel interview, and she had not been told that in advance. When she met with her boss, Denise Hunter, a few days later, Hunter offered her the job, but did not seem very happy. Masterson found out later that Hunter had wanted to offer the position to a friend of hers, but the rest of the panel voted for Masterson. That same day, Masterson was given a tour of the offices and experienced a pang of disappointment—the volunteer programs were housed in a warehouse-like facility at the back of the Community Organization (CO) headquarters, with cubby-holes and no private offices. Since she was going to be supervising three staff members plus volunteers, Masterson wondered where she was supposed to hold staff and personnel meetings. Also, she noticed that her cubbyhole was situated near the SVP staff, but Hunter told her that was going to be changed. Masterson's cubbyhole was going to be right next to Hunter's, across the warehouse from the SVP staff. Hunter said she wanted all her directors to be together. The fact that no one except Masterson had staff to supervise did not seem to be important to Hunter.

Masterson had been hired to replace the retiring director, a man who had run the program for more than twenty years. Her first inclination that something was not quite right happened the day she met the retiring director before he left the position. Hunter told her that, due to (unexplained) time constraints, they could only have twenty minutes together. The former director told Masterson that she had to fight for the senior program because CO's Volunteer Center wanted to incorporate it entirely into the Center. The SVP's federal funds could not be mingled with other resources so it made sense to keep the SVP somewhat autonomous from the rest of the Volunteer Center's programs. The Volunteer Center and the CO knew that autonomy was important, but they kept trying to encroach on the SVP's autonomy and cherished federal funds and volunteer resources.

SIGNS OF TROUBLE

Masterson started on January 2. During the first week she encountered several problems. First was the question of the SVP fiscal year (FY) and staff raises. The SVP's parent organization—CO—operated on a July 1–June 30 FY, yet both of the SVP's sources of funding functioned on different FYs. The county used a FY of October 1–September 30 and the federal grant used a January 1–December 31 FY.

> **Hunter:** Julia, I want you to sign these letters for your staff. Normally they would receive a raise at the start of every grant year, but we have incorporated your FY into the FY of the CO, and therefore raises will not be given until June.
>
> **Masterson:** (thinking that, on the one hand, I really don't want to sign these until I find out what is going on; on the other hand, it is only my first week and I do want to be a team player). Does my staff know their raises will be postponed?
>
> **Hunter:** Yes, this has been discussed with them.

So, Masterson signed the letters, only to find out later that week, from a very angry staff, that the issue had never been discussed with them. The staff raised such a fuss that raises were reinstated. Masterson called Angela Dixon, her state monitor, to find out what was going on regarding the changing of the FY.

Dixon: Julia, I am sorry to tell you, but the CO in general, and Hunter in particular, have been trying to make this change for a couple of years now. It is almost impossible to change the grants for the SVP projects. No formal requests have ever been sent to us. If you want to send us a letter with your request, we will look into it.

A letter was sent, and the response was that it was not possible to change the FY of the SVP. The SVP operation and records would remain as they were. The second problem Masterson encountered involved a special events coordinator.

Hunter: I am going to hire a special events coordinator, to be paid jointly by SVP and the Volunteer Center. Fifty-fifty. This person will work half-time for me and half-time for you. I need her to plan and coordinate the community events we sponsor in the spring and summer, and you will need her for your annual fall raffle. The salary will be $15,000 and you will pay half, which can come out of your non-federal funds.

Masterson: Well, honestly, my experience has been that it is difficult for one person to work for two supervisors. Besides, as I understand it, the SVP staff handles all the activity for the raffle. So, I'm not sure we need an extra person to do it.

Hunter: Well, I have decided, and I have just the right person in mind.

Masterson: How much does the SVP raffle typically raise? From looking over the books, it looks like it brings in only about $8,000–10,000 annually. So what you are proposing is that I pay $7,500 to bring in $10,000?

Hunter: Oh, with her working for you, the amount of the raffle will double. Besides, you will be able to use her for lots of other things. This is really going to help both of our programs.

Masterson brought the issue up again with Dixon, who said it did not sound quite right, but that non-federal funds could be used in a variety of ways.

The third issue was where Masterson's "office" would be located. True to her word, Hunter had the SVP Director's office moved next to her office, and away from the SVP staff. Masterson therefore had no privacy when it came to phone calls and visitors. Because there was still an empty space near the SVP staff and before she got too settled, Masterson asked Hunter if she could move closer to her staff. Hunter insisted that Masterson remain with her and her other directors. Masterson's staff told her they were sure Hunter wanted to keep tabs on all Masterson's conversations and work.

At that time, Masterson decided she could overcome all those obstacles because she was generally happy with the position and wanted to do a good job. However, other issues surfaced in the next few months.

One was the issue of the SVP newsletter, which was sent out quarterly to all volunteers and community agencies. Hunter wanted Masterson to discontinue the newsletter and incorporate any SVP news within the Volunteer Center's newsletter, which went out sporadically, when there was enough money to print it. Including any SVP news would permit the Volunteer Center to legitimately use SVP money to print their newsletter.

Masterson conferred with her staff, who told her this had been proposed before. Masterson thus declined to change the newsletter process.

Another issue was the use of computer databases. SVP had their own computers with their own database. Hunter wanted Masterson to give up her database (of 2,500 volunteers) and incorporate it into the one the Volunteer Center utilized (200–300 volunteers). Again, the Volunteer Center could then use SVP monies to maintain their computers and utilize SVP's volunteers. Masterson fought hard against this. She was helped by the fact that the programs of the Volunteer Center rarely worked.

Yet another issue was project costs. Hunter had told her that the SVP and Volunteer Center always shared some costs. After reviewing the telephone and copier costs, Masterson realized that SVP was paying more than half of the expenses, even though it was only one of seven programs run by the center.

> **Masterson:** Denise, I'd like to discuss these invoices with you. First of all, why are we charged for half the phone bill instead of being charged for each telephone line assigned to SVP? Also, why are we paying half the copier expenses when we are designated as one program out of seven in the center? Why aren't we paying one-seventh of the copier costs?
>
> **Hunter:** Oh, I am sure your staff make more copies than you think they do. And, they are always on the phone.
>
> **Masterson:** They are on the phone because that is how they recruit and place the volunteers and keep in touch with the agencies they serve. I would prefer that we look at each of the phone lines dedicated to SVP and allocate the costs that way. As for the copier, let's assign copy codes to each program. That way we can really keep track of the copies made. Then, costs can be allocated in a fairer manner.
>
> **Hunter:** Oh, the copier is just too old for that, and we don't need to do that at this time. We can look over the telephone bill if you want to, but sometimes your staff uses my staff phones.

Masterson realized that what her staff had been saying was true: the center wanted to use as much SVP money as possible. The center had a much smaller budget than her project, and it apparently did not have enough money to cover its costs, thus it used the SVP's resources.

Masterson again called the state monitor and expressed her concerns about the problems she was facing. Dixon said she would be down soon for a monitoring visit, and would bring the SVP State Director Ethan Washington with her. They would spend a couple of days listening to Masterson's concerns, and then they would submit their report.

THE REMEDY PROVES UNSUCCESSFUL

After spending several weeks getting ready for the visit and then spending two days with the monitors answering questions, going over files, and trying to find meeting places to discuss the issues in private, Masterson was hopeful that she would receive support for trying to retain some autonomy for SVP. She had no argument with Hunter, but she was tired of the constant badgering and just wanted to be left alone to run the senior project. She could barely contain her disappointment when the state monitors failed to issue a report. When she questioned Dixon about it, she was told that Washington did not want to issue a negative report and that he would probably not do anything. Masterson thought, "Now what do I do?"

Toward the end of her first six months, Masterson encountered a dilemma: As she was passing Hunter's cubbyhole, she noticed an envelope addressed to 'Julia Masterson, Director, SVP' in Hunter's mail basket. The envelope had been opened. Hunter was on vacation.

ROLE-PLAY ASSIGNMENT

You are Masterson. You have several decisions to make.

QUESTIONS FOR DISCUSSION

1. Identify the problems Masterson is facing. What examples of tension exist between Masterson and her boss, Hunter, and between the SVP and the Volunteer Center? Do these problems justify Masterson taking the envelope addressed to her that she found in Hunter's mailbox?

2. Is there any evidence that Hunter is trying to use the SVP resources to run the Volunteer Center? Is there any evidence that Hunter has a personal problem with Masterson?

3. What obligations does one have to follow the orders of a supervisor if one feels the supervisor or the orders are unethical?

4. What do you do if you "blow the whistle" on another employee and nothing happens? But what if that "other employee" is your boss? How far up the organizational chart should Masterson go to get someone to listen to her concerns?

5. At what point should one resign from a program as a way of drawing attention to the problems? Does such a resignation merely push the problem off to someone else? And what are the consequences to one's own career?

SOURCES FOR FURTHER READING

Adams, G. B., and D. L. Balfour. *Unmasking Administrative Evil.* Los Angeles: Sage, 1998

Dalton, S. L., and N. J. Cayer. *Supervision for Success in Government.* San Francisco: Jossey-Bass, 1994.

Gortner, H. F. *Ethics for Public Managers.* New York: Praeger, 1991.

- stay in current position
- quit job
- request ethics committee, document everything, whistle blow
- to whistle blow

14 Public Scrutiny and Accountability: An Ethical Dilemma in State Administration

Geralyn M. Miller

ABOUT THE AGENCY

The *Department of Occupational Licensing* is a state agency charged with oversight of the occupational licensing activities in the state. It is a mid-sized department comprised of five bureaus, each organized around a major function of the agency, one of which is the *Bureau of License Enforcement*.

ABOUT THE CHARACTERS

Mike Daniels is the bureau chief, Bureau of License Testing, Department of Occupational Licensing.

William J. Smith, the state's governor, is in the midst of a reelection campaign.

Art Springer is the bureau chief, Bureau of License Enforcement, Department of Occupational Licensing. Springer is a relatively new administrator and is caught between political pressures and ethical behavior.

Anne Trotter is the director of the Department of Occupational Licensing and is a political supporter of the governor.

POLITICS AND THE DEPARTMENT OF OCCUPATIONAL LICENSING

Art Springer has headed the Bureau of License Enforcement for three years and during that time, has enjoyed a relatively free reign. Springer reports to the agency director, Anne Trotter, who in turn reports directly to the Office of the Governor. Although there have been a few instances in which the director has intervened in matters to give Springer some guidance in his work, in general, all decisions for the Bureau of License Enforcement are left strictly up to him. Those instances in which the director has stepped in and given him an indication of the course of action he was expected to take were ones involving a potentially high profile issue or ones in which the administration had some partisan interest at stake. Even so, these directives from Trotter to Springer were ones involving courses of action he most likely would have taken on his own. Furthermore, Springer had no ethical problems with his actions or the outcomes.

110

Governor William J. Smith is a charismatic leader who runs the state with a tight rein, primarily, through his own personal style. He is used to getting his way and quite adept at negotiating high-powered deals between legislative leaders and special interest groups. Although his easy-going demeanor serves him well in his negotiations, his reputation for getting even with those who cross him also helps him get his way. He is a man who seldom takes *no* for an answer and does not take kindly to those who stand in his way. The governor expects those around him to "tow the line." He also makes it clear that loyalty to him means putting the best light on his administration, something his closest aides know means covering for him in the event of any negative publicity. The opportunity to be a part of the administration comes with the cost of being willing to sacrifice one's own career for Governor Smith's record.

When Springer moved to the state, he quickly realized that surviving as a state administrator meant demonstrating support for the governor. Springer was also quite aware that his boss, Trotter, would go along with whatever she perceived as potentially beneficial to the governor, and, of course, her own standing within the governor's administration. Smith was elected governor shortly before Springer came into his position. When Smith appointed Trotter—his longtime political supporter—to head the department, her first move was to recruit what she believed were the best in the field to head the department's five bureaus. Trotter recruited individuals she believed were stars who would make her department and the governor's administration shine. Trotter's nationwide search for her new bureau chiefs resulted in the appointment of Springer to head the Bureau of License Enforcement. Now, just over three years later, Smith was in a tough reelection campaign.

Since the campaign began, the media have covered state government more intensively, with the apparent hope of finding sensational material to present to the voting public. Sensationalism sells newspapers and attracts viewers, so stories that create more of a "horse race" between the gubernatorial candidates became fodder for the press and state administrators must thus consider public relations and media scrutiny as part of their jobs. Springer has experienced the presence of the media within his job. Recently, his director of medical enforcement noted several calls to the investigative unit regarding specific ongoing investigations. Furthermore, the agency's public information officer reported at the last staff meeting that media inquiries regarding licensing and enforcement activities were up more than 20 percent from last year at this time. At that same meeting, the public information officer cautioned the bureau chiefs to take extra care in ensuring that nothing occur within the agency that the media could construe as scandalous or improper.

Governor Smith likes to be surrounded by his supporters and likes to know that his administrative team is behind him, even though in public he is careful to display a healthy respect for non-partisan approaches to state government. His administrators understand the importance of supporting the governor to their standing within the administration. In a couple of weeks, the governor's reelection committee is hosting a gala fundraiser in the state capital. Many of the agency's mid-level administrators have expressed a desire to attend the event. Three of the other four bureau chiefs are holding meetings in their state capital offices on the day of the event so that the mid-level administrators in their bureaus' district offices can attend the event and get reimbursed for their travel expenses to and from the state capital.

THE DILEMMA

The state statutes are very clear about prohibiting partisan activity by employees on state time. Springer is certain this particular activity taking place within the agency is a violation of the spirit of the statutes if not, in fact, the letter of the statutes, especially since the other chiefs have privately admitted to him there is no legitimate reason for the meetings. The meetings appear to be called solely as a "perk" for bureau employees so that the employees can be seen at the event and have a chance to network with other state administrators. The gala fundraiser is also one of the important *career* functions within state government.

When Springer first heard about the meetings, he was shocked and certain that the bureau chiefs were acting on their own. Perhaps they saw it as a way to garner some additional favor by the director and the governor. Springer reasoned that they were probably trying to build support in the upper rungs of the administrative ladder they hoped to climb. At the outset he wanted nothing to do with the whole mess. In a conversation with the director after a recent staff meeting, however, Springer realized the bureau chiefs' actions were not self-initiated. Trotter pointedly mentioned to Springer that she was aware of planned attendance at the fundraiser of the bureau chiefs. From the tone of her voice, Springer got the distinct impression that she wanted him to "go along with the program." In other words, the director expected him to call his own meeting to cover for his employees. Springer's loyalty to the Smith Administration was being put to the test.

That same afternoon, one of the other bureau chiefs, Mike Daniels, asked Springer if he intended to call his own meeting in the state capital. Springer dodged the question, but did express his concern to Daniels that since the media had increased their scrutiny of the agency, he felt there was some risk to doing so. Daniels scoffed at the idea, doubting the media would "latch onto the scheme" and pointing out that the media usually had to be "led to the problems." Daniels felt that nothing would come of it.

Later that day when Springer was driving home from the office, he began to think about how much his job meant to him at this particular point in his life. He had worked hard to get to this level and made sacrifices along the way including working in some less desirable positions and communities. This job allowed for a lifestyle both he and his wife considered ideal. Furthermore, with two kids—and another on the way—and a stack of medical bills from some serious health problems of his youngest child, this would not be a good time to be unemployed. Springer had friends who faced the difficult challenge of looking for a job after leaving a senior-level administrative post only to find that there were few employers eager to hire them.

On the other hand, Springer had always tried to live up to a high moral code of behavior. He was an active and respected member of his local community who people sought out for advice on ethical decisions. Calling an unnecessary meeting at the taxpayers' expense was definitely not what Springer considered to be an ethical course of action.

ROLE-PLAY ASSIGNMENT

Imagine you are Springer faced with this situation.

QUESTIONS FOR DISCUSSION

1. Identify and discuss the ethical dilemmas you face.

2. What are some of the possible alternative courses of action you can take?

3. Would you discuss the situation and possible alternative courses of action with anyone and, if so, who would that be? Justify your rationale.

4. What are the primary considerations that will affect your decision in this situation, and how would you prioritize them? How would each decision relate to your career standing, the state's codes of conduct, and your own conscience?

5. What would you do if you were formally requested to schedule a meeting in the state capital and attend the fundraiser by a senior aide to the governor? What would you do if the media called your office to inquire about the appropriateness of such meetings?

SOURCES FOR FURTHER READING

Carter, S. *Integrity*. New York: HarperCollins, 1996.

Cooper, T. L. *The Responsible Administrator*. San Francisco: Jossey-Bass, 1998.

Sophocles. *Antigone*. Edited by Mark Griffith. New York: Cambridge University Press, 1999.

15 Eliminating Disability-Associated Employment Discrimination: Deciding the Future of Safe Haven

Gary E. May

ABOUT THE AGENCY

Safe Haven was founded in 1964 "for the purpose of providing job-training employment to persons with epilepsy and other disabilities, who are otherwise employable." The production employees in the factory are persons with disabilities, and the managers and support staff are non-disabled. This nonprofit organization serves business and industry in the Hometown, Indiana, area by providing contractual services and products for businesses, including equipment cleaning, uniform laundering, inspection services, and other services.

ABOUT THE CHARACTERS

Adam Male, president of the board of directors, is also an executive of one of the client companies and his company was instrumental in founding Safe Haven. Male has been a board member for approximately ten years and is very dedicated to the mission and programs of the organization.

Barney Barrister is chair of the strategic planning committee and a prominent attorney who has been involved with the organization for several years. Barrister is a dynamic leader, who has led the committee to consider a wide variety of options, mostly focused on increasing the workforce and bringing more contracts into the organization. He seeks the involvement in the organization of Xavier Pert, a member of the community who has a background in disability-related services and management, as he feels Pert will have suggestions as to how they might recruit more workers with disabilities.

Herb Jefe is the plant manager, brought in to manage the company when it was experiencing serious financial problems, and its future was very much in doubt. He and his assistant implemented a consistent management system, bid jobs appropriately, and aggressively sought new accounts for the organization. Their attempts at a turnaround were met with success to the point that now they were having trouble meeting the expectations of their long-standing, reliable corporate customers. Jefe is very loyal to Safe Haven, but he is approaching retirement age and wishes to retire soon. He has no definite retirement date in mind.

Harry Jefe, assistant plant manager and Herb's son, is less committed to the organization than his father and aspires to own his own construction business.

Xavier Pert, consultant and disabled Vietnam veteran, has been very visibly involved in developing Vietnam veteran programs nationally. He has also served as the director of the state's Vocational Rehabilitation agency.

SAFE HAVEN: A SUCCESSFUL DISABILITY EMPLOYER   *financial +
labor probs*

Safe Haven has a good track record among the businesses using its services. Their services are dependable and their pricing is reasonable. Many organizations contracting with Safe Haven also feel strongly about being a socially responsible business, in that they both feel good about working with an employer of those with disabilities and are seen in the community and among their customers as doing the right thing by supporting Safe Haven. The organization also enjoys ample public and political support.

Safe Haven employs approximately forty-five people, thirty-five of whom are client/ employees who have a variety of disabilities. Several of the employees have worked at Safe Haven since it was established. Most of the employees expect to remain in the employ of Safe Haven, and the majority of those who have worked or attempted to work in integrated settings in the past report experiencing discrimination and deferential treatment. In most instances, the employees are single and reside with their family. Safe Haven has cultivated a relationship with employees' families and many of the families report a close identification with Safe Haven.

THE BOARD'S DILEMMA

Safe Haven is headed by a board of directors. The board is a typical community board for a nonprofit organization. It includes corporate executives, professionals, retirees, volunteers, prominent members of the media, and others. Most are strongly identified with the organization and feel that it is helping to promote appropriate employment for people with disabilities. They are actively involved in the leadership of the organization. Wishing to do what is right, they are open to suggestions and guidance. They have concerns about the future of the organization, since Herb Jefe, the plant manager, has indicated he is entertaining retirement plans.

Safe Haven is facing the challenge of competition from other segregated employment organizations for people with disabilities (the sheltered workshops at Hometown Association for Retarded Citizens, Goodwill Industries, and the Hometown Association for the Blind). Unlike other disability organizations, Safe Haven has not received Vocational Rehabilitation or other state/federal funds. Rather, workers are paid prevailing minimum wage, receive a benefit package, and occasional bonuses, whereas the salary of their competitors' workers is subsidized by government grants and aid.

Moreover, there is changing public sentiment regarding segregated disability employers. An increasing number of political leaders and others feel it would be best to integrate disabled employees into the general workforce. As a result, Safe Haven's board is concerned that the organization's days are numbered.

THE CONSULTANT'S PLAN

Barney Barrister, chair of the board's Strategic Planning Committee, sought the advice of Xavier Pert, a well respected consultant on disability employment issues. Pert told Barrister that the movement in employment for people with disabilities was toward employment in integrated settings with existing companies, rather than in segregated organizations comprised of disabled workers. He pointed out that it has been demonstrated that people with disabilities prefer this arrangement and that, with proper supports, they can effectively compete in such integrated settings. Pert said that recruiting more workers with disabilities for employment in a segregated setting was not desirable. Barrister invited Pert to attend a meeting of the Strategic Planning Committee, which he did. At the meeting, Pert told the committee the same things he had told Barrister in their discussions. The Strategic Planning Committee invited Pert to attend the next meeting of the full board. They, too, were attentive and interested.

Pert has identified the following factors that seem to contribute to the labor shortage: (1) the need for prospective employees to identify themselves as persons with disabilities (the emergence of the Disability Rights movement and disability pride notwithstanding, disability is still a low status and avoided identity); (2) the need for relatively high skill levels when compared with sheltered workshops (according to Safe Haven, "The employees at Safe Haven demonstrate every day that persons with epilepsy are capable of working in an industrial environment and of producing quality work."); (3) the efficacy of current medications that control the symptoms of epilepsy; (4) the fact that epilepsy is among the categories of disabilities for which relatively low unemployment is experienced; (5) the region is experiencing a strong economy with growth in new industries and an expansion of existing industries; (6) the trend in public policy for people with disabilities has been toward community inclusion in all spheres of living; (7) the difficulty in finding a niche market or product; and (8) structural barriers to employment (employees lose SSI, Medicaid, food stamps, etc.).

Pert suggested that the board liquidate the organization's assets and assist the workers in finding jobs in the private, for-profit sector.

Management's Plan

The actual management of the organization is centralized in a plant manager and his son, Harry Jefe, who serves as his assistant. Management has investigated several possibilities for developing a unique product that could be manufactured by the organization and marketed through an existing retail establishment. (Another facility for persons with disabilities in Hometown has negotiated such an arrangement for one of their products that is sold at K-Mart.) Several products have been tried, but failed to attract the attention of retailers. Recently, the board has become increasingly impatient with these failed attempts. But the facility is still in decent financial health, having accumulated a sizeable cash surplus over the years. The managers propose continuing the effort to find a marketable product to manufacture for a major retail firm.

THE BOARD'S DECISION

Several months ago, the board created a Strategic Planning Committee to investigate possible alternatives to assure ongoing employment for its workers, solvency for the organization, and assure customers' expectations were being met. This committee has been charged with soliciting the opinions of consultants and key informants in the community, including conferring with Safe Haven's "competitors"—some of the sheltered workshops in this market. The board is giving very serious consideration to Pert's recommendations, but they have concerns about "abandoning" their employees.

ROLE-PLAY ASSIGNMENT

As a member of Safe Haven's board, what course of action do you recommend. The Strategic Planning Committee, on which you also sit, is preparing the report to the board.

QUESTIONS FOR DISCUSSION

1. What are the problems and issues before the board?
2. How important is public opinion to the direction of such an organization? To what extent do political developments shape the direction of nonprofit organizations such as Safe Haven? Should such factors as the move away from "segregated," disability organizations to integrated work environments play a role in shaping the mission of organizations like Safe Haven? How might Safe Haven utilize its image to its benefit?
3. Whose input should the board seek in weighing its options and making its decision?
4. What ethical obligation does the board have to Safe Haven's employees? Does this ethical obligation remain if most prospective workers with disabilities prefer working in integrated environments?
5. What role should ethics play in the decision with respect to other factors such as competition, cost of the production process, trends in society on disabilities, and so on?

SOURCES FOR FURTHER READING

Kosciulek, J. G. "Implications of Consumer Direction for Disability Policy and Rehabilitation Service Deliver." *Journal of Disability Policy Studies* 11 (2000): 80–89

Shapiro, J. P. *No Pity: People with Disabilities: Forging a New Civil Rights Movement.* New York: Times Books, 1994.

Trupin, L., D. S. Sebesta, E. Yelin, and M. P. LaPlante. *Trends in Labor Force Participation Among Persons with Disabilities, 1983–1994.* San Francisco: University of California Press, 1997.

- do nothing - no change
- go fully disabled & apply for gov't funding
- close Safe Haven
- move direction of Safe Haven in service offerings and use a different organization as a benchmark to live up to.

Cultural Diversity and Social Justice: Racial Profiling in a Police Department

James D. Ward

ABOUT THE AGENCY

The city of *Onate,* population 60,000, is a small but growing college town in rural southeastern New Mexico. The chief of the *Onate Police Department,* a transplanted Bostonian, was an assistant chief in Lowell, Massachusetts, before arriving in Onate five years ago. The chief has a reputation for running his department with an iron fist. According to him, northeastern "snowbirds," of whom he is only one of many, came to the quiet Southwest to escape the crime-laden streets of New York and Boston. So, he believes that his zero tolerance policy for gang activity and drug trafficking is not only appreciated but expected.

ABOUT THE CHARACTERS

Charles Johnson is African American and is assistant professor of government at Southwest College in Onate, New Mexico.

Leland Smith is Caucasian and is a Boston transplant and Onate's Chief of Police.

Frank Ortiz is Hispanic and is a cop with a shady past. Few know Ortiz was fired by the Los Angles Police Department for yelling racial slurs at a man he was attempting to apprehend.

Mayor Gus Russo is Caucasian and is an ambitious mayor in a council-manager system.

Fred Booker is African American and is the local NAACP president.

THE INCIDENT

It was 10:30 on a hot September night in southern New Mexico. Charles Johnson still felt his feet pounding against the pavement as he spotted his black BMW ahead in the Freeman Hall parking lot. He was nearly finished with his three-mile jog. It was a good feeling Johnson had, having gotten this run in after teaching a two-and-a-half hour graduate seminar; not bad, he reasoned, for a thirty year old.

On his way home he drove to Jones Supermarket to refill a plastic water jug. Standing at the coin operated water dispenser adjacent to Jones' dimly lit parking area, Johnson watched the water pouring into the clear, plastic jug, allowing his mind to wander. The dispenser suddenly stopped and a little water dribbled down the sides of the container. The instant the water stopped pouring a strange feeling came over Johnson. He felt like someone was watching him just as he had watched the water flow into the jug. He glanced around but saw no one. The dimly lit parking lot seemed empty.

It had been less than a month since Johnson moved to Onate to begin his teaching job. Even so, he was at the point of feeling somewhat comfortable in this western town of Mexican and Old West heritage, but with very few other African Americans. As Johnson drove back onto Lowes Avenue he did not see the other car that was quietly parked at the far end of the darkened lot. It was about fifty yards away. Nor did he see the car's headlights pop on as it too began to move toward Lowes Avenue. As Johnson casually drove toward busier Zelcor Boulevard, the car behind him sped up and Johnson, looking in his rearview mirror, got his first glimpse of it as it seemed to get closer and closer. Even from the distance, Johnson sensed it was a police cruiser. Seconds later he realized his assumption was correct. It was a dark blue cruiser. But, this did not bother him as he waited at the intersection of Lowes and Zelcor. Why should it? He had already switched on his turn signal. His seat belt was buckled.

Johnson's apartment was left on Zelcor, less than a mile away. So, he signaled to get into the left lane. Shortly after changing lanes flashing lights from the police cruiser spun on. "What?" he exclaimed to himself. "Tell me what I have done?" Charles pulled off Zelcor and into an empty office park. As he sat in the car, he saw the cruiser pull up behind him and turn its lights on bright. "Why are they stopping me?" he pondered. A single cop approached him while shining a flashlight through the back windshield of his car and then gradually into his side mirror.

"Why did you stop.....? Oh my God! Oh!" Johnson exclaimed, seeing the barrel of a handgun pointed directly at his face.

"Get out of the car and keep your hands where I can see them!" shouted an Hispanic-looking officer, as he tightly gripped his weapon with both hands.

Johnson hurriedly exited the vehicle as the officer slowly backed up. "Why did you pull your gun on me?" Johnson demanded. "Why did you stop me?"

"Keep your hands down by your side!" shouted the officer, slowly placing his gun back into its holster. "I wanna see your driver's license and insurance card."

"This is racial harassment!" Johnson proclaimed. "You should know that I will be filing a complaint."

"You're gonna have a ticket with my name and badge number to help you do it! ID! Now!" Officer Frank Ortiz retorted, his hand poised to unholster his weapon. "And keep your hands down by your side!"

In his frustration, Johnson suddenly realized he had gestured with his hands. He could not help it. It's something he had always done, especially when teaching. "All that's in the trunk," he explained, his palms now tightly gripping his sweaty, oversized white T-shirt and cotton shorts. "I've just finished running. Everything's in the trunk."

"Get them!" demanded the cop, continuing to rest his hand on the holstered gun.

Johnson opened the unlocked trunk and retrieved his wallet and a large envelope from out of his brief case. "Here. Here's my driver's license," he told the officer, handing him the whole wallet.

"You have proof of insurance?" asked the cop, as he observed the license.

"Yes. It's in this envelope," said Johnson, holding the large white parcel with both hands. "I just got them renewed."

Johnson attempted to open the envelope but his hands began to tremble. "Here, you take the whole thing," he offered the cop, extending the paper towards him. "I'm too nervous."

"Fine," the cop remarked sarcastically, quickly removing the driver's license from Johnson's wallet. As the cop attempted to hand the wallet back to Johnson in exchange for the insurance papers, the wallet slipped through Johnson's fingers and dropped to the ground.

"Why are you nervous?" demanded Officer Oritz, his face exulting the power of his position.

"Because no one has ever pulled a gun on me before," Johnson replied, stooping to retrieve the black leather wallet resting next to his jogging shoes. His voice cracked in hapless despair.

"You changed lanes without signaling," noted the cop. "Ah, and you have an out-of-state license plate. We assumed you were lost or intoxicated." To Johnson, the explanation seemed to be made-up on the spot. The officer avoided making eye contact.

"I'm not lost. And, I am not drunk," cautiously replied Johnson.

"You have a criminal record?" the cop imprudently asked while perusing the items in the envelope.

"No!" Johnson asserted, frightened but defiant.

"What's your social security number?"

"555-222-5774."

"Wait here," ordered the cop, as wrote down the number and walked away with the driver's license and insurance papers.

Johnson could not believe this was happening to him. He had never had any trouble with the law. He had never been arrested. As Johnson waited, he saw a plain-clothed officer standing next to the cruiser as the cop got inside and made several calls. To Johnson, it seemed as if the wait was forever; however, it was only about fifteen minutes before the officer returned.

"So, you're clean, huh?"

"Yes," replied Johnson. "Why are you surprised? Is it because I am Black?"

"I didn't even know you were black until after I stopped you," argued the cop, his countenance having mellowed. "I saw that parking sticker on your car. I figured you were probably a student."

"I'm not a student," responded Johnson. "I am a professor."

"What do you teach?"

"Government."

"I was a government major," replied Oritz. "But I'm not in class this semester. Hey, I'm sure we can put this all behind us. I told you why I stopped you. You changed lanes without signaling. It's no big deal. I'm not even gonna give you a ticket. So, we're clear on why I stopped you, right?"

RACIAL PROFILING

Johnson remembered having met Fred Booker, the local NAACP chapter president, a week earlier. He called Booker early the next morning and arranged to meet with him at Booker's office.

"What you say is not unusual," replied Booker, as Johnson fought unsuccessfully to suppress the tears that flowed freely down his masculine cheeks. "You're a young Black man driving an expensive car late at night. And, you've got out-of-state license plates. It happens all the time. In fact, I'm surprised this hasn't happened to you before," Booker remarked. "It's a real big problem back on the East Coast. Have you heard about the 'Traffic Stops Statistics Study Bill'?"

Johnson replied that he had not so Booker explained that it dealt with racial profiling. The bill had passed the House and was now in the Senate. Booker stated that the NAACP was lobbying for its passage. The initiative would force police departments to record the race, ethnicity, gender, and age of every person stopped, even if no ticket is issued. This information would thus enable the justice department to study police behavior to determine if they are stopping people based on their race. Johnson admitted that he was surprised he had not heard of the bill. Booker reassured him and suggested that there could be some good in it. He recommended they contact Mayor Gus Russo and fill him in on what happened and see what he has to say.

Johnson returned home, and Booker placed the call to Russo's office. By the late afternoon Booker had not heard back from the mayor's office. When Johnson talked to Booker later that afternoon, he agreed with Booker's suggestion that they put out a press release on the matter. Booker warned that the action would be "a major step" and that "there will be no turning back." Johnson read the release and saw that Booker had captured the entire essence of his encounter in one double spaced, typewritten page. The release was immediately faxed to all major newspapers and broadcast stations in New Mexico and west Texas. It read:

The Onate NAACP is gravely concerned over the numerous occurrences of police abuse of minority motorists. Dr. Charles Johnson, an assistant professor at Southwest College, was pulled over at gun point for no reason other than he was a young, Black man driving an expensive car late at night. The officer, Frank Ortiz, gave Johnson no justifiable reason for the stop but detained him for fifteen minutes while a criminal background check was performed. The NAACP has lobbied Congress to pass the Traffic Stops Statistics Study Bill that we believe is the first step in attacking racial profiling and in eliminating pretextual traffic stops where police officers stop motorists on the pretext of some minor traffic violation but the real motivator is race.

The Police Department's Perspective

Police Chief Leland Smith first heard about the press release when he received a telephone call that evening from a reporter for one of the Albuquerque television stations. "This is my first time hearing of this," said Smith. "But, I can guarantee you that the Onate Police Department does not tolerate racial discrimination in any fashion. I'll initiate my own investigation into the matter and hold a press conference tomorrow."

The two police officers, Ortiz, the rookie officer that pulled Johnson over, and training officer Kurt Grange were questioned separately on video tape. Sergeant Paul Lucero of the Internal Affairs Department, assisted in the investigation. Ortiz and Grange both stated that the driver was stopped after he signaled to drive the wrong way down an interstate off ramp. They also stated that, seeing the out-of-state license plate, they assumed the motorist to be either lost or intoxicated.

"We need to get that press release out ASAP," Chief Smith said to Sgt. Lucero, as they wrapped the investigation. "I think we know what happened. Don't forget to mention the five o'clock press conference in there."

"OK chief. It's in there," responded Lucero. "It's printing now."

"It says Charles Johnson was stopped because he signaled to turn the wrong way down an exit ramp," read Smith, as he picked up the freshly printed release. "I think we want to say that he drove down the exit ramp."

"But that's not what Ortiz and Grange said," argued Lucero.

"I'm running the show here Lucero! I've handled Blacks like this before. You give them an inch and they take a mile."

Sgt. Lucero protested but Smith talked him down. Then, without Lucero's knowledge, Chief Smith rewrote the press release and had his secretary fax it to the area news media. Lucero, Ortiz, and Grange would not know about the rewrite until the press conference later that day. With members of the press crowded around the conference table at police headquarters and with camera lights brightly shining on his face, the chief stated:

Charles Johnson was stopped after officers saw him driving the wrong way down an interstate exit ramp. Johnson then made a U-turn and crossed several lanes of traffic without signaling. The officers reported seeing his out-of-state license plate, and they assumed he could be lost or intoxicated. Furthermore, Ortiz noticed suspicious activity in Johnson's car. He twice ordered Johnson to show his hands but Johnson refused. At that time, and in accordance to proper procedure, Ortiz drew his weapon and pointed it to the ground. The officer was justified in drawing his weapon because he feared for his safety. Johnson was belligerent, uncooperative, and accused the officer of stopping him only because he was Black. In conclusion, my thorough investigation has exonerated both officers of any wrongdoing. They both acted properly and in accordance with police procedure.

The Situation Escalates

Johnson became extremely upset after seeing the reports on television and reading the chief's accusations in the newspapers. So, he decided not to talk to any reporters. Behind the scenes, Mayor Russo called Booker at the NAACP office and blasted him for going public with a matter that could have been resolved without media intervention. Booker argued back, indicating that he went public only after Russo failed to return his phone call and that the matter demanded immediate action. One week later, and after consulting with an attorney, Johnson composed an official complaint and sent it through certified mail to Chief Smith and Mayor Russo.

After two additional weeks had passed and Johnson still had not received a response from the mayor, he called the city to ask if the city would be continuing its investigation. He was told that the matter had already been resolved; an investigation had shown that the officers acted properly. As a result, Johnson and Booker issued a second press release informing the news media that Johnson had filed an official complaint against Chief Smith, Frank Ortiz, and Onate City. Thus, in response to a new flurry of questions from the press, the city reopened the internal investigation based on alleged "new evidence." Nevertheless, a couple of weeks later the city reached its same conclusion: The police officers had acted properly. Johnson filed a law suit.

ROLE-PLAY ASSIGNMENT

You are the mayor's assistant and have been assigned the task of dealing with this matter.

QUESTIONS FOR DISCUSSION

1. What is your first action in dealing with this issue? What individuals might you want to interview or invite to provide you with information on the situation?

2. How should city officials have responded to the initial allegation of racial profiling by Johnson and the local chapter of the NAACP? Did Mayor Russo have grounds to blast Booker later that evening for not making it clear what he wanted to talk to him about? How should the mayor deal with the allegation that the police chief fabricated his version of the story?

3. Assess the need to assure that all citizens are treated fairly regardless of characteristics such as race with the need to provide public safety. To what extent do you feel police officers use racial profiling in stopping motorists? Why is this done and what type of "profile" do some officers use to justify police intervention? Did Officer Ortiz invent the charges against Johnson as a pretext to justify pulling him over, or did Johnson overreact and read something into the officer's actions?

4. What would be the impact of the NAACP press release and Johnson's lawsuit, and the corresponding media exposure of his incident, on relations between the Onate Police Department and the city's African-American community? What course of action would you recommend to address any resulting image problems and the wider issue of racial animosity in the community?

5. What are the ethical, social, and legal problems resulting from the use of racial profiling?

SOURCES FOR FURTHER READING

Harris, D. A. "The Stories, the Statistics and the Law: 'Why Driving While Black Matters.'" *Minnesota Law Review* 84 (1999): 265–326.

"Racial Profiling is Seen as Widespread, Particularly Among Young Black Men." *Gallup News Service* (2000).

"Special Section on Racial Profiling: Implications for Public Policy." *Public Administration Times* 24 (2001).

Planning and Implementing Public Programs

THE CHALLENGE OF PLANNING AND IMPLEMENTATION FOR MANAGERS

The Planning Function

Proper program or project management begins with the *planning* process. Planning involves careful attention to a number of matters, such as identifying goals and the resources required to achieve the goals, and considering alternative approaches to the delivery of the program or service. The plan is the basis for implementing the program and specifying all actions to be undertaken. Implicit within planning is the time component that planning obviously take place at the outset of the process, before formulating and implementing the program.

The key components of planning are *forecasting*—or assessing future scenarios—and specifying goals in operational formats. *Strategic planning,* a comprehensive and long-range approach to planning, involves identifying not only the goals and resources needed for goal attainment, but also the forces acting on the program or policy environment and alternative courses of action. Each potential course of action is then evaluated with respect to environmental forces and goals. Managers must be careful to focus their planning efforts on the entire policy area rather than just a single program. It must be remembered that the program under consideration is but a part of larger agency goals and missions, so it is beneficial to view the program's place and role within the larger system and not as simply a facet of it. Likewise, although strategic planning models recommend long-range plans, the reality of politics and administration compels managers to consider the more immediate needs and results of their efforts. As such, while targeting long-range objectives, many planners balance ideal and comprehensive scenarios with medium-range plans.

Most approaches to planning assume that the process is a rational one. The basic steps involved in planning are: (1) identify problems, (2) identify possible opportunities and objectives to be achieved, (3) design several possible courses of action, (4) compare and evaluate each alternative, (5) develop the plan, and (6) seek feedback from evaluators on the outcome of the plan.

The Implementation Function

Once policies and programs are formulated, perhaps the most difficult task arises: carrying them out. *Implementation* involves putting the program in place or into effect. The implementation phase of policies and programs is the primary focus of the field of public administration. The actual implementation of public programs and services confronts numerous challenges. Even the best plans can go awry, and it is impossible to predict and plan for all hurdles and scenarios. As such, program administrators typically face a number of decisions, many of them absent from the planning document. Also, the language used by policy makers as well as the statutes governing public programs are often vague or unclear, meaning street-level administrators must interpret the meaning of statutes and make decisions about the actual implementation of programs.

Implementation has been plagued by a lack of scholarly attention historically. In fact, it has been called the "missing link" in social theory and more attention to this stage in the policy or program cycle is needed.[1] So too have policy makers and planners at times ignored implementation considerations and the street-level managers involved in the actual implementation of programs were not consulted during the formulation stage of the process. Not surprisingly, traditional practices of implementation were insufficient, leading to an array of shortcomings.[2]

Scholars now recognize that this phase in the life cycle of policies and programs has unique demands and challenges, and the lack of consideration given to implementation might explain the failure of many public programs and services. This appears to have been the case in the 1960s and 1970s when numerous programs were created in one of the most active legislative periods in the nation's history.[3] Public officials were dismayed to note that many of these programs did not appear to accomplish their intended tasks, and improper approaches to implementation seemed to be part of the problem.

THE POLITICS OF PLANNING AND IMPLEMENTATION

It is a tricky and sensitive dilemma, but managers must attempt to keep program analysis and planning free from political manipulation or from solely serving goals of a political nature. At the same time, because the process exists within a political setting, the planning function must consider the reality of politics while remaining neutral and objective. Ultimately, the goal of both planning and implementation is to produce viable public programs and services. Therefore, while considering political imperatives the focus should be, as the saying states, "Good government is good politics."

The astute scholars of policy implementation, Jeffrey Pressman and Aaron Wildavsky, noted that a core complexity of the implementation process is the multiplicity of perspectives and multiplicity of participants.[5] The many stakeholders in the outcome of the program have different perspectives on how the program or service should be delivered, how much priority should be given to it, and other concerns, and will exert pressures on both the planning and implementation phases of the program. The pressures from clients and special interests interfere with crafting and implementing programs. But street-level managers must be free from such interference. Giving managers the resources and tools necessary to implement programs helps them avoid political influence.

Because of the give-and-take of the legislative process, public programs are often the byproduct of compromise. They are thus not always the "best" way to realize the intended goal. Moreover, programs are designed with politics in mind and multiple objectives. As a result, the language underlying public programs often mandates "reasonable" approaches or administrators acting to the best of their abilities. The existence of such vagaries places the manager in the role of policy maker. While filling in the blanks inherent in legislative language, managers are confronted with ample discretion and making important decisions. Thus, implementation is not a matter of simply following the letter of the law to provide public programs.

Planners should consider a number of alternatives and accept inputs from an array of sources and perspectives. An advantage of this is that programs will not be developed that are controlled or captured by one interest or individual. Moreover, planners have the responsibility of providing policy makers with a variety of options. As the new president, John F. Kennedy made uninformed decisions about the disastrous Bay of Pigs invasion in Cuba. He would later admit that he did not receive or solicit enough perspectives on the issue and listened to only a few advisers.

DECISION-MAKING ISSUES TO CONSIDER AS YOU READ THE CASES

Implementation is a Political Endeavor

The many models of or approaches to implementation reflect the complexities of the issue and paint the process as overtly political. Eugene Bardach, author of *The Implementation Game*, sees the implementation process as defined by such elements as bargaining, uncertainty, and persuasion.[6] As such, implementation mirrors many political processes, although it is thought of as a neutral administrative activity. Managers employ a number of "gamesmanship" strategies to carry out their programs. Another approach, by scholar Milbrey McLaughlin, also views the process of implementation as inherently political.[7] The competition of interests bringing pressure to bear on administrators requires that senior administrators and elected officials provide street-level managers with the necessary political supports to minimize outside influence on the process or administrators.

Robert T. Nakamura and Frank Smallwood, in their book, *The Politics of Implementation*, view the stages in the policy process or program life cycle as interrelated. It is problematic to approach the planning and development of programs as well as the formulation, implementation, and evaluation of public programs and services as linear, step-by-step processes. The actors involved in formulating, implementing, and evaluating programs—and the stages of the process themselves—comprise a larger process that must be coordinated and integrated in order to be successful. Each stage shares similar interests and must be thought of as an interdependent, larger system. The stages in this larger process are depicted in the table below.

The Policy/Program Process

Agenda Setting ⟶ Formulation ⟶ Implementation ⟶ Evaluation

Delivering Programs and Services to Society

The scope of government's authority has increased over time to cover nearly every social and economic ill facing society. As a result, managers must consider such questions as the nature and role of government in society and plan for nearly every contingency and issue. And those attempting to plan or implement programs to alleviate these many problems will find that some issues are not easily addressed or may not be solvable at all. Consider the issue of homelessness or crime. Regardless of how well programs are administered, it is doubtful the problems will be completely remedied.

But this is not to suggest that partial successes are not worthwhile. Many problems are resolved one step at a time. To better assure the success of programs, managers must consider, prior to undertaking implementation, whether sufficient resources and expertise exist for the endeavor. Administrators might need to be retrained if the program area is new or involves a degree of technical proficiency. Relatedly, managers must consider whether an existing agency can assume responsibility for implementing a program or whether a new agency should be created for the task. Managers should also recognize that their attempts at planning for change and implementing new programs will often be met with institutional resistance to change, stemming from entrenched interests in the bureaucracy. They will also face a variety of political pressures before, during, and after carrying out the program. Indeed, developing plans and implementing programs are complex undertakings.

17 Developing a New Policy: A Police Department Responds to Street Gangs

Mike Carlie

ABOUT THE AGENCY

The Midvale Police Department consists of 300 police officers serving a community of nearly 300,000 residents. It is funded with a combination of revenues from local sales and property taxes (the bulk of the budget) as well as by federal grants and local contributions. The police chief's position is appointed by the city manager with the advice and counsel of the city council.

ABOUT THE CHARACTERS

Chief Alex Buckner, Midvale Police Department, reports directly to, and takes orders from the city manager.

City Manager Sandro Taft is a hard-line manager with little patience for inaction, yet Taft rarely takes an initiative himself or responsibility for his actions. He is dependent on those under him.

Major Max Carson, one of several majors under the Police Chief, is in charge of officers in several divisions, including: juvenile; patrol (cars, bikes, motorcycles, foot); homicide; robbery; burglary; and narcotics.

THE PROBLEM

Midvale, a community that has experienced steady growth over its history, is currently being invaded by street gang members from nearby larger cities. While Midvale has a history of having several local street gangs, those gangs have typically only been involved in protecting their neighborhood (turf gangs) or misdemeanor crimes (theft, underage drinking, vandalism, and occasional assault through inter- and intra-gang conflicts).

To date, patrol officers have been handling the community's gang problem at the same time as all non-gang-related crime problems (traffic violations, disorderly conduct, calls for service in regard to theft, burglary, and rape). However, it is now clear that the work of the patrol officers has become overwhelming because gang-related crimes have increased dramatically. In fact, the Midvale citizens now view the gang problem as out of control.

One year ago some gang members from a nearby city visited Midvale and, much to their delight, found a ready market for the sale of illegal drugs (marijuana, crack cocaine, etc.). As their sales increased, members of other intruder gangs also moved to Midvale. The influence of these gangs on the local gang situation has become apparent. Feeling their turf is being invaded by intruder gangs, acts of violence between gangs are increasing. And some local gang members, seeing the profits to be made from the sale of illegal drugs, have begun to join the intruder gangs in their activities. In order to get money to buy drugs to sell, gang members are committing income-producing crimes all over town. As a result, police have noticed a significant increase in both residential and commercial burglaries, street robberies (muggings, purse snatchings, etc.), thefts (from cars and car theft), and the use of drugs by the community's youth.

A growing number of residents on the west side of town, where the increase in gang activity is most noticeable, are alarmed and have begun calling the police department and the city manager to complain about the problems they are having with gangs and their criminal behavior. A few of the residents have written hard-hitting editorials about the problem and have begun attending city council meetings to voice their concerns.

Under growing pressure from west side residents and many of the victims of the burglaries, robberies, and thefts, Midvale City Manager Sandro Taft has instructed Midvale Police Chief Alex Buckner to "do something about these gangs! And don't ask for any additional funds!" More specifically, Taft told Chief Buckner that the city council wants to see two outcomes: (1) a reduction in the number of crimes being committed by gang members, and (2) a corresponding reduction in the number of gangs and gang members. And they want to see the results soon.

Given the way in which bureaucracies work, Buckner then ordered Major Max Carson to "do something about these gangs! And don't ask for any additional funds!" He also told Carson to prepare an action proposal for dealing with the two problems Taft identified. So Major Carson is confronted with a dilemma: How, with no additional funds, might one organize the department to deal effectively with the gang situation and its resulting crime problems? Carson asked the lieutenants reporting to him to develop some points to consider. The lieutenants issued the following points.

Issue A. From an organizational perspective, one might consider, (1) creating a new division in the police department (a gang unit) to deal with the problem, (2) inserting a special unit into an existing division, or (3) giving gang training to all police officers, or train only a select few in how to deal with gangs and gang-related problems.

Issue B. If a gang unit were to be developed, where should the unit be placed within the structure of the department (within narcotics, the juvenile division, etc.)? Likewise, there is the issue of where the officers should come from? Given the budget limitations, it would be difficult to hire new officers, but it would also be problematic to transfer them from other existing units.

Issue C. If a new unit is created, some thought must be given to, (1) how it would be organized in terms of hierarchy, (2) its relationship to other units, and (3) its position within the police department.

Issue D. The police department must develop goals for their gang policy/operation. For instance, should the gang unit be an intelligence gathering operation only, allowing other units to conduct arrests? If so, what kinds of intelligence should be gathered on the gangs, and how might it be most effectively used? Or, should the gang unit collect intelligence *and* make arrests? The unit must give some thought to whether it wants to try and arrest all gang members, only the most violent, or only the leaders.

Issue E. The issue of prevention must be considered if the police department is to fully address the issue of gang violence. What prevention efforts should be developed (anti-gang programs in the schools, sports activities for at-risk youth, etc.)? What units or which officers should be responsible for prevention? Remember, prevention takes a different mind set than arrests.

Issue F. In what ways can the existing units and officers in the department be utilized?

Issue G. What organizations within the community should be consulted, and what should their role be?

ROLE-PLAY ASSIGNMENT

Acting as Carson, you have just received the report from your lieutenants. Now you must propose your plan to the police chief and city council.

QUESTIONS FOR DISCUSSION

1. Evaluate the merits and weaknesses of each issue (A–G) your lieutenants presented.
2. What is your proposal for addressing crime? Assuming the proposal you forward is successful, what can be done to prevent gang problems from returning to the community?
3. How will the police officers respond to your proposal?
4. What role do the media, local activist groups, and elected officials play in the development of your proposal? How do you involve them in your decision making and plan of action?
5. How might you present your proposal to the police chief and city council to make sure it is accepted? No matter what proposal you present, adequate public and political support must be a part of your consideration. Do you consider promoting a plan that requires increases in the budget, even though the mandate was to address the gang problem without corresponding increases in funds?

SOURCES FOR FURTHER READING

Celline, H. D. *Youth Gang Prevention and Intervention Strategies*. Albuquerque, NM: University of New Mexico Training and Research Institute, 1991.

Knox, G. W. *An Introduction to Gangs*. New York: Wyndham Hall Press, 1994.

———. "Preliminary Finding from the 1992 Law Enforcement Mail Questionnaire Project." *The Gang Journal: An Interdisciplinary Research Quarterly* 1 (1993): 11–37.

Maxson, C. L. "Investigating Gang Migration: Contextual Issues for Intervention." *The Gang Journal: An Interdisciplinary Research Quarterly* 1 (1993): 1–8.

Feasibility Analysis: Hurricane Mitigation and Beach Nourishment in Coastalville

William R. Mangun, Amy K. Blizzard,
& Sheridan R. Jones

ABOUT THE ORGANIZATION

The town of Coastalville is a community located on the North Carolina coast, with a population of approximately 6,500 permanent residents and more than 25,000 seasonal residents. The town has a council-manager form of government.

ABOUT THE CHARACTERS

Janet James is Coastalville homeowner's association representative.

Jimmy Roberts is the mayor of Coastalville and a local restaurant owner.

Oliver Roscoe is a retired town council member.

Karen Wilson is the Coastalville town manager.

Frank Smith is an environmental engineer with the U.S. Army Corps of Engineers.

Jill Thomas is a high school biology teacher.

Linda Garcia is an environmental activist.

Dr. David Bean is a university professor.

Vera Mann is a retired citizen of Coastalville.

PLANNING FOR HURRICANES

The town of Coastalville has been developing plans for a beach nourishment/storm mitigation project, but before the plans could be completed Hurricane George viciously pounded the coast. Most of the property near the coast was demolished, resulting in millions of dollars in property damage. Fortunately, because of early planning actions by county and state governments, all of the town's resident and tourist populations were evacuated successfully and there was no loss of life. The remainder of the tourist season, upon which many of the full-time residents' jobs are dependent, will be curtailed substantially. Unlike Coastalville, Milleniatown, less than fifty miles down the coast, experienced very little damage. Geographically and ecologically speaking, Milleniatown is virtually identical to Coastalville. The only significant difference is that Milleniatown adopted a beach nourishment strategy five years ago and recently completed a major nourishment project.

The economic consequences of Hurricane George on Coastalville included: $8.92 million in direct property damage; $5.96 million loss in beach tourist expenditures; $1.42 million in local payroll losses; a reduction of $597,240 in local tax receipts; and an overall decline in retail sales of $7.64 million, which was the only decline in the past decade. In contrast, oceanfront damage in Milleniatown amounted to less than $250,000.

The Players and the Proposals

Janet James, a representative from the Coastalville Homeowner's Association, presented the town council with a petition signed by more than one-half of the residents. James and her husband moved to Coastalville from Pennsylvania after her husband retired from his job as a business executive. They lived in an oceanfront home and their property had been experiencing moderate erosion, but wave action associated with Hurricane George severely damaged their property. The Homeowner's Association demands that the town council agree to establish a beach nourishment program for Coastalville.

After briefly examining the petition, Mayor Jimmy Roberts accepted it and asked James to make a presentation to the town council. Mayor Roberts is a local restaurant owner who has been mayor for twelve years and has lived most of his life in Coastalville. He has always believed that his political success was tied to "giving the people what they want." Although Mayor Roberts is an avid sport fisherman and loves the natural beach environment, he is well aware of the need for economic development in the community. In fact, he is almost always swayed by public opinion and consistently seeks out "opportunities for growth" for Coastalville.

On the basis of her extensive research into beach nourishment projects, James made a strong presentation in favor of beach nourishment to the town council. She started off by handing several reports to the council from Dr. James Stronge, a renowned authority on tourism at the University of Miami, which clearly demonstrate how nourishment projects can enhance tourism. While town council members perused these documents, James pointed out the potential of beach nourishment to mitigate the impact of storms, using Milleniatown as proof of its potential. She also recited facts from the "Hutchinson Island Study" on turtle nesting that demonstrated that nourishment does not disturb these endangered animals. Relatedly, in anticipation of concerns about the need to dredge local waters for sand for the nourishment project, James referred the council to the "Reily Study," which found a benign impact on the local littoral environment from dredging and pumping sand. In concluding, James acknowledged that the cost for implementing the project may be high, but argued that the costs of not doing the project were very steep. Again, she pointed to the contrast in effects of Hurricane George on Coastalville and Milleniatown.

The tentative budget for a beach nourishment project for Coastalville involves an estimated 48,720 feet of shoreline and is reflected in the table on the next page.

Estimated Initial Project Costs:

Total Cost	$30,102,000
Federal Share	$19,566,300
State Share	$ 7, 901,775
Local Share	$ 2, 663,925
Annual Debt Service	
With 5 Year Note	($ 608,370)
With 10 Year Note	($ 349,437)
Annual Cost of Periodic Maintenance	$ 485,982
Total Annual Cost of Beach Preservation	
With 5 Year Note	$1,094,353
With 10 Year Note	$ 788,439

While listening to James make her presentation, council member Oliver Roscoe, who has lived his whole life in Coastalville and is now retired, reflected about how much he missed the "good old days" before all the tourists and the "damn Yankees" moved into town. Roscoe sees all this growth destroying the town that he loves. As a member of the town council, he has been the board member that has voted against anything that he perceived as costing the town money. To win his approval for the plan, proponents must demonstrate how such a project will benefit the town financially.

Immediately after James completed her presentation, Helen Cooper, a prominent local business owner, asked to be heard. Cooper is active in the community and Coastalville politics and is the leader of the Beach Preservation Association (BPA), a local grassroots organization. The majority of BPA members are local business people who strongly support beach nourishment as a way of promoting economic development for the community. Cooper concluded her impassioned speech with: "No sand equals no beach equals no tourists equals no jobs."

The mayor asked Karen Wilson, the town manager, who is responsible for drafting the beach restoration plan and sending it to the Army Corps of Engineers for approval, to respond to the presentations. Wilson is a professional with no personal attachment to the beach nourishment issue, but is concerned with ensuring that rules and regulations are upheld and that the project not break the town's budget. Wilson realized that the start up costs for beach nourishment can be high. Also, because a nourishment project needs to be nourished at periodic intervals, the whole process requires long-range planning that addresses sand sources, financing, and land uses. One of the most difficult problems will be where to get the sand. The sand must be compatible with the existing sand and economically feasible to procure. Sources like inland sand pits can sometimes offer economically viable sand but quality is often lacking.

Details of the Dilemma

In anticipation of the probable need to inform the town council about the technical and intergovernmental aspects associated with beach nourishment, Wilson had invited Frank Smith to attend the meeting. Smith has been with the Army Corps of Engineers since he graduated from college. He knows practically everyone on the coast and has worked on every state beach project over the past twenty years. Smith sees the Corps' role as one of protecting the quality of life for beach community residents and believes that the Corps is the only organization qualified to determine the validity and scope of beach nourishment projects.

The town manager asked Smith to explain to the town council and members of the community some of the technical and cost issues associated with beach nourishment. Smith discussed beach nourishment as a mitigation construction project, showing slides on a number of cases where the Corps has completed nourishment projects. He argued that a lot of so-called "experts" claimed these projects were a waste of money until a major storm event came along, like Hurricane George, and millions of dollars in property damage were avoided because of the projects.

Smith also acknowledged that there are problems of sand sources. But this problem can be minimized through a feasibility planning study because an appropriate source must be identified before a project can be funded. The source can be from a federal dredging project, an off-shore borrow area, or a combination of sources. Smith pointed out that getting sand from "upland sources" is a good news/bad news situation. If the source of the sand is close enough to the project area, the cost of mining and trucking would be minimal compared to dredging, thus reducing the overall cost of the project considerably. But sand material from upland sources is frequently inadequate for a "fill" project in terms of grain size and composition, and inappropriate materials must often be mixed in. Increased use of heavy equipment also raises the cost, may damage the road system, disrupt the flow of beach traffic, and therefore, interfere with beach recreation.

With regard to sand from "inlet areas," Smith stated that although such sand sometimes has too many fine grains for nourishment purposes, it usually can be used. Like the upland sources, there also are problems associated with sand from inlets. Obtaining dredging permits has become more difficult, as research studies increasingly demonstrate the fragility of the nearshore and estuarine communities. On a positive note, however, if the nourishment project can be tied to a navigational dredging project, the cost of obtaining the sand drops considerably, and an economically marginal project becomes possible. Also, with nearshore deposits—the most used source of sand for nourishment projects—the dredges have the capacity to work nearly year round, which might be important if seasonal breeding habitats of endangered species are impacted.

The Community Weighs In

After listening attentively to Smith's long presentation, Jill Thomas, a local high school teacher and environmentalist, stood and vigorously protested against the nourishment project. She said that she is concerned that a beach nourishment project will harm the endangered seaturtle nesting sites. Thomas is compassionate and dedicated, but some townspeople see her as a zealot and refer to her as the "Turtle Lady." Thomas has conducted a highly passionate campaign against the project since it was initially discussed, enlisting the aid of many of her biology class students, who have threatened to conduct a sit-in on the beach to prevent the project from ever being carried out.

No sooner had Thomas concluded her remarks than Linda Garcia and David Bean asked to be heard. Garcia is the president of Citizens Rallied Against Beach Sand (CRABS), a grassroots organization opposed to the beach nourishment project. She and her group see this project as wasting money, damaging to the environment, and benefiting only wealthy oceanfront property owners. CRABS has been active in a public campaign to raise awareness of the problems with nourishment, and some recent polls show that their work has been effective. CRABS has enlisted the support of Bean, a professor at East Coast University and prominent expert on coastal geologic processes and erosion patterns, who sees beach nourishment as a waste of money and time. He argued before the audience that it is nearly impossible to find a source of sand that will match a particular beach, that renourished beaches simply wash away during the next storm, and that such projects waste taxpayers' money.

Bean's presentation excited Vera Mann, the town's conservative finance watcher, who screamed out that the plan was just another tax busting proposal that must not be permitted. Displaying the town budget, Mann claimed that the town has increased property taxes 20 percent over the past five years and that it simply cannot afford the additional tax burden of the beach nourishment project. She also identified all of the new capital improvement projects initiated over the past five years: $500,000 for a highway extension; $3 million for the new Natatorium; $15 million for the new high school; and $60,000 for a Memorial Park, as well as salary increases for town employees.

ROLE-PLAY ASSIGNMENT

Mayor Roberts and Wilson, the Town Manager, have appointed you to head a special task force to make a decision on the plan. They want your report as soon as possible.

QUESTIONS FOR DISCUSSION

1. Who do you invite to serve on your task force? What interests should be represented?
2. What are the major problems facing decision makers?
3. The task force is asked to provide a recommendation on: a) Should the project be initiated? b) Who should pay and where should the money come from? c) Where should the sand come from (without sand the project is doomed)? d) Will the project harm the environment (sea turtles and other coastal flora and fauna); and e) Do economic stability issues outweigh environmental conservation issues?
4. What course of action would you recommend to the mayor and town manager to address the politically charged situation involving Thomas and her students who threaten a beach sit-in? Is there a way to assuage Thomas' concerns while still getting the beach nourishment project initiated?
5. How might Mayor Roberts and Wilson effectively address the high costs of the proposals and the budget concerns expressed by members of the community?

SOURCES FOR FURTHER READING

Leonard, L. A., T. Clayton, and O. H. Pilney. "An Analysis of Replenished Beach Design Parameters on U.S. East Coast Barrier Islands." *Journal of Coastal Research* 6 (1990): 15–36.

Leonard, L. A., K. L. Dixon, and O. H. Pilney. "A Comparison of Beach Replenishment on the U.S. Atlantic, Pacific, and Gulf Coasts." *Journal of Coastal Research* 6 (1990): 127–140.

National Research Council. *Beach Nourishment and Protection.* Washington D.C.: National Research Council, 1996.

19

Dealing with Inmates and Image: A Prison Town's Dilemma

Pat Nation

ABOUT THE ORGANIZATION

Huntsville, Texas, is a unique town in that it houses the largest prison population in the world, confined to one community area. This town leads the United States in executions each year. In any given month there are typically at least two executions scheduled, sometimes more. Within the close vicinity of Huntsville are eight different prisons. The "Walls Unit," where the actual executions actually take place, is located in the heart of downtown Huntsville and can be seen from the Sam Houston State University dorms, less than two blocks away. And it is within close walking distance to the courthouse. By all standards, Huntsville, Texas, is a prison town.

ABOUT THE CHARACTERS

Don Gravestone is the newly elected mayor of Huntsville and a professor at Sam Houston State University. Gravestone appreciates the small-town atmosphere of Huntsville and is one of the town's residents that is openly concerned about the overall image of the town as "a prison town." Gravestone would like to see the university replace the prison in defining the town image.

Alice Ragby is the director of the Huntsville Chamber of Commerce, a position she has held for almost five years. Ragby is a native of Huntsville, going back six generations. She would like to update the town's image and has been actively attempting to do so, but she is publicly cautious about her stance due to the town's economic concerns.

David Hallowday is the director of the Texas Department of Criminal Justice, which is headquartered in downtown Huntsville. Hallowday has been director for fourteen years and is very proud of the worldwide attention Huntsville attracts because of the prison system. Hallowday would actually like to see several new prisons built in the vicinity.

Roger Johnson is the owner of the largest furniture store in town, located just across from the courthouse in downtown Huntsville. Johnson is eighty-four years old and his family has owned this furniture business for more than 100 years. A member of the chamber of commerce, Johnson has been known to threaten members of the media when they have camped out in front of his store to cover the prison executions.

Katie McDade, owner of a restaurant located just across from the courthouse, constantly complains to anyone who will listen about how difficult it is to find parking by her restaurant during a publicized execution, which can last for up to three weeks. But McDade admits that she would have to shut down business if it was not for the people coming into town for the executions.

Linda McDade is Katie's sister and part-owner of the family restaurant. Linda is greatly disturbed with all the attention the town gets because of the executions and is strongly opposed to the death penalty on moral grounds.

Richard Duvall, head of the Huntsville Parole Board, has political aspirations and comes to every town meeting to further his career, as well as to appease the community and their concerns over paroled prisoners.

John Edwards has been Huntsville Police Chief for twenty-four years and will be the first to tell you that the town has diverse beliefs about anything pertaining to the prisons.

Angela Bakersfield, an employee of the City of Huntsville, works at the courthouse and is leading an effort to draw attention to the problems of traffic in the downtown area.

Arnold Kitchens is the new superintendent of schools for Huntsville, Texas. Kitchens is concerned about safety issues stemming from having so many prisoners in the community and the proximity of the prisoner release site to the town—both issues brought up by several parents at the PTA meeting last week.

A PRISON TOWN

The City of Huntsville is part of Walker County in east Texas. Even though the town has various other potential interests to both the community and to visitors, the prisons continue to dominate the town. Upon entering Huntsville, visitors are offered several walking and driving tours of the various prison sites, all offered by the Huntsville Chamber of Commerce. The town has several museums, one of which is the world famous "prison museum," located in the town square just behind the courthouse. This museum has "Old Sparky," the actual Texas electric chair used for decades to execute prisoners, confiscated inmate weapons, relics of escape attempts, and countless facts about the characters on both sides of the prison bars. Pictures of the deceased Bonnie and Clyde, complete with close-ups of the bullet holes, are among the numerous photographs displayed throughout the museum. If a souvenir of a visit to Huntsville is desired, it is possible to purchase one of several T-shirts that displays various statements that reflect the general atmosphere of Huntsville, such as "I spent time in Huntsville, Texas." If you prefer a more hands-on remembrance, for a fee you can have your picture taken with one of the notable prisoners out at the Ellis Unit. The Ellis Unit houses death row inmates and lifers.

The City of Huntsville and the Texas prison system have forged a partnership that has existed for well over 150 years. The prison system is an integrated element of life in this city. An illustration of this is "The Walls," an old red brick prison located in downtown Huntsville, which has served continuously as a state penitentiary since 1848. Huntsville is the home of the Texas Department of Criminal Justice, even though it is not the state's capitol. The prisons have the capacity to house 15,250 prisoners, most of which are considered part of the official census, and the prison system is an integral part of the economy of Huntsville and Walker County. The Texas Department of Criminal Justice is the largest employer in the county, with more than 7,143 employees, followed by Sam Houston State University, also located in Huntsville, with 2,130 employees, the Huntsville Independent School District, and Wal-Mart. With the prison system as the major employer in the community, a majority of the town either works for the prison system or has a close family member that does. For generations, families have continued to work for the prison system in this community. Downtown Huntsville is the home of Sam Houston State University, the first teacher-training institution in the southwestern United States. This university is very well regarded for its criminal justice department, which dominates the university and is the largest criminal justice learning facility in the United States. To further illustrate Huntsville's "prison town" identity is the newest prison built—the Holliday Unit—located directly on Interstate 45. The Holliday Unit is near the large "Welcome to Huntsville" sign on the interstate. Even though Holliday Unit is noticeable to all that pass along the main interstate during the day, it is unmistakably apparent at night when illuminated. Given the visibility and dominance of the prisons in the community, many of the citizens of Huntsville have become concerned with the perceived image of their town and would like community leaders to do something about it.

PUBLIC DISCONTENT

In spite of the economic benefit to Huntsville of the prisons, recently there has begun a publicized movement as a result of a community concern. The city council wants to change the image of Huntsville from that of recognized prison town to a more typical small-town image. The town's mayor wants the town to shift its focus away from the prison and concentrate more on the university. The majority of the town supports the mayor and the city council, recognizing the negative perception of the town by outsiders as a prison town. Although residents would like to see this image changed, they do not know how it can be done. However, the director of the Texas Criminal Justice System believes that the town is doing fine with the current image, seeing no problem, and prison officials applaud the town's fame as the site of so many prisons. Likewise, most business owners fear economic repercussions if the prisons are not highlighted, due to the large influx of tourism the prisons bring. The debate continues between the two groups.

Further dividing the town on this issue is the fact that every time there is a scheduled execution—especially if the prisoner is a publicized case—traffic in town increases dramatically. Traffic is most problematic in the town square area where many small businesses are located, along with government buildings and Sam Houston State University. Traffic in the downtown area is impassable for hours at a time, and it is reported that the traffic problems are constant, both day and night, during times of high influx of visitors. During high-profile executions, crowds of reporters, television crews, journalists, human rights groups, and others from around the world gather in the downtown area.

Not surprisingly, there is debate among the community as to how to handle this situation. Most businesses claim that their local customers cannot get to their businesses, which harms their profits. On the other hand, restaurants claim that it is a huge asset for business, and they would financially go under without the constant flow of outsiders coming for the executions. Government employees state that they have to get to their jobs at least an hour and a half to two hours early each morning so that they can have a place to park. Employees complain that leaving the vicinity is equally challenging and highly stressful. Everyone in the town reports being adversely affected by the traffic and driving conditions in the downtown area because of the prisons.

About the only point of agreement is the universal disdain for the media and the image that their town has consistently received as a result of the "media's construction." When an execution takes place, the citizens complain that the cameras and microphones are constantly an intrusion in the community and some residents have literally run from reporters to avoid being photographed or filmed. When contacted about this problem, the media claim they have a right to a story. While some residents understand this, they just want the media to be more "polite or respectful" of the town's citizens when they pursue their stories and wish the town would be portrayed for something other than an execution. Thus, there is widespread desire for the media to "leave the town alone" and let the town develop a more "normal, hometown image."

To add further concern to the image of the town is the daily routine of the prison system itself. Each day around noon the prisons let out inmates that are scheduled for release. The ex-prisoners are released on town square, just a block or two from the bus station. Next door to the bus station is a clothing exchange shop, in which inmates being released can trade their prison uniforms for street clothes. The prisoners get out of prison, change their clothes, and then typically wait around downtown for three to five hours to catch their bus out of town. Many members of the community are concerned about the resulting problems with image and safety. Customers and business owners are afraid of the inmates and parents of grade-school children who attend school just a few blocks from the bus station are outraged. Parents have estimated that approximately 225 children have to walk past the release area each day. Prison officials claim that the release is not harming the town's image and that the prisoners are free citizens with rights. At one point, policing was increased to appease citizens, but there were complaints from the prisoners of harassment by police and so the monitoring was reduced.

ROLE-PLAY ASSIGNMENT

Mayor Gravestone has appointed you to coordinate his office's commission to study and recommend a plan of action on this issue.

QUESTIONS FOR DISCUSSION

1. Why is a town's image so important? Why would it be something government would be called on to address? What are the problems of having an image as a prison town?

2. Who should serve on the mayor's commission studying the issue? What perspectives do you think each of the characters mentioned at the beginning of this case would have on this dilemma? The characters reflect the community's varying perspectives on the issue; so how would you bring the community together to support your commission and subsequent plan?

3. Should the town attempt to change its "prison town" image? On what factors would you base your decision? If a change of image is called for, what is your proposal? If a change of image is not needed, what are the reasons you are going to give the town for your decision?

4. What potential economic impacts on the community will result from your proposal? How are you planning on addressing this impact? What can be done to ease the traffic problems of this community? Would you address the media concerns and why?

5. When considering the issue of prisoners being released in downtown, what are your main concerns? Who are the stakeholders? If you give more consideration to one group over another in your plan of action, how do you justify this?

SOURCES FOR FURTHER READING

Conrad, J. P., and R. A. Myren. *Two Views of Criminology and Criminal Justice Definitions, Trends, and the Future*. Chicago: Joint Commission on Criminology and Criminal Justice Education and Standards, 1979.

President's Commission on Law Enforcement and Administration of Justice. *The Challenge of Crime in a Free Society*. Washington, D.C.: U.S. Government Printing Office, 1967.

Roth, M. *Fulfilling a Mandate: A History of the Criminal Justice Center at Sam Houston State University*. Huntsville, TX: Sam Houston Press, 1997.

Schichor, D. *Punishment for Profit: Private Prisons/Public Concerns*. New York: Sage Publications, 1995.

Welch, M. *Punishment in America: Social Control and the Ironies of Imprisonment*. New York: Sage Publications, 1999.

Note: Special thanks are given to Middle Tennessee's Faculty Research and Creative Activity Grant for their generous support in this research. Also thanks are given to the citizens of Huntsville, Texas, for their openness and willingness to participate in this research about their hometown. This case is based on actual research findings conducted in Huntsville. The case presented involves actual expressed concerns and issues of the Huntsville community. All names and identities of individuals in the case profile have been altered.

To Privatize or Not to Privatize? A City Prepares to Contract Out Services

Robert P. Watson

Centraltown is an old, industrial, mid-sized city in the Northeast. After two decades of factory closings and a gradual loss of population—as residents fled to the warmth of sun-belt states—Centraltown is facing financial difficulties. A new mayor is promising to shrink government through privatization, but powerful unions and entrenched public employees oppose the plans.

ABOUT THE CHARACTERS

Nancy Martin, newly elected mayor of Centraltown, has promised to shrink government and contract out public services. She is opposed by the city's public employee union, but she is determined to move forward as soon as possible, beginning with city garbage collection.

Salvatore Pavone is the long-time head of the city's public employee union. He has always opposed privatization, as he sees it as his duty to save city jobs.

Claudia Alvarado, head of the city's management and budget office and trusted confidante of the new mayor, is charged with developing a plan to implement the privatization of municipal services.

A CITY IN DECLINE privatization

Throughout the 1980s and 1990s, Centraltown experienced several painful factory closings. The way of life in this old industrial city is coming to an end. Making matters worse, many residents joined those fleeing the "rust belt" for the "sun belt," further contributing to the city's shrinking tax base. In response to the tough times, the voters of Centraltown elected a new mayor who promised to shake things up, beginning with cuts in government programs. Mayor Martin is a political newcomer, but rode a wave of voter resentment—toward the high costs and poor quality of municipal services—into office.

One of Martin's campaign pledges was to privatize municipal services. Privatization—the practice of contracting out public services provided by government to businesses who perform the service for government—has been a widely used "solution" to problems associated with the cost and quality of public programs and services. While privatization has been used in many communities, it has not been attempted in Centraltown owing to the city's powerful municipal employee's union, who oppose any cuts in public jobs. The traditional character of the community has also led to opposition to such changes. Most residents, after all, either worked for the city or knew someone who did, and the boom years of industrial production up through the 1970s translated into economic good times for Centraltown. There was never a need to cut government programs. This has changed and both taxpayers and political reformers are now supportive of cutting what they see as the high costs of a bloated, inefficient bureaucracy.

Mayor Martin wants to begin by privatizing the city's garbage collection and use that as a model to aggressively pursue privatization of other municipal programs and services.

THE SANITATION DEPARTMENT

The Centraltown Sanitation Department is responsible for collecting garbage and does so twice weekly through the door-to-dump collection of residents' garbage. Trucks collect garbage from every home in the municipality and, once weekly, the trucks pick up garbage from large commercial dumpsters located behind or near the city's businesses. This is an expensive service that requires a staff of sanitation workers and fleet of garbage trucks. The department also collects recyclable materials (newspaper, steel cans, and plastics) biweekly from special color-coded recycling containers provided for residents. To obtain recyclable containers, Centraltown residents need only go to the sanitation department offices, fill out a request, and show a valid state ID. They are then given recyclable containers to use.

The sanitation department has been overspending its budget for several years in a row and its marginal service record has resulted in an increasing stream of complaints from citizens. These complaints include careless emptying of trash cans, trash spilled on city streets, sanitation workers being too loud, and tardy trash pick up. The department recently procured new garbage trucks, which was an expensive purchase for the city. With the acquisition of new trucks, roughly half the fleet of garbage trucks is new, the other half is very old and in immediate need of replacement. Several of the older trucks are breaking down and are expensive to maintain.

Mayor Martin has asked her trusted adviser and head of the city's management and budget office, Claudia Alvarado, to convene the mayor's new Privatization Task Force, charged with developing a plan for contracting out municipal garbage collection.

THE PROPOSALS

The mayor is serious about fulfilling her campaign pledge. She gave Alvarado a short memo that included some issues and questions to be answered. The mayor's memo to Alvarado follows.

Memorandum

TO: Claudia Alvarado, Director, Management and Budget

FROM: Nancy Martin, Mayor

RE: Plan for Privatization

DATE: June 19

I am asking you to convene a Privatization Task Force to study the issue of privatization of our municipal services, beginning with garbage collection. When I announce the formation of this Task Force in one month at my press conference, I want to be prepared to answer questions about privatization and our plan for contracting out services. I would like you to have answers to these questions on my desk one week prior to the press conference.

Issue A. How do we privatize garbage collection? I need to know the "nuts and bolts" of the process. Most governments advertise the contract and then require prospective contractors to submit sealed bids to the government. Officials then select the lowest bidder providing that prospective contractor is deemed "responsible and responsive." Is this the process we should adopt? Would this guarantee us an ethical process and a competent, affordable contractor? We need to give some thought to how we define "responsible and responsive."

Issue B. There are three sanitation service companies in the region who expressed interest in working with us: (1) General Waste, Inc., whose work is excellent but they have a record of charging high amounts; (2) Northern Waste, whose price is very affordable, but their service record is questionable; and (3) Disposal Services, a new company listing moderate prices for their services, but they are an unknown entity. What criteria should we employ in deciding which contractor to use: cost or quality? How many contractors should be encouraged to submit bids, and how should the contract be announced to the public?

Issue C. Should the city consider contracting municipal garbage collection out to the county? The county appears to do a good job of collecting garbage, and its resources are greater than those of Centraltown.

Issue D. I am already receiving severe opposition from Salvatore Pavone, head of our municipal employees union. He is going on record saying that no city job should be cut or lost and our economy would suffer from privatization. What do we do about Sal and the employees in our sanitation department? In "marketing" privatization, can we capitalize on the overwhelming public support I received during my recent campaign for cutting government?

Good luck, Claudia. I am depending on you!

ROLE-PLAY ASSIGNMENT

You are Alvarado's assistant. As the mayor's adviser and head of the city's management and budget office, Alvarado asks you to join her on the Privatization Task Force and make some preliminary recommendations to her regarding the privatization of the municipality's garbage collection.

QUESTIONS FOR DISCUSSION

1. What individuals and groups would you invite to join the Privatization Task Force? Why?

2. What are your answers to the mayor's stated concerns and issues (A–D) listed in the memo?

3. If the mayor moves forward with the privatization of garbage collection, what criteria should be used for selecting a private contractor to provide the service? What individual or office should be charged with administering the bidding process and the actual contract itself? Should a separate office be created, and what would be the responsibilities of this person or office?

4. What problems do you foresee in implementing a new privatization plan? Could privatization of garbage collection be avoided? Can you recommend any changes to current garbage and recyclable materials collection as a remedy to the problem?

5. What other municipal services could be considered for privatization? Is there one approach or model (for instance, the plan you develop for garbage collection) that could be followed in privatizing other municipal services?

SOURCES FOR FURTHER READING

Cooper, P. J. "Government Contracts in Public Administration: The Role of Environment of the Contracting Officer." *Public Administration Review* 40 (1980): 460–461.

Kettl, D. F. *Sharing Power: Public Governance and Private Markets*. Washington, D.C.: Brookings, 1993.

Salamon, L. M. *Beyond Privatization: The Tools of Government Action*. Washington, D.C.: The Urban Institute Press, 1989.

Sharkansky, I. "Government Contracting." *State Government* 53 (1980): 23–24.

- "privatize
- keep it public
- allocate responsibility to residents - take their own to dump
- hybrid public/private - contract by section

Part VI
Evaluating Public Programs and Organizations

THE EVALUATION CHALLENGE FOR MANAGERS

Evaluation can be considered as a systematic process that gathers information about and measures the results of programs, policies, and organizations. Evaluation also contributes to the public's understanding of what it is government does and informs the development of both new and existing programs and procedures. The systematic evaluation of public programs and agencies is a relatively new phenomenon, beginning only in the 1970s.[1] However, the call for reform and accountability in government and the need to cut the costs of wasteful programs has made the evaluation process a central concern of managers, elected officials, and the public.

Managers must consider the effects of the programs they administer, both short-term and long-term. Certain programs and services may not fulfill their intended mission and unsuccessful programs should not be permitted to continue without revisions. Even if the program appears to be successful, however, an evaluation is recommended, as without the evaluation there is no basis for reliably ascertaining whether the program is a success or a failure. Moreover, evaluations help the organization and managers learn valuable lessons from successful programs. The evaluation process should be an educational process. The ultimate goal of the evaluation is to drive decisions about the program's status and future such as whether the effort was successful, whether it should be continued, discontinued, or modified, and how to plan future strategies, tactics, and resources for the program.

The evaluation process can be considered to involve five basic steps: (1) identifying problems pertaining to the program or organization, (2) setting goals and making the goals of the program or organization the basis for the evaluation and decision making about their result, (3) determining before hand what is being evaluated and the measurement criteria, (4) conducting the actual evaluation, and (5) using the findings to inform any action about the program or organization.

THE POLITICS OF EVALUATION

Political Consequences of Evaluations

Conducting a thorough evaluation of a public agency or program requires a serious commitment. Unfortunately, the evaluation process is often little more than an afterthought and ends up being neglected or under-prioritized in many organizations and by many managers.

There are a number of possible reasons for this. Two common reasons are that not all managers are trained in evaluation techniques and conducting a thorough evaluation takes time, resources, and a commitment from the agency.

The findings of the evaluation might have political consequences. For instance, should the findings be negative, the evaluation could result in the reduction of funds and staff or the elimination of the program altogether. Such evaluations could reflect negatively on elected officials who championed the program and, as such, there might be political pressures placed on managers to produce a more positive evaluation, especially during election years. Or, a negative evaluation could reduce political and public confidence in the agency. In other circumstances, managers conduct evaluations simply because they are required to do so by law, because it is the policy of the agency to conduct periodic evaluations, or because the terms of the grant or policy mandate an evaluation at the conclusion of the program's life cycle. Even if managers are committed to the evaluation process and to using the results to deliver a better service, they must still contend with the powerful bureaucratic force of maintaining the status quo. Even in the face of compelling findings, the bureaucracy will resist change, especially if it means reducing or eliminating programs, personnel, or funds.[2]

It is important to develop both institutional and political support for the evaluation process and devote the necessary resources to the process. This involves conducting evaluations more often than simply at the ending date for the program or when forced to evaluate. Instead, evaluations should be on-going throughout each step or stage in the policy process or program's life. The same should occur for agencies and units of the organization, where the goal is to create self-evaluating organizations. This requires not only institutional support and adequate resources for the process, but the development of an organizational culture that is open to evaluations. A commitment to evaluation will be reflected in the frequent analysis of all facets of the organization. It is equally important to start the evaluation early enough in the process to be effective and to incorporate the evaluation into a *feedback loop*. As such, the results of evaluations should be shared with others in the organization and should continually inform the various actors and stages in the process, including the program formulation and implementation stages.

Evaluation Procedures

There are many ways to conduct an evaluation but every approach involves several preconditions that must be met. The manager must specify exactly what is to be evaluated, how it is to be evaluated, when the evaluation should take place, and who should conduct it. Because of problems in measuring the results of public programs, it is important to identify the basis and instrument for measurement. It is also vital to make sure the analysis avoids the problem of bias.

Evaluation requires that sufficient data be collected in order to conduct the analysis. The agency or manager charged with overseeing the evaluation must make sure that evaluators are trained in data collection and analysis and that adequate management information systems are in place to support this task. During the data analysis phase, a frequent error is to make a cause-and-effect determination where there is no such relationship. Given the complexities and countless forces acting on the program, it is possible that some force other than the program caused the apparent outcome, producing a spurious result.

Among the various approaches to the actual evaluation is a before-and-after comparison that considers the conditions previous to the implementation of the program and those present after the program. The assumption is that any change after the program can be attributed to the program. It is necessary to find an appropriate time before and after implementation to conduct the analysis and the manager must be careful to make sure the conditions before the program were the same as after implementation. Another method of evaluation involves comparing the actual results to anticipated results. Program models and projections can be used to calculate anticipated results. The projections could be for the optimal outcome or a realistic outcome and used to determine whether the program achieved its desired outcome. Evaluators could also compare the program with similar programs in other agencies or communities, or against cases where no program was attempted to determine the success or impact of the program. There are many other qualitative and quantitative approaches from which to choose but no one approach is best and managers must decide which method best serves their purposes. Many evaluators prefer to utilize more than one method and to first attempt an experimental or pilot program to test the feasibility of the program.[3]

DECISION-MAKING ISSUES TO CONSIDER AS YOU READ THE CASES

In undertaking the evaluation of programs and organizations, there are several basic questions that must be considered. Initially, it is important to ask a variety of questions about the organization that provide insights on the performance of the program or agency, such as their goals, resources, personnel, clients, and so forth. This also includes obtaining all the necessary facts and data about the program and agency so as to allow for an adequate evaluation.

Overt or "Covert" Evaluations?

The evaluator and program manager must also be aware of what amounts to "covert" reasons for conducting an evaluation. Not all evaluations are undertaken purely to obtain the true results of the program. Nor will the results of the evaluation always be used to guide decisions about the program's future. For instance, stakeholders in the program might evaluate simply to justify the program or its budget allocation, or there might be political pressures to prove that the program or organization has been successful. On the other hand, opponents of the program might encourage an evaluation that justifies terminating the program.

What Measures Will be Used to Evaluate?

Other basic questions or concerns in the evaluation process include *what* to evaluate and what measures to use in evaluating. Numerical or quantitative measurements are typically used as the basis for an evaluation. Unfortunately, not all public services and programs can be easily quantified. It might be easy to quantify the goals if the program under evaluation involved manufacturing shoes or hamburgers or producing a film where quantitative output measures are straight forward. But, it is hard to come up with a dollar amount for such issues as a human life or the cost of a quality education. In such cases, other facets of public programs or organizations serve as the basis of the actual evaluation. This includes such measures as the timeliness or cost of the program, its efficiency or ability to come in at or under cost, the degree of citizen input or public satisfaction regarding the program, or the accountability of public officials in implementing the program, as measured by their adherence to stated rules and procedures during the program's existence.

Often, a primary consideration is politics. This is manifested through polls of public satisfaction with the program, its visibility or ability to generate positive public perceptions, avoidance of scandal, and, of course, re-election. More generally, in the public sector there is an absence of reliable performance measures and indicators because of the complexity of the tasks and the many factors acting at any one time on the situation. Because of this, managers must be careful to avoid spurious findings whereby the apparent cause of the finding turns out, in fact, not to be the source of the result. Some other factor caused the phenomenon.

Multiple Outcomes

There are multiple beneficiaries and multiple goals of public programs and services, so the idea that there is a single satisfactory measure is misleading. As such, the output of the program might have been positive for some beneficiaries but negative for other clients. Or, one aspect of the goal might have been realized while another was not. In such cases, would the program be deemed a success or a failure? Such uncertain scenarios are common in government where programs and services include building and maintaining roads, regulating foods, providing safe streets, and expanding economic opportunities to as many people as possible.

Who Should Conduct the Evaluation?

Still another question is *who* should conduct the evaluation. There are, for instance, benefits to conducting the evaluation within the organization. In-house evaluations offer the advantage of the evaluator being familiar with the organization, its history and practices, and other pertinent facts. But such closeness to the program and people under evaluation might pose inherent biases. An individual too close to an organization and its service may lack objectivity and perspective, or may have a vested political interest in seeing a particular finding promoted.

If the organization lacks the technical capacity or means to conduct a viable evaluation, it may have no choice but to seek outside help. External evaluations by consultants might be costly, but might also bring neutrality and expertise to the process. A further benefit is the legitimacy derived from an outside evaluation. The public is more likely to believe the results of an evaluation performed by those not involved in the program or invested in the result of the evaluation. Managers should keep in mind, however, that evaluations conducted internally often focus on the successes of the program or organization, whereas external evaluators tend to point out or stress the deficiencies.[4]

When to Evaluate and the Time Frame for Evaluation?

The question of the time frame for the evaluation is another important issue. Evaluations conducted too soon after the program's initiation might not permit the program enough time to accomplish its intended purpose. But waiting too long to look into the program's results might miss opportunities to modify the program or prevent its continuation long after its effectiveness has ended. The issue of the time frame for evaluation involves whether to measure program *outputs* or *outcomes*. The output is the immediate result of the program; for instance, providing a child from a low-income family a nutritious lunch during the school day. The outcome is the ultimate result of the program's existence. The outcome of the school lunch program might be the existence of healthy, educated, productive members of society twenty years after the program. Regardless of whether one is measuring outputs or outcomes, the evaluation process should begin early enough in the program's life cycle to be effective and guide the development of the program.

The process of evaluating a public program or organization is complex and not free from potential problems. Unfortunately, the lack of straightforward measures and the history of shoddy evaluations have cast public doubt as to the reliability of many evaluations. Managers must commit themselves to a goal of conducting continual, periodic, and reliable evaluations, whose results are fed back to all stakeholders and participants in the program so as to inform decisions about offering better programs and services.

Strategic Planning and Performance Measurement: Setting Goals and Tracking Achievement in the City of Glenville

Donald P. Moynihan

ABOUT THE AGENCY

The mission of the Glenville *Office of Management and Budget* (OMB) is to ensure effective, efficient allocation and management of city resources to enable the mayor and city departments to provide quality services for the *City of Glenville.*

ABOUT THE CHARACTERS

Pam Herd is a senior analyst in the planning division of OMB.

Mayor Sean Casey is a successful local businessman whose only previous public sector experience was in managing an unsuccessful Senate campaign. He was elected mayor six months ago.

Keith Cook is the president of the powerful city workers union.

Maureen Alpert is a staff assistant to Mayor Casey, and frequently acts as an intermediary between the mayor's office and the OMB.

Buckley Jones is the director of OMB.

Susan Sieg heads Citizens for a Safer Glenville (CSG), and is traditionally critical of the efforts of the city and the police and fire departments.

Phil Kangas is the longtime chief of the fire department.

BACKGROUND: A NEW STRATEGIC PLAN?

[handwritten note: establish a plan to assess ea. agency's strategic goal by setting specific goals]

Mayor Sean Casey's campaign platform promised a "change in how we do things in city hall" and a "more efficient, accountable government." In particular he proposed that Glenville badly needed "a strategic vision for the new millennium." However, once elected, the promise of the strategic plan slipped off the radar. So, after being pressed by the media and local interest groups, the mayor called a press conference last week to unveil his strategic plan, six months into his term. It was not a successful effort. With the aid of political advisers and appointees, a slim document, titled "Glenville: A New Millennium," was presented, which did little more than elaborate on the mayor's campaign platform. During the press conference the mayor appeared at a loss when pressed for specifics of the plan. The local paper, *The Glenville Post*, ran an editorial chastising the mayor for "preferring rhetoric over content. . . . If this is the best strategic plan Mayor Casey can produce for Glenville, we are in worse shape than we thought. Mayor Casey needs to understand that governing means more than rehashing campaign catch phrases. He needs to consult citizens, action groups, academics, and city employees to deliver a real strategic plan."

Many members of the city council also criticized the plan, reminding the mayor that they too had an interest in the future of the city. Two days later The *Post* ran another article under the title of "Mayor's Plan Weak, Say Critics." A professor in the School of Public Management at Glenville University, labeled the plan ". . . a little fluffy. It is too broad to really provide direction and offers no guide as to how results will be measured."

The mayor is reported to be furious. There has been talk of little else in city hall in the last week. After the editorial, the mayor's office issued a press release stating that "Glenville: A New Millennium" was merely a vision statement for the City, meant to set the framework for a more detailed strategic plan. Mayor Casey promised a more fully developed plan "based on the concerns of our citizens and the expertise of our workers."

PERFORMANCE MEASURES

While all this transpired, "Citizens for Better Government," a task force appointed by the mayor and made up primarily of local business and community leaders, issued their report on performance measurement. The existing performance measurement process allows city agencies to report a set of self-selected performance measures in their budget. The task force was critical of the current process, believing that improved tracking of performance is the key to more efficient government and greater accountability to the public. Two specific criticisms stood out: (1) performance measures vary in quality among agencies, and (2) measures are not used to motivate employees or hold them accountable.

The task force recommended the following: (1) performance measures be linked to the goals laid out in the mayor's strategic plan, (2) agencies focus on outcome measures and create performance targets, (3) all agency measures be reviewed by the OMB for quality and consistency, and (4) a pay-for-performance system be created, linking employee pay and/or agency budgets to agency outcome measures.

BLUEPRINT FOR A STRATEGIC PLAN

The following Monday morning, senior staff at OMB met with Maureen Alpert, an aide to the mayor. Alpert said that the mayor expects OMB to take a leading role coordinating a more detailed strategic planning process and creating a more rigorous performance tracking system. She summarized, "Look, a lot of stuff has come together at once, and we are definitely feeling pressure to get the job done. But you guys should see this as an opportunity. Now you can create an integrated strategic planning and performance measurement process."

After the meeting, Buckley Jones, OMB director, commented to his staff, "Well, new administration but the same old story. They create a mess and we are supposed to clean it up." Jones then asked Pam Herd, one of his senior analysts and planners, to head up the "Blueprint Task Force." Jones charged the task force with examining the most feasible strategic planning options, given the relatively short time available, and developing a set of performance measures to track strategic goals. Herd previously worked with another city, one widely admired for its strategic planning process and one that utilized planning teams composed of political appointees and high-ranking agency officials. Their strategic planning decisions were also preceded by widespread consultation with citizens and employees. Herd knows that the ability to coordinate a series of consultative meetings with stakeholders and any other outreach to citizens will be tough to pull off in a limited period of time.

Herd decides to look for feedback from various stakeholders before making a decision. Her first phone call is to union representative Keith Cook, who is especially critical of the Citizens for Better Government report. He said, "Workers will be held to a higher level of accountability and can expect little in return. Tying pay to outcomes is grossly unfair, since workers cannot control outcomes." Herd has worked closely before with Phil Kangas, the fire chief, so she met with him to discuss the mayor's plan. Kangas' take on the plan notes its broad nature, saying that the only goal relevant to the fire department is that: "safer communities in Glenville means less crime, safer streets, and safer homes." Kangas accepts the need for a better performance measurement system, but is also skeptical about relying exclusively on outcome measures. While he feels output measures are useful as efficiency indicators and for tracking performance over time, he is worried about linking budgets to performance. He said, "Our committee on the city council will not stand for any cut in our budget. We are hard pressed for resources as it is. They are not going to start cutting our budgets if we do not make performance targets." He also expressed concern about the loss of discretion: "Other people, who do not know the business, should not be telling us what to do. Look, you should really let the departments drive this process. We know our jobs better than anyone else, and that includes you folks at the OMB. We are already measuring a lot of what we do and can come up with a series of goals."

Herd also receives a phone call from Susan Sieg, longtime head of Citizens for a Safer Glenville, who informed her: "At long last we can get some control over the safety of our citizens in Glenville. The mayor's office told me you were in charge of the strategic planning process, and I expect you will keep the mayor's promise that citizens will get a real say here. We are not going to see better service until bureaucrats believe they are going to be held publicly accountable for their performance."

ROLE-PLAY ASSIGNMENT

Acting as Herd, head planner for OMB who has been put in charge of leading the "Blueprint Task Force," you must put together a proposed plan for establishing strategic goals for every city agency and setting performance measures to assess the goals. Jones, head of OMB, wants to meet with you next week about your approach to the plan and task force.

QUESTIONS FOR DISCUSSION

1. Identify the stakeholders in this process. How should the stakeholders be involved in the two proposals (strategic plan and performance measures) under development?
2. What groups or individuals do you invite to offer input to your task force? How do you assure continued input from these groups to the on-going process?
3. What are the benefits of strategic goals and performance measures for the city agencies?
4. What are the different types of strategic planning processes Herd could recommend?
5. Suggest a series of strategic goals and outcome measures appropriate for the fire department.

SOURCES FOR FURTHER READING

Hatry, H. *Performance Measurement: Getting Results.* Washington, D.C.: The Urban Institute Press, 1999.

Rabin, J., G. J. Miller, and W. B. Hildreth. *The Handbook of Strategic Management.* New York: Marcel Dekker, 1989.

Halachmi, A., and G. Bouckaert. *Organizational Performance and Measurement in the Public Sector: Towards Service, Ef-* *fort and Accomplishment Reporting.* Westport, CT: Quorum Books, 1996.

Moore, M. H. *Creating Public Value Strategic Management in Government.* Cambridge, MA: Harvard University Press, 1995.

- 4 stage Performance Measurement System for ea. agency
  ↳ strategic planning, budget development, budget implementation, and performance monitoring

- task force - set goals for agencies

- OMB to implement strategic plan

- Performance Measures Review Board
  ↳ set performance measures & strategic goals
  ↳ then monitor

Restoring Mystic Lake: Program Choices When Science is Ambiguous

R. Edward Bradford & Dwight C. Kiel

ABOUT THE AGENCY

The *Central Florida Water Management District* (CFWMD) is one of four such districts created in 1970 by the state legislature. Its goals are to protect Floridians from flooding, to provide adequate water for farming and industry, to assure the quality of Florida's drinking water, and to protect the state's environment. The CFWMD has a budget that is funded partly through its own taxing district and thus is able to hire a large professional and scientific staff. The legislature almost always takes the advice of the CFWMD and the legislature grants it considerable autonomy in decision making.

ABOUT THE CHARACTERS

Bob English, project manager for Mystic Lake, Central Florida Water Management District (CFWMD), is responsible for recommending how the lake should be restored.

Isabel Forge is the president of the Friends of Restoration (FOR), an environmental group that lobbies for restoration and advocates purchasing the muck farms to accomplish this.

Leon Wells is a lawyer/lobbyist for the muck farm owners.

Gabe Taylor is a spokesperson for the chamber of commerce in Mystic Village.

Juan Orson is a spokesperson for the Florida Farm Workers Union and thus speaks for the muck farm workers.

Marco Burke represents the CFWMD scientists and other scientists who argue that Mystic Lake's degradation is the result of the muck farms.

Wendy Castle represents the scientists who argue that the condition of Mystic Lake is largely due to natural events.

BACKGROUND

Mystic Lake in central Florida was once a scenic, clear water lake that provided some of the best bird watching and bass fishing in North America. After World War II, as the new vacationing middle-class discovered Florida, Mystic Lake became a popular tourist destination. From 1950 until the late 1960s the town of Mystic Village grew rapidly in response to the tourist boom. Birders and anglers poured over $2 million into the local economy each year, and signs that the health of the lake was in jeopardy were ignored.

By 1970, however, thick green algae blooms—sighted occasionally for more than ten years—began to overrun Mystic Lake. The clear, shallow waters of the lake became pea green, reducing dramatically the number of birds and bass living in the lake's ecosystem. And without them, the number of bird watchers and fishermen coming to Mystic Lake also declined. Within ten years the tourist dollars generated by Mystic Lake had fallen to almost zero. Today, Mystic Village, which had grown to a population of 9,000 during its boom years, has just 1,000 persons more now than its pre-tourism population of 4,000. Mystic Lake, devoid of all plant life except the thick green algae, attracts few visitors except for lake biologists. These "limnologists" come to examine a classic example of shallow lake eutrophication, a lake so rich in nutrients that green algae choked the water.

Back in 1990, ten citizens of Mystic Village met and created Friends of Restoration (FOR), a group dedicated to cleaning up the lake and returning it to its former splendor. FOR, under the leadership of Isabel Forge, quickly expanded the group's membership by drawing together young people who were interested in preserving wilderness areas and older citizens who were conservationists and birders. The group grew rapidly to 300 members and had many sympathetic supporters and donors from around the state. Forge has been involved in an aggressive and highly public lobbying campaign to convince the Florida legislature and the Central Florida Water Management District (CFWMD) that it was in the interests of all Floridians to restore Mystic Lake, even if the costs were high.

The Issues at Hand

One of the first goals of FOR was to determine the source(s) of the nutrients that were responsible for the decline of the lake's vitality. FOR's analysis claimed that the main source of "nutrient loading" was the phosphorous pumped into the lake by the muck farms at the southern end of the lake. FOR was careful in leveling this charge, because the muck farms were a major source of employment and income for Mystic Village. The muck farms had, as all the locals realized, provided jobs and revenues before, during, and after the boom years of tourism.

Like several other lakes in central and south Florida, Mystic Lake has a large marshy shoreline that was drained during World War II to provide very rich soil for agricultural production. Vegetable production on this rich muck was twice that of excellent soils, and in Florida there were three growing seasons each year. The muck farms lay below the now diked lake, and the farms constantly pumped rain and seepage water off their lands and into the lake. This water, claimed FOR, carried fertilizer in the form of phosphorous into Mystic Lake, thus damaging the health of the entire lake.

The three muck farms on Mystic Lake, each almost 2,000 acres in size, recognized that they were under attack by FOR so they sought the services of lawyer/lobbyist, Leon Wells. In his public pronouncements, Wells emphasized the economic contributions that the farms made to the region, noting the 100 employees working directly on the farms and the indirect employment created by these jobs. The farmers made purchases in Mystic Village, reminded Wells, and the produce from the muck farms fed many. The economic benefits of the muck farming to the local economy was estimated at easily $2 million annually.

Wells did not deny that the farms have pumped phosphorous-laden water into the lake, but he clearly pointed out the disagreement among limnologists concerning the exact cause of the lake's demise. One group of scientists, including those who work for the CFWMD, believed that FOR is correct in blaming the phosphorous from the farms for the lake's current troubled condition. Marco Burke is the spokesperson for these scientists and has argued for years that the lake had been able to absorb the phosphorous, but finally the phosphorous load became so great that the algae blooms appeared. These blooms prevented sunlight from reaching the native plants in the lake and reduced the oxygen in the water, leading to fish kills. The native plants that had helped absorb and bond the phosphorous were killed off and the fish kills then further reduced oxygen levels. The only solution, according to Burke, is to stop the farms from polluting the lakes by buying the farmland and turning it back into the marsh it had once been. The restored marsh would thus serve as a natural filter to reduce the phosphorous already in the lake.

However, the other group of scientists, led by Wendy Castle, contends that Mystic Lake had a historically high level of phosphorous. The lake, in fact, was quite good at handling high phosphorous levels, including the phosphorous pumped into the lake from the muck farms. But Castle views the demise of the lake not as the result of human acts, but as the result of a natural disaster. In this case the disaster was a hurricane in 1960, which swept through central Florida and hit the lake with eighty-five-mile-per-hour winds. The result, according to Castle, was that many of the plants from the lake bottom were destroyed. The scientific community and the two opposing spokespersons—Burke and Castle—are in agreement that the plants had absorbed and bonded phosphorous; but they differ on why the plants died. Castle argues that the hurricane had ripped up many plants, and in the ensuing years more were ripped from the lake floor by waves that had previously been muted by the plant growth. The muck farms, in her opinion, are not the cause of the problems in Mystic Lake and the restoration of the old marshland is therefore not the solution. Rather than spend tens of millions of dollars on purchasing the farms, it would be more prudent to set up a water treatment plant on the lake to remove the phosphorous through chemical treatment.

Bob English is the CFWMD project manager for Mystic Lake. The Speaker of the House recently informed English that he is confident that the state legislature would budget at least $35 million this session for cleaning up Mystic Lake. Thus, English has money for a project, but he lacks a clear scientific answer to lake restoration and even a clear mandate from the citizens of Mystic Village.

While many citizens are supportive of FOR and its goal of purchasing the muck farms, there are other citizens with serious doubts about this strategy. At a recent CFWMD-sponsored public hearing, the spokesperson for the Mystic Village Chamber of Commerce, Gabe Taylor, argued against shutting down the farms. He warned that many businesses, especially agricultural supply stores, would be hurt and that as many as thirty jobs in town would be lost. Juan Orson, speaking for the muck farm workers, was also critical of any proposed purchase of the farms. Almost all of the muck farm workers had been migrant laborers and they had no other skills. Purchasing the farms would leave the farm owners well off, but the workers would be left without jobs or other opportunities. As is the case with the scientific community, the citizens of Mystic Lake are split regarding how to address the problem.

ROLE-PLAY ASSIGNMENT

English will have sufficient funds from the legislature to either purchase the farm land as part of the lake restoration plan or to build a water treatment plant. You are English, the CFWMD project manager for Mystic Lake, and you must develop a plan of action.

QUESTIONS FOR DISCUSSION

1. How should English weigh the alternatives? What criteria should he use?
2. How would you try to evaluate the economic benefit of the scenic beauty of a restored lake or the ideals of restoring an ecosystem for purposes beyond human utility?
3. If the muck farmers and the CFWMD agree to a buyout of farmland, how should the price paid for the land be determined? Should the state also pay for the equipment and buildings on the farm land? What about the costs of retraining the muck farm workers?
4. How would you build support for your decision? What individuals or groups would you need to convince that your plan has merit?
5. To what extent do you base decisions purely on science as opposed to considering other factors like the jobs and livelihood of the farmers, the interests and political power of the home owners living on the lake, and so on in evaluating your options?

SOURCES FOR FURTHER READING

Blake, N. M. *Land into Water—Water into Land: A History of Water Management in Florida.* Tallahassee, FL: University Presses of Florida, 1980.

"Flow-way Allows Nature to Cleanse Lake Apopka." *Streamlines* (Summer 1999). Can also be accessed by website: http://sjr.state.fl.us/info/streamln/99summer/su99sln2.htm

Land Acquisition Program. St. Johns River Water Management District (FL) Publication, website: http://sjr.state.fl.us/about/plan/planhome/landacq/landacq.html

Case 23

The Role of Benchmarking in Performance Appraisals: Lessons from State Workers' Compensation Programs

Sharon E. Fox

ABOUT THE AGENCY

The *Georgia Bureau of Workers' Compensation* is the agency with primary responsibility for administering the workers' compensation laws in the state. The primary responsibilities of a state workers' compensation agency include informal and/or formal dispute resolution, organizing education and training programs, monitoring statutory compliance with the law, collecting data, and evaluating workers' compensation programs.

ABOUT THE CHARACTERS

Joe Health, head of the administrative agency (Bureau of Workers' Compensation) in Georgia, is responsible for overseeing the state workers' compensation program. His is a senior management position that was politically appointed by the governor.

BACKGROUND

need to improve timliness of worker's comp payments

The use of benchmarking studies, organizational report cards, and other performance measurement tools have become more common in public policy settings as a means for increasing accountability and improving performance. Generally, benchmarking reports compare organizations to the "best in class" or to standards established by knowledgeable professionals. A central component of a benchmarking effort is the identification of process differences that account for gaps in performance and the adaptation or implementation of processes in one's own organization in an effort to close these gaps.

A national public policy research organization has conducted a study that benchmarks the performance of workers' compensation programs in eight states. The study addresses three basic questions: (1) How do state workers' compensation systems compare on standard measures of performance? (2) Which states have positive outcomes that others might want to replicate? and (3) What are realistic goals for states seeking to improve their systems? As head of his state's program, Joe Health is faced with a number of challenges and opportunities when the findings of the report are released. Various state government officials and policymakers, as well as representatives of key interest groups, naturally expect him to take a leadership role in interpreting and responding to the study's findings.

AN OVERVIEW OF STATE WORKERS' COMPENSATION PROGRAMS

Workers' compensation is a form of social insurance that provides coverage for workplace injuries and illnesses. Under workers' compensation, eligible workers receive medical care and rehabilitative treatment, as well as cash payments to partially replace lost wages for time spent away from work. In nearly all states, employer participation is mandatory and, as a result, more than 95 percent of the workforce is covered by workers' compensation insurance. Benefits are financed almost entirely by employer premiums paid to commercial insurers or through self-insurance. The insurer has primary responsibility for managing and paying injured workers' claims for benefits. The state provides the regulatory and administrative framework that ensures compliance with the law and the timely resolution of disputes between the parties when they arise. In essence, the state oversees the application of the statute to ensure that its objectives are being met.

Myriads of other powerful stakeholders are interested in workers' compensation issues and policies. These include leaders of business and organized labor, as well as representatives of the insurance industry, the medical and legal communities, and grassroots injured worker organizations. Given the multitude of special interests involved in workers' compensation, policymaking tends to be partisan and contentious.

Workers' compensation systems were originally envisioned to be self-administering. They are based on a no-fault principle that specifies that employers are responsible for the costs of all workplace injuries and illnesses, without regard to fault. In return for these protections, employees relinquish the right to sue their employers for damages. However, the complexities of the system have necessitated that state governments assume more active roles in the administration of their laws.

COMPARING WORKERS' COMPENSATION SYSTEM PERFORMANCE ACROSS STATES

In the past decade, many states have made significant statutory and regulatory changes to their workers' compensation programs in the areas of administrative organization, insurance coverage, benefit eligibility requirements, benefit rates, and dispute resolution processes. However, policymakers and agency administrators often lack basic data and information about current or emerging problems, making it hard to target opportunities for improvement. Adding to this difficulty is the fact that most states have not been able to examine their programs in a reliable manner, relative to those of other states. Without this broader context, states are unable to set realistic goals or fully appreciate the magnitude of their program's strengths and weaknesses. In an effort to help state policymakers and administrators fill these gaps, the Workers Compensation Research Institute, an independent nonprofit research organization located in Cambridge, Massachusetts, initiated a new research program that provides benchmark comparisons of state workers' compensation systems. The first study was released by the program this year and it provides comparisons of eight states on more than 75 performance measures, including timeliness of injury reporting, timeliness of benefit payments, and the cost of claims.

Policy debates about workers' compensation reform and so many other policy issues are often driven by perceptions that a state is a higher or lower cost state. For example, a state's reputation as having high or low workers' compensation costs may have implications for attracting and retaining business and whether there is sufficient political interest in increasing benefits for injured workers.

MANAGING REACTIONS TO THE STUDY'S FINDINGS

Medical-legal exams are often used in workers' compensation to determine a worker's eligibility for benefits, the extent of permanent disability that a worker may have suffered, or a worker's ability to return to work. In 1993, California made significant changes to its medical-legal system, and subsequent studies confirm that the state successfully reduced both the frequency and the cost of medical-legal examinations. But the benchmarking study was the first to put California's experience in a broader perspective. It showed that 25 percent of claims in California had expenses for medical-legal examinations—more than twice the average rate across other states. At one extreme were Connecticut, Florida, Georgia, and Texas, where fewer than 10 percent of claims had medical-legal costs. And at $1,025 per claim, the cost of the average medical-legal examination in California was considerably higher than that cost in the other states, more than twice the cost in Georgia.

In Pennsylvania, employers and insurers have twenty-one days from the date they have knowledge of a worker's disability to investigate and either accept or deny the worker's claim, or begin payment of benefits without admitting liability. The results of the benchmarking report indicate that nearly 60 percent of injured workers in Florida and Massachusetts received their initial benefit payment within twenty-one days of injury; in Pennsylvania, the rate was much lower at about 40 percent. These results have raised concerns, especially in the labor community, about the reasons for Pennsylvania's poor performance. Georgia's performance is also below average.

In an effort to improve the timeliness of benefit payments to injured workers, two alternative strategies are being proposed in Georgia. First, members of organized labor have urged the agency (Bureau of Workers' Compensation) to take a more active role in imposing penalties on employers or insurers who make late payments. However, representatives of the business and insurance industries are strongly resisting additional regulation and oversight. As an alternative, they propose a more pro-active educational effort that informs employers and insurers of their reporting requirements and responsibilities. Clearly some action must be taken and the governor, to whom Health reports, has promised the public that an improvement in performance will be shown in the subsequent benchmarking study.

According to the benchmarking report, Georgia has the highest average cost per claim ($10,474 versus an average of $8,843) based on a subset of claims with more than seven days of lost time from work. However, based on the broadest perspective that accounts for all claims in the system, Georgia's costs are considerably lower than average ($1,833 versus $2,152). The study cautions that characterizing Georgia as a high- or low-cost state depends on the base of claims that are used in the calculation of the measures.

In January 2001, the governor of Georgia created a Workers' Compensation Advisory Commission. The advisory commission is charged with reviewing the workers' compensation system and making additional legislative and/or regulatory modifications, as warranted. The commission is considering making a recommendation that benefits in Georgia be increased, although the business community is resisting. The chair of the governor's commission has received a copy of the complete report and is considering using some of the information in helping the task force frame its recommendations. As the head of the agency, the chair is interested in Health's assessment of the study and the validity of the findings. In particular, he has asked Joe to clarify whether, in his opinion, Georgia is a high- or low-cost state and whether he thinks a benefit increase is warranted.

ROLE-PLAY ASSIGNMENT

You are Health, head of the Bureau of Workers' Compensation in Georgia—the state indicted by the report as having the highest costs of workers' compensation claims. The governor and the governor's task force on the issue have asked for your recommendation.

QUESTIONS FOR DISCUSSION

1. What are the pros and cons of using reports from policy think tanks? How would you use the report of the Workers Compensation Research Institute?

2. Based on the results of the report, how might you approach investigating whether there is additional room for improvement? How might this study be used to set goals for your state and monitor performance? Should the agency make specific policy recommendations based on the evaluation (study findings)?

3. What information from the other states might you use to make your recommendation?

4. What do you say to the governor and the governor's task force regarding the "high" costs of workers' compensation in Georgia? The head of the governor's task force has contacted you requesting to know more about how other states have achieved such low rates. How would you go about handling this situation? Specifically, as the agency director who is responsible for monitoring compliance with the law, which of the two approaches outlined in the case do you favor—a more active role by the agency in imposing penalties on employers and insurers who are late making payments or educating employers and insurers about reporting requirements? How do you explain your choice to those that favored the alternative? What other steps might you take to demonstrate your agency's commitment to improving the timeliness of payments to injured workers?

Australian

Benchmarking
- 8 step procedure
audits, partners,
re-est.

Performance
Measurement
for gov't
- strategic plan,
program plan,
set priorities, allocate
resources, activity
plan & organization,
mgt + operations,
monitor operations
- measure result,
analysis + reporting
results, obtaining
feedback of results

- Benchmarking groups
  └ exchange info about
  effectiveness of diff.
  organizational practices

- Balanced Scorecard
  └ strategy based balances
  efficiency, infrastructure +
  financial + non financial views of performance

performance

5. Identify some political considerations you would face as you approach the evaluation of Georgia's workers' compensation system?

SOURCES FOR FURTHER READING

Ammons, D. *Municipal Benchmarks: Assessing Local Performance and Establishing Community Standards*. Thousand Oaks, CA: Sage Publications, 1996.

Fox, S. E., C. A. Telles, and C. Casteris. *Benchmarking the Performance of Workers' Compensation Systems: CompScope Multistate Comparisons*. Cambridge, MA: Workers Compensation Research Institute, 2000.

Gormley, W. T., and D. L. Weimer. *Organizational Report Cards*. Cambridge, MA: Harvard University Press, 1999.

Holzer, M., and K. Callahan. *Government at Work: Best Practices and Model Programs*. Thousand Oaks, CA: Sage Publications, 1998.

Walters, J. *Measuring Up*. Washington, D.C.: Governing Books, 1998.

Assessing the Organization: Accountability and Public Appeal

Alton M. Okinaka

ABOUT THE ORGANIZATION

The *Strategic Management Committee* of *West Island Services for Humanity* (WISH) is a private, nonprofit chapter of a nationwide organization. WISH serves an entire island in Hawaii through its mission as a fund-raising agency for social and charitable causes.

ABOUT THE CHARACTERS

Kelly Kobata is the chair of the WISH Strategic Management Committee and a volunteer who is an urban planner by profession.

Annie Doright, coordinator of WISH, runs the office staff and the day-to-day operations of the agency. She is also responsible for implementing the action plans and directives of the board of directors.

Ebeneezer Taylor is an old volunteer who has served continuously for two decades on committees and the board. Taylor's main focus and concern is in fund-raising—advocating ways to improve fund-raising through solicitation of employees of large organizations.

Mary Belog is the director of one of the community programs that has traditionally received funds from the agency and serves on the committee as the representative of the various programs receiving funds.

ACCOUNTABILITY AND PUBLIC APPEAL

· should change mission statement

As a private, nonprofit organization that raises and distributes funds, West Island Services for Humanity (WISH) serves as the central or umbrella organization for fund-raising agencies on the island. As the "clearinghouse" for social services, WISH helps avoid duplication of requests in the community for donations. As such, WISH has led the way in collecting private donations for community benefit programs on the island for many years. WISH works somewhat independent of its national affiliate and only a small portion of the monies collected are forwarded to the national organization; otherwise, all monies raised by the chapter are kept to meet the agency's expenses and to provide funds for local community service agencies. Historically, the majority of fund raising has occurred by soliciting donations from individual employees of large employers on the island. This has allowed for relatively focused and effective fund-raising.

However, increasing demands for funds for a variety of community service programs has lead to a reconsideration of the way funds are raised, with an eye to increasing the base of donations while keeping costs minimized. In addition, public opinion has shifted. The public is demanding accountability of all public contributions and its service programs. These changes in public opinion both nationally and locally have come, in part, from a scandal at the national level that harmed the parent organization's reputation. As a result, donations have decreased at a time of increasing demands for funds. In response, the national organization came up with a slight change in mission. The change calls for a shift from primarily fund-raising to a joint mission of, (1) more effective and targeted fund raising, and (2) fund allocations to programs that demonstrated benefits to the community. Member chapters were asked to consider the proposal for adoption.

In response, Annie Doright, WISH coordinator, feels a change is needed to increase the appeal of the agency in order to collect donations. The same motivation for change at the national level has resulted in a suggestion by the national organization that member chapters make changes to their mission in ways that will increase their appeal to their local constituencies. To help member chapters make these changes, the national organization created a sample mission statement that represented a shift from the old mission statement. Agencies would attempt to meet the changes in public opinion and address the concerns regarding accountability. WISH's Strategic Management Committee, headed by Kelly Kobata, has been charged with completing a report on whether the agency should comply with the national organization's suggestion about modifying their mission statement and how this should be done. This report will then be presented to the board of directors for consideration for adoption.

NEW MISSION STATEMENT

The old mission statement had, as its primary focus, fund-raising. While the notion of "community benefit" is in the old mission, it was broadly worded and purposely left vague to allow for flexibility by the board of directors in identifying worthy issues and allocating funds. This type of mission statement created flexibility but also made accountability almost impossible, as too many things could fit under the mission and there was no real means for judging both the relative merits of programs and criteria for ranking priorities for programs.

What was suggested by the national organization was a change in the mission statement to a dual mission of both fund-raising and targeted resource allocation based on community needs and input. Changes to fund-raising were seen as necessary to increase the target population and donation base. Changes to resource allocations required creating more specific criteria for choosing which programs were funded and requiring recipient programs to be accountable for the funds received.

Fund-raising

In the area of fund-raising, many members of the community who had made donations in the past had stopped donating because they objected to certain programs funded by the agency. More input on fund allocations in the form of targeted donations ear-marked for certain programs was suggested as a response to this problem. The new mission has received mixed reviews. Many in the community are pleased with the emphasis on funding community programs, but some former community beneficiaries are concerned about how the "community benefit" criterion will be defined. Mary Belog, for instance, the head of an organization that has received WISH funding in the past, worries that her organization might not qualify or that further WISH guidelines will be attached to the donation that will interfere with her ability to spend the funds as she sees fit. She does not want WISH telling her how to spend the money.

Others, like Ebeneezer Taylor, who has served on WISH's board for many years, thinks it is easier to simply get funds from large employers just as they have always done. And, he does not want to change WISH's policies, which will, in his opinion, only complicate things.

In addition, the traditional fund-raising approach of using large employers was felt to be limiting in both target population and means of making donations. Greater flexibility was suggested in creating a campaign targeted at new donors—such as self-employed individuals or employees of small businesses—as well as adopting more creative means of making donations, such as estate gifts in wills or donations of goods or property. It was believed that broadening the appeal base in both numbers of people and in types of donations accepted would result in an increase in the amount of donations collected.

The major constraint in broadening the appeal base was to find ways to accomplish these things without increasing the proportion of funds used in fund-raising efforts. It would be self-defeating to raise more funds only to end up spending more of those funds than is raised.

Resource Allocation

Changing the allocation of resources was a much trickier issue. This required not only the creation of new procedures, but also a change to the agency's mission statement to include more specific goals or objectives that could be used to create criteria by which decisions of what programs to fund could be made. First of all, the goals and objectives needed to be clearly stated so that procedures and criteria could be developed in a way that priorities could be identified. These would provide an initial screening mechanism for identifying programs that addressed the most critical need areas in the immediate community. In addition, the goals and objectives needed to be stated so that criteria and procedures for accountability could be developed to determine which programs were making effective use of their resources to meet the community's needs. This would enable the agency and programs to demonstrate to the community that not only were needs being addressed, but that resources were being put to good use in addressing those need areas.

THE PROBLEMS

The Strategic Management Committee is faced with a two-fold task. The first challenge is to decide whether changes are needed to the mission statement. The second problem pertains to what changes to make.

The national organization's suggestion for changes include the following items: (1) address community priorities and identifiable need areas, (2) give priority to programs that create long-term changes toward program or community self-sufficiency, (3) develop partnerships and a commitment to resource sharing that increase effectiveness, and (4) develop criteria by which need and effectiveness can be judged.

ROLE-PLAY ASSIGNMENT

As Kobata, convener of WISH's Strategic Management Committee, your job is to organize the members and tackle the problem. Various members within the committee, representing different interest groups, will present their opinions in ways that may seem to contradict each other and have their own priorities.

QUESTIONS FOR DISCUSSION

1. To what degree does WISH want to become the leader in setting the direction for social service providers in the community? Or does it simply aspire to be a support agency for social service programs?

2. How can the mission statement be worded in order to be flexible enough to meet the variety of social needs, yet specific enough to create criteria for prioritization and assessment? Develop a definition of "community benefit" as well as criteria for awarding funds to social service providers and a policy for raising funds.

3. If the agency is going to insist on more accountability on the part of recipient programs, to what degree are they going to need to spend more resources on helping these programs develop and implement effective accountability and assessment measures? How might this be done without imposing rules that burden recipients or beneficiaries of WISH funds?

4. How should the agency assess community needs and the conditions necessary for setting priorities and funding decisions? What would you recommend, and should WISH dedicate money or resources to this task?

5. How would you overcome resistance to change among board members, beneficiaries of WISH funds, and the community? How would you present the changes so that they are acceptable and welcomed by the recipient programs, donors, and the community at large?

SOURCES FOR FURTHER READING

Bryson, J. M. *Strategic Planning for Public and Non-Profit Organizations*. San Francisco: Jossey-Bass, 1988.

Drucker, P. F. *Managing the Non-Profit Organization*. New York: HarperCollins, 1990.

Espy, S. N. *Handbook of Strategic Planning for Non-Profit Organizations*. New York: Praeger, 1986.

[handwritten notes:]

- mission-based marketing
- no change & hope for incr. donations
- keep mission statement - w/new strategic plan to raise donation levels
- chang mission statement

NOTES

The Case Analysis Approach

1. Charles E. Lindblom, "The Science of Muddling Through," *Public Administration Review* 19 (1968): 79–88.

Introduction

1. Budget of the United States Government, Fiscal Year 2001.

2. Daniel J. Elazar, *American Federalism: A View from the States* (New York: Harper & Row, 1984); Morton Grodzins and Daniel J. Elazar, *The American System* (Chicago: Rand McNally, 1966).

3. Deil S. Wright, "Federalism, Intergovernmental Relations, and Intergovernmental Management: Historical Reflections and Conceptual Comparisons," *Public Administration Review* 50 (1990): 168–178; Deil S. Wright, *Understanding Intergovernmental Relations* (Monterey, CA: Brooks/Cole, 1988).

4. David H. Rosenbloom and Deborah O. Goldman, *Public Administration: Understanding Management, Politics, and Law in the Public Sector* (New York: McGraw-Hill, 1997).

5. Marshall Dimock, Gladys Dimock, and Douglas Fox, *Public Administration* (New York: Holt, Rinehart and Winston, 1983).

6. Melvin J. Dubnick and Barbara S. Romzek, *American Public Administration: Politics and the Management of Expectations* (New York: Macmillan, 1991).

7. Grover Starling, *Managing the Public Sector* (Chicago: The Dorsey Press, 1986).

8. Charles H. Levine, B. Guy Peters, and Frank J. Thompson, *Public Administration: Challenges, Choices, Consequences* (Glenview, IL: Scott, Foresman, 1990).

9. Richard J. Stillman, II, *Public Administration: Concepts and Cases* (New York: Houghton Mifflin, 2000).

10. Charles T. Goodsell, *The Case for Bureaucracy: A Public Administration Polemic* (Chatham, NJ: Chatham House, 1994).

11. Graham T. Allison, "Public and Private Management: Are They Fundamentally Alike in All Unimportant Respects?" In *Current Issues in Public Administration*, ed. F. S. Lane (New York: St. Martin's Press, 1994): 16–32; Graham T. Allison, *Essence of Decision* (Boston: Little, Brown, 1971).

12. Grover Starling, *Managing the Public Sector* (Chicago: The Dorsey Press, 1986). 14–18.

13. Gerald Garvey, *Public Administration: The Profession and the Practice* (New York: St. Martin's Press, 1997), 17–20, 312.

14. Charles E. Lindblom, "The Science of Muddling Through," *Public Administration Review* 19 (1959): 79–88; Charles E. Lindblom, "Still Muddling, Not Yet Through," *Public Administration Review* 39 (1979): 517–526.

Part I. Managing Public Organizations and Employees

1. H. H. Gerth and C. Wright Mills, *From Max Weber: Essays in Sociology* (New York: Oxford University Press, 1946), 196–203.

2. The Office of Personnel Management website (2000) provides detailed information on this and other related personnel matters.

3. See the Budget of the United States Government, Fiscal Year 1999.

4. W. Richard Scott, *Organizations: Rational, Natural, and Open Systems* (Englewood Cliffs, NJ: Prentice Hall, 1992).

5. Frederick W. Taylor, *The Principles of Scientific Management* (New York: Norton, 1967). Taylor's book was first published in 1911.

6. Chester I. Barnard, *The Function of the Executive* (Cambridge, MA: Harvard University Press, 1938).

7. Mary Parker Follet, "The Giving of Orders," reprinted in J. M. Shafritz and A. C. Hyde, eds. *Classics of Public Administration* (Pacific Grove, CA: Brooks/Cole, 1992): 66–74.

8. Henri Fayol, *General and Industrial Management* The book was first published (in French) in 1916 and first translated into English by Constance Storrs (New York: Pitman, 1949).

9. Elton Mayo, *The Human Problems of an Industrial Civilization* (Boston: Harvard Business School, 1933); Frederick J. Roethlisberger and William J. Dickson, *Management and the Worker* (Cambridge, MA: Harvard University Press, 1939).

10. Douglas McGregor, *The Human Side of Enterprise* (New York: McGraw-Hill, 1960).

Part II. Managing Human Resources

1. N. Joseph Cayer, *Public Personnel Administration in the United States* (New York: St. Martin's, 1986); Steven W. Hays and Richard C. Kearney, *Public Personnel Administration: Problems and Prospects* (Englewood Cliffs, NJ: Prentice Hall, 1995).

2. Robert S. Lorch, *State and Local Politics* (Englewood Cliffs, NJ: Prentice Hall, 1992); Clarence N. Stone, Robert K. Whelan, and William J. Murin, *Urban Policy and Politics* (Englewood Cliffs, NJ: Prentice Hall, 1979).

3. Steven W. Hays and Richard C. Kearney, *Public Personnel Administration: Problems and Prospects* (Englewood Cliffs, NJ: Prentice Hall, 1995), 24–25, 277–278.

4. President Jimmy Carter was assisted in designing and promoting his reforms by his Civil Service Commissioner, Alan K. Campbell. See, Alan K. Campbell, "Testimony on Civil Service Reform and Reorganization," In *Classics of Public Personnel Policy*, Frank J. Thompson ed. (Pacific Grove, CA: Brooks/Cole, 1991): 82–104.

5. The 1896 U.S. Supreme Court ruling in *Plessy v. Ferguson* codified the "separate but equal" clause into law.

6. Bill Conti and Brad Stetson, "Affirmative Action is Harmful," In *Minorities*, Mary E. Williams ed. (San Diego: Greenhaven Press, 1998):105–110; Timur Kuran, "A Backlash Against Affirmative Action is Growing Among Whites," In *Race Relations*, Paul A. Winters, ed. (San Diego: Greenhaven Press, 1996): 29–35.

7. Kathleen Staudt, *Policy, Politics & Gender: Women Gaining Ground* (West Hartford, CT: Kumarian Press, 1998); Amber Coverdale Sumrall and Dena Taylor, *Sexual Harassment: Women Speak Out* (Freedom, CA: Crossing Press, 1992).

Part III. Managing Budgets and Financial Resources

1. Thomas D. Lynch, *Public Budgeting in America* (Englewood Cliffs, NJ: Prentice Hall, 1990).

2. Aaron Wildavsky and Naomi Caiden, *The New Politics of the Budgetary Process* (New York: Longman Publishers, 1997).

3. Thomas D. Lynch, *Public Budgeting in America* (Englewood Cliffs, NJ: Prentice Hall, 1990): 3, 10–11, 47.

4. John Maynard Keynes, *The General Theory of Employment, Interest and Money* (New York: Harcourt Brace, 1936).

5. Aaron Wildavsky, *The Politics of the Budgetary Process* (Boston: Little, Brown, 1964).

6. Aaron Wildavsky and Naomi Caiden, *The New Politics of the Budgetary Process* (New York: Longman Publishers, 1997), 45–49.

7. Irene S. Rubin, "Budget Reform and Political Reform: Conclusions from Six Cities," In *Current Issues in Public Administration*, F. S. Lane ed. (New York: St. Martin's Press, 1994): 306–326.

Part IV. Managing Ethics

1. Dennis Thompson, "The Possibility of Administrative Ethics," *Public Administration Review* 45 (1985): 555; Dwight Waldo, *The Administrative State: A Study of the Political Theory of American Public Administration* (New York: Holmes and Meier, 1984).

2. Joel Fleischman et. al., *Public Duties: Moral Obligations of Government Office* (Cambridge, MA: Harvard University Press, 1981); Thomas Nagel, "Ruthlessness in Public Life," In *Public and Private Morality*, S. Hampshire ed. (Cambridge, UK: Cambridge University Press, 1978): 82–90; John R. Rohr, *Ethics for Bureaucrats* (New York: Marcel Dekker, 1989): 4–6, 64–65.

3. Gerald Garvey, *Public Administration: The Profession and the Practice* (New York: St. Martin's, 1997): 305–306, 320–334.

4. Barbara S. Romzek and Melvin J. Dubnick, "Accountability in the Public Sector: Lessons from the Challenger Tragedy," *Public Administration Review* 47 (1987): 227–238.

5. Stephen K. Bailey, "Ethics and the Public Service," In *Public Administration and Democracy*, R. C. Martin ed. (Syracuse, NY: Syracuse University Press, 1965): 283–298; George J. Gordon and Michael E. Milakovich, *Public Administration in America* (New York: St. Martin's, 1995): 183–184.

6. Grover Starling, *Managing the Public Sector* (Chicago: The Dorsey Press, 1986): 115–124.

Part V. Planning and Implementing Public Programs

1. Edwin C. Hargrove, *The Missing Link* (Washington, DC: Urban Institute, 1975).

2. Jeffrey L. Pressman and Aaron Wildavsky, *Implementation* (Berkeley, CA: University of California Press, 1973).

3. Ibid.

4. Ibid.

5. Eugene Bardach, *The Implementation Game* (Cambridge, MA: MIT Press, 1977).

6. Milbrey McLaughlin, "Implementation as Mutual Adaption," In *Social Program Implementation*, Walter Williams and Richard Elmore eds. (New York: Academic Press, 1976).

7. Robert T. Nakamura and Frank Smallwood, *The Politics of Implementation* (New York: St. Martin's, 1980).

Part VI. Evaluating Public Programs and Organizations

1. William N. Dunn, *Public Policy Analysis* (Englewood Cliffs, NJ: Prentice Hall, 1994).

2. Ralph P. Hummel, *The Bureaucratic Experience: A Critique of Life in Modern Organization* (New York: St. Martin's, 1994).

3. Allen D. Putt and J. Fred Springer, *Policy Research: Concepts, Methods, and Applications* (Englewood Cliffs, NJ: Prentice Hall, 1989).

4. Putt and Springer, 1989.

BIBLIOGRAPHY

Adams, Guy B., and Danny L. Balfour. *Unmasking Administrative Evil*. Los Angeles: Sage, 1998.

Allison, Graham T. "Public and Private Administration: Are They Fundamentally Alike in all Unimportant Respects?" In *Current Issues in Public Administration*, F. S. Lane ed. New York: St. Martin's, 1994, 16–32.

Allison, Graham T. *Essence of Decision*. Boston: Little, Brown, 1971.

Ammons, D. *Municipal Benchmarks: Assessing Local Performance and Establishing Community Standards*. Thousand Oaks, CA: Sage Publications, 1996.

Anderson, A. "Nurse-Physician Interaction and Job Satisfaction." *Nursing Management* 27 (1996): 33.

Bailey, Stephen K. "Ethics and the Public Service." In *Public Administration and Democracy*, R. C. Martin ed. Syracuse, NY: Syracuse University Press, 1965, 283–298.

Banovetz, James M. *Managing Local Government: Cases in Decision Making*. Washington, D.C.: International City/County Management Association, 1998.

Bardach, Eugene. *The Implementation Game*. Cambridge, MA: MIT Press, 1977.

Barnard, Chester I. *The Function of the Executive*. Cambridge, MA: Harvard University Press, 1938.

Barrier, Michael. "Sexual Harassment: The Supreme Court's Message." *Nation's Business* December (1998): 1–20.

Beach Nourishment and Protection. Washington, D.C.: National Research Council, 1996.

Berry, L. M. *Psychology at Work: An Introduction to Industrial and Organizational Psychology*. Boston: McGraw-Hill, 1998.

Blake, Nelson Manford. *Land into Water—Water into Land: A History of Water Management in Florida*. Tallahassee, FL: University Presses of Florida, 1980.

Bland, Robert L., and Irene S. Rubin. *Budgeting: A Guide for Local Governments*. Washington, D.C.: International City/County Management Association, 1997.

Bryner, G. C. *Bureaucratic Discretion: Law and Policy in Federal Regulatory Agencies*. New York: Pergamon Press, 1987.

Bryson, John M. *Strategic Planning for Public and Non-Profit Organizations*. San Francisco: Jossey-Bass, 1988.

Burke, J. P. *Bureaucratic Responsibility*. Baltimore: Johns Hopkins University Press, 1986.

Carter, Stephen. *Integrity*. New York: HarperCollins, 1996.

Castelle, George P., and Robert L. Bee. *States and Reservations: New Perspectives on Federal Indian Policy*. Tucson, AZ: University of Arizona Press, 1992.

Cayer, N. Joseph. *Public Personnel Administration in the United States*. New York: St. Martin's, 1986.

Cellini, Henry D. *Youth Gang Prevention and Intervention Strategies*. Albuquerque, NM: University of New Mexico Training and Research Institute, 1991.

Condrey, Stephen, and Stephen B. Condrey. *Handbook of Human Resource Management in Government*. San Francisco: Jossey-Bass, 1998.

Conrad, John P., and Richard A. Myren. *Two Views of Criminology and Criminal Justice Definitions, Trends, and the Future*. Chicago: Joint Commission on Criminology and Criminal Justice Education and Standards, 1979.

Cooper, Phillip J. "Government Contracts in Public Administration: The Role and Environment of the Contracting Officer." *Public Administration Review* 40 (1980): 460–461.

Cooper, Terry L. *The Responsible Administrator*. San Francisco: Jossey-Bass, 1998.

Dalton, S. Lee, and N. Joseph Cayer. *Supervision for Success in Government*. San Francisco: Jossey-Bass, 1994.

Deloria, Vine, and Clofford Lytle. *The Nations Within: The Past and Future of American Indian Sovereignty*. New York: Pantheon, 1984.

Dimock, Marshall, Gladys Dimmock, and Douglas Fox. *Public Administration*. New York: Holt, Rinehart and Winston, 1983.

Drucker, Peter F. *Managing the Non-Profit Organization*. New York: HarperCollins, 1990.

Dubnick, Melvin J., and Barbara S. Romzek. *American Public Administration: Politics and the Management of Expectations*. New York: Macmillan, 1991.

Dunn, William N. *Public Policy Analysis*. Englewood Cliffs, NJ: Prentice Hall, 1994.

Elazar, Daniel J. *American Federalism: A View from the States*. New York: Harper & Row, 1984.

Espy, Siri N. *Handbook of Strategic Planning for Non-Profit Organizations*. New York: Praeger, 1986.

Fayol, Henri. *General and Industrial Management*. New York: Pitman, 1949.

Fleischman H., et. al. *Public Duties: Moral Obligations of Government Office*. Cambridge, MA: Harvard University Press, 1981.

"Flow-way Allows Nature to Cleanse Lake Apopka." *Streamlines* (Summer 1999).

Follet, Mary Parker. "The Giving of Orders" In *Classics of Public Administration*, J. M. Shafritz and A. C. Hyde eds. Pacific Grove, CA: Brooks/Cole, 1992, 66–74.

Forte, P. "The High Cost of Conflict." *Nursing Economics* 15 (1997): 119.

Fox, R. L., and R. A. Schuhmann. "Gender and the Role of the City Manager." *Social Science Quarterly* 81 (2000): 604–621.

Fox, S. E., C. A. Telles, and C. Casteris. *Benchmarking the Performance of Workers' Compensation Systems: CompScope Multistate Comparisons*. Cambridge, MA: Workers Compensation Research Institute, 2000.

Garvey, Gerald. *Public Administration: The Profession and Practice: A Case Study Approach*. New York: St. Martin's, 1997.

Gerth, H. H., and C. Wright Mills. *From Max Weber: Essays in Sociology*. New York: Oxford University Press, 1946.

Goodsell, Charles T. *The Case for Bureaucracy: A Public Administration Polemic*. Chatham, NJ: Chatham House, 1994.

Gordon, George J., and Michael E. Milakovich. *Public Administration in America*. New York: St. Martin's, 1995.

Gormley, W. T., and D. L. Weimer. *Organizational Report Cards*. Cambridge, MA: Harvard University Press, 1999.

Gortner, Harold F. *Ethics for Public Managers*. New York: Praeger, 1991.

Grodzins, Morton, and Daniel J. Elazar. *The American System*. Chicago: Rand McNally, 1966.

Gruber, J. E. *Controlling Bureaucracies: Dilemmas of Democratic Governance*. Los Angeles: University of California Press, 1987.

Halachmi, Arie, and Geert Bouckaert. *Organizational Performance and Measurement in the Public Sector: Towards Service, Effort and Accomplishment Reporting*. Westport, CT: Quorum Books, 1996.

Hampshire, S. *Public and Private Morality*. Cambridge, UK: Cambridge University Press, 1978.

Hargrove, Edwin C. *The Missing Link*. Washington, D.C.: Urban Institute, 1975.

Harris, David A. "The Stories, the Statistics and the Law: 'Why Driving While Black Matters.'" *Minnesota Law Review* 84 (1999): 265–326.

Harrison, M. Trice. *Occupational Culture in the Workplace*. Ithica, NY: ILR Press, 1995.

Harrison, M. Trice, and Janice M. Beyer. *The Cultures of Work Organization*. Englewood Cliffs, NJ: Prentice-Hall, 1993.

Hatry, Harry. *Performance Measurement: Getting Results*. Washington, D.C.: The Urban Institute Press, 1999.

Hays, Stephen W. "Staffing the Bureaucracy: Employee Recruitment and Selection." In *Handbook of Human Resource Management in Government*, Stephen Condrey ed. San Francisco: Jossey-Bass, 1999.

Hays, Stephen W., and Richard C. Kearney. *Public Personnel Administration: Problems and Prospects*. Englewood Cliffs, NJ: Prentice Hall, 1995.

Herzberg, Frederick. *Work and the Nature of Man*. Cleveland, OH: World Publishing, 1966.

Hird, John. *Superfund: The Political Economy of Environmental Risk*. Baltimore: Johns Hopkins University Press, 1994.

Holzer, Mark, and K. Callahan. *Government at Work: Best Practices and Model Programs*. Thousand Oaks, CA: Sage Publications, 1998.

Hummel, Ralph P. *The Bureaucratic Experience: A Critique of Life in Modern Organization*. New York: St. Martin's, 1994.

Kelly, Rita Mae and Phoebe Morgan Stambaugh. "Sexual Harassment in the States." In *Current Issues in Public Administration*, Frederick S. Lane ed. New York: St. Martin's Press, 1994.

Kettl, Donald F. *Sharing Power: Public Governance and Private Markets*. Washington, D.C.: Brookings, 1993.

Keynes, John Maynard. *The General Theory of Employment, Interest and Money*. New York: Harcourt Brace, 1936.

Knox, George W. *An Introduction to Gangs*. New York: Wyndham Hall Press, 1994.

———. "Preliminary Findings from the 1992 Law Enforcement Mail Questionnaire Project." *The Gang Journal: An Interdisciplinary Research Quarterly* 1 (1993): 11–37.

Kosciulek, J. G. "Implications of Consumer Direction for Disability Policy and Rehabilitation Service Delivery." *Journal of Disability Policy Studies* 11 (2000): 80–89.

Larson, E. "The Impact of Physician-Nurse Interaction on Patient Care." *Holistic Nursing Practice* 13 (1999): 38.

Lemoncheck, Linda, and Mane Hajdin. *Sexual Harassment: A Debate.* New York: Rowman & Littlefield, 1997.

Leonard, L. A., T. Clayton, and O. H. Pilney. "An Analysis of Replenished Beach Design Parameters on U.S. East Coast Barrier Islands." *Journal of Coastal Research* 6 (1990): 15–36.

Leonard, L. A., K. L. Dixon, and O. H. Pilney. "A Comparison of Beach Replenishment on the U. S. Atlantic, Pacific, and Gulf Coasts." *Journal of Coastal Research* 6 (1990): 127–140.

Levine, Charles H., B. Guy Peters, and Frank J. Thompson. *Public Administration: Challenges, Choices, Consequences.* Glenview, IL: Scott Foresman, 1990.

Lindblom, Charles E. "Still Muddling, Not Yet Through." *Public Administration Review* 39 (1979): 517–526.

———. "The Science of Muddling Through." *Public Administration Review* 19 (1968): 79–88.

Lipsky, M. *Street-level Bureaucracy: Dilemmas of the Individual in Public Services.* New York: Russell Sage Foundation, 1980.

Lorch, Robert S. *State and Local Politics.* Englewood Cliffs, NJ: Prentice Hall, 1992.

Luke, Jeffrey. *Catalytic Leadership: Strategies for an Interconnected World.* San Francisco: Jossey-Bass, 1998.

Lynch, Thomas D. *Public Budgeting in America.* Englewood Cliffs, NJ: Prentice Hall, 1990.

Martin, G. E., and T. Bergman. "The Dynamics of Behavioral Response to Conflict in the Workplace." *Journal of Occupational and Organizational Psychology* 69 (1996).

Masmanian, Daniel A., and Michael E. Kraft. *Toward Sustainable Communities: Transitions and Transformations in Environmental Policy.* Cambridge, MA: MIT Press, 1999.

Maxson, Cheryl L. "Investigating Gang Migration: Contextual Issues for Intervention." *The Gang Journal: An Interdisciplinary Research Quarterly* 1 (1993): 1–8.

Mayo, Elton. *The Human Problems of an Industrial Civilization.* Boston: Harvard Business School, 1933.

McGregor, Douglas. *The Human Side of Enterprise.* New York: McGraw-Hill, 1960.

McLaughlin, Milbrey. "Implementation as Mutual Adaption." In *Social Program Implementation,* Walter Williams and Richard Elmore eds. New York: Academic Press, 1976.

Meyers, Roy T. *Handbook of Government Budgeting.* San Francisco: Jossey-Bass, 1998.

Mikesell, John L. *Fiscal Administration.* New York: Wadsworth Publishing, 1995.

Moore, Mark H. *Creating Public Value: Strategic Management in Government.* Cambridge, MA: Harvard University Press, 1995.

Nakamura, Robert T., and Frank Smallwood. *The Politics of Implementation.* New York: St. Martin's, 1980.

O'Leary, Rosemary, Robert F. Durant, Daniel J. Fiorino, and Paul S. Weiland. *Managing for the Environment: Understanding the Legal, Organizational, and Policy Changes.* San Francisco: Jossey-Bass, 1999.

Pressman, Jeffrey L., and Aaron Wildavsky. *Implementation.* Berkeley, CA: University of California Press, 1973.

President's Commission on Law Enforcement and Administration of Justice. *The Challenge of Crime in a Free Society.* Washington, D.C.: U.S. Government Printing Office, 1967.

Putt, Allen D., and J. Fred Springer. *Policy Research: Concepts, Methods, and Applications.* Englewood Cliffs, NJ: Prentice Hall, 1989.

Rabin, Jack, Gerald J. Miller, and W. Bartley Hildreth. *The Handbook of Strategic Management.* New York: Marcel Dekker, 1989.

Rachlin, Robert. *Handbook of Budgeting.* New York: John Wiley & Sons, 1998.

"Racial Profiling is Seen as Widespread, Particularly Among Young Black Men." *Gallup News Service* (2000).

Rohr, John R. *Ethics for Bureaucrats.* New York: Marcel Dekker, 1989.

Roethlisberger, Frederick J., and William J. Dickson. *Management and the Worker.* Cambridge, MA: Harvard University Press, 1939.

Rosenbloom, David H., and Deborah O. Goldman. *Public Administration: Understanding Management, Politics, and Law in the Public Sector.* New York: McGraw-Hill, 1997.

Roth, Mitchel. *Fulfilling a Mandate: A History of the Criminal Justice Center at Sam Houston State University.* Huntsville, TX: Sam Houston Press, 1997.

Rubaii-Barrett, N., and A. C. Beck. "Minorities in the Majority: Implications for Managing Cultural Diversity." *Public Personnel Management* 22 (1993): 503–521.

Rubin, Irene S. *The Politics of Public Budgeting: Getting and Spending, Borrowing and Balancing.* New York: Chatham House, 2000.

Salamon, Lester M. *Beyond Privatization: The Tools of Government Action.* Washington, D.C.: The Urban Institute Press, 1989.

Scott, David, John D. Martin, and Arthur J. Keown. *Basic Financial Management.* Englewood Cliffs, NJ: Prentice-Hall, 1999.

Scott, W. Richard. *Organizations: Rational, Natural, and Open Systems.* Englewood Cliffs, NJ: Prentice Hall, 1992.

Shapiro, J. P. *No Pity: People with Disabilities: Forging a New Civil Rights Movement*. New York: Times Books, 1994.

Sharkansky, Ira. "Government Contracting." *State Government* 53 (1980): 23–24.

Shichor, David. *Punishment for Profit: Private Prisons/Public Concerns*. New York: Sage Publications, 1995.

Sophocles. *Antigone*. (Edited by Mark Griffith). New York: Cambridge University Press, 1999.

"Special Section on Racial Profiling: Implications for Public Policy." *Public Administration Times* 24 (2001).

Starling, Grover. *Managing the Public Sector*. Chicago: The Dorsey Press, 1986.

Staudt, Kathleen. *Policy, Politics, & Gender: Women Gaining Ground*. West Hartford, CT: Kumarian Press, 1998.

Stillman, Richard J. *Public Administration: Concepts and Cases*. New York: Houghton Mifflin, 2000.

Stone, Clarence N., Robert K. Whelan, and William J. Murin. *Urban Policy and Politics*. Englewood Cliffs, NJ: Prentice Hall, 1979.

Sumrall, Amber Coverdale, and Dena Taylor. *Sexual Harassment: Women Speak Out*. Freedom, CA: Crossing Press, 1992.

Suzuki, Peter T. "Pan-Indianism, Ethnicity, and Omaha Tribe of Nebraska." *Contemporary Society: Tribal Studies* 1 (1994): 103–114.

———. "The Rebirth of a Nation: The Winnebago Tribe of Nebraska." *Contemporary Society: Tribal Studies* 4 (1999): 71–83.

Taylor, Frederick W. *The Principles of Scientific Management*. New York: Norton, 1967.

Thompson, Dennis. "The Possibility of Administrative Ethics." *Public Administration Review* 45 (1985): 555.

Thompson, Frank J. *Classics of Public Personnel Policy*. Pacific Grove, CA: Brooks/Cole, 1991.

Trupin, L., D. S. Sebesta, E. Yelin, and M. P. LaPlante. *Trends in Labor Force Participation Among Persons with Disabilities, 1983–1994*. San Francisco: University of California Press, 1997.

Vroom, Victor. *Work and Motivation*. New York: John Wiley & Sons, 1964.

Waldo, Dwight. *The Administrative State: A Study of the Political Theory of American Public Administration*. New York: Holmes and Meier, 1984.

Walters, J. *Measuring Up*. Washington, D.C.: Governing Books, 1998.

Welch, Michael. *Punishment in America: Social Control and the Ironies of Imprisonment*. New York: Sage Publications, 1999.

Wildavsky, Aaron, and Naomi Caiden. *The New Politics of the Budgetary Process*. New York: Longman Publishers, 1997.

Wildavsky, Aaron. *Budgeting: A Comparative Theory of Budgetary Processes*. New York: Transaction Books, 1986.

Wilkens, David E. "Tribal-State Affairs: American States as 'Disclaiming' Sovereigns." *Journal of Federalism* 28 (1998): 55–81.

Williams, Mary E. *Minorities*. San Diego: Greenhaven Press, 1999.

Witt, Stephanie L., and W. David Patton. "Recruiting for a High-performance Workforce." In *Human Resource Management in Local Government: An Essential Guide*, Siegrun Fox Freyss ed. Washington, D.C.: International City/County Management Association, 1999.

Winters, Paul A. *Race Relations*. San Diego: Greenhaven Press, 1996.

Woodard, B., and B. House. "Nurse Physician Communication: Women and Men at Work." *Orthopaedic Nursing* 16 (1997): 39.

Wright, Deil S. "Federalism, Intergovernmental Relations, and Intergovernmental Management: Historical Reflections and Conceptual Comparisons." *Public Administration Review* 50 (1990): 168–178.

Wright Deil S. *Understanding Intergovernmental Relations*. Monterey, CA: Brooks/Cole, 1988.

Yaffe, J. "Latina Managers in Public Employment: Perceptions of Organizational Discrimination." *Hispanic Journal of Behavioral Sciences* 17 (1995): 334–346.

ABOUT THE CONTRIBUTORS

Jeffrey S. Ashley, Ph.D. is Assistant Professor of Political Science at Eastern Illinois University where he teaches American government and public administration, focusing primarily on human resource management and organization theory. He taught previously at Saginaw Valley State University and is the co-author of *Indian Tribal Governments and the U.S. Federal System* (Praeger Press, forthcoming) and co-editor of *Groundwater Management in the West* (University of Nebraska Press, 1999).

Kimberly Bejcek is a graduate student in organizational leadership and administration at Saginaw Valley State University and is employed with the Michigan Family Independence Agency.

Amy K. Blizzard is a student in the Ph.D. program in Coastal Resources Management at East Carolina University. She is a certified (AICP) planner with ten years experience in coastal community planning.

R. Edward Bradford received his M.A. in political science from the University of Central Florida, where he serves as an instructor in the Department of Political Science. His most recent research interests are on Florida environmental issues, especially land acquisition policies.

Pamela Tarquinio Brannon received her Ph.D. in public administration from Florida Atlantic University and is an adjunct professor in the Organizational Management Program at Warner Southern College, where she teaches courses in diversity, human resources, and business law. Her research interests include race and diversity issues, public administration education, and collaborative solutions to public problems. She has been an administrator in both the nonprofit and governmental sectors in the areas of elderly services, volunteers, and criminal justice and is a member of the American Society for Public Administration and the Conference of Minority Public Administrators.

Michael Kaye Carlie completed his Ph.D. at Washington University in St. Louis and is a Professor of Sociology and Criminal Justice in the Department of Sociology and Anthropology at Southwest Missouri State University. He lectures, speaks publicly, and publishes articles on prisons, corrections, and the gang phenomenon.

Sharon E. Fox, Ph.D. is Assistant Professor and Research Scientist at the University of Massachusetts Medical School in Worcester. She is also Deputy Director of the Robert Wood Johnson Foundation Workers' Compensation Health Initiative, a national grant program based at the university's Center for Health Policy and Research. Her professional and scholarly interests involve comparative state politics and policy in the areas of workers' compensation and health.

Mark Funkhouser, Ph.D. has been City Auditor of Kansas City, Missouri since 1988. Before that he headed the performance audit group in the Division of State Audit, State of Tennessee. Funkhouser has a B.A. in political science from Thiel College, an MSW from West Virginia University, an MBA from Tennessee State University, and a Ph.D. in public administration and sociology from the University of Missouri at Kansas City. He was editor of *Local Government Auditing Quarterly* from 1990–1998 and continues to serve as a columnist for the journal. He is a Certified Government Auditor and speaks frequently on topics related to government performance and accountability.

W. Bartley Hildreth, Ph.D. is the Regents Distinguished Professor of Public Finance in the Hugo Wall School of Urban and Public Affairs and the Frank Barton School of Business at Wichita State University and director of the Kansas Public Finance Center. He is the editor-in-chief of the quarterly journal, *Municipal Finance Journal,* and the lead editor of the *Handbook on Taxation.* Among his many professional activities, he has served as Director of Finance for the City of Akron, tax policy advisor to the governor of

Kansas, member of the National Advisory Council on State and Local Budgeting, and Chair of the Association on Budgeting and Financial Management, a section of the American Society for Public Administration. Hildreth has held tenured, senior faculty positions at Kent State University and Louisiana State University.

Sheridan R. Jones is a student in the Ph.D. program in coastal resources management at East Carolina University. He has an M.A. in maritime history and nautical archaeology from ECU and has served as an underwater archaeologist and a construction manager.

Dwight Conrad Kiel received his Ph.D. in political science from the University of Massachusetts, Amherst and is Associate Professor of Political Science at the University of Central Florida. He teaches courses on American politics, political theory, and public policy, and his research interests include environmental policy, education policy, and the history of liberalism.

J. Gary Linn, Ph.D., is a medical sociologist, and professor in the School of Nursing at Tennessee State University where he designs and teaches courses in nursing and hospital management. Linn is currently conducting funded research on the effectiveness of HIV prevention programs for special populations in the United States and Brazil. He worked previously as a senior administrator in a Veterans Administration hospital.

William R. Mangun, Ph.D. is Professor of Political Science and Coastal Resources Management at East Carolina University. He served as the Project Manager for Policy Analysis and the National Resource Management Coordinator for the U.S. Fish and Wildlife Service. He also worked for the U.S. Environmental Protection Agency. Mangun has published several books on environmental and natural resources management. His books include *Managing the Environmental Crisis* (Duke University Press, 1999), *American Fish and Wildlife Policy* (Southern Illinois University Press, 1992), *Public Policy Issues in Wildlife Management* (Greenwood Press, 1991), and *The Public Administration of Environmental Policy* (Indiana University, 1977). He has also published articles on pollution control and natural resources policy in *Public Administration Review, Policy Studies Journal, Policy Studies Review, Evaluation Review, Environmental Conservation, Journal of Environmental Studies, Environmental Review,* and other journals.

Gary E. May, MSSW, is Assistant Professor of Social Work in the Graduate Social Work Program at the University of Southern Indiana where he teaches social welfare policy. Additionally, he is the director of the USI/Epi-Hab Center for Disability Studies and has led many workshops on disability and veterans issues. He is a member of the Indiana Governor's Planning Council for People with Disabilities, several boards, and learned societies.

Geralyn M. Miller is Assistant Professor in the School of Public and Environmental Affairs at Indiana Purdue University in Fort Wayne. She earned her Ph.D. from the University of Illinois at Chicago and returned to academia after a lengthy career in the public sector. Her main interests include public administration, political communication, state and local governance, and public policy analysis.

Donald P. Moynihan, is a Ph.D. candidate in the Maxwell School of Citizenship and Public Affairs at Syracuse University. As a research associate with the Alan K. Campbell Public Affairs Institute, he has worked on the Government Performance Project, an analysis of public management in federal, state, and local government and his research has focused on managing for results, strategic planning, performance measurement, performance information use, comparative administration, and public sector reform.

Pat Nation, Ph.D. is Assistant Professor of Sociology at Middle Tennessee State University where she serves as a criminology advisor. Her interests include: crime; family; stratification; gender; deviance; mental health; and oral history of women sociologists. She is a community counselor and therapist for marriage, individuals, and families, specializing in victimology with an emphasis on working with battered spouses and children. A specialist in serial homicides, Nation also works as a consultant with federal, state, and local law enforcement agencies in the profiling and apprehension of predators.

Lisa S. Nelson, Ph.D. is Associate Professor in the Department of Political Science at California Polytechnic University, Pomona, where she coordinates the Masters in Public Administration degree program. Her interests include environmental policy and administration, intergovernmental relations, community participation, and public administration theory. She is the past vice president of the Western Social Science Association.

Alton M. Okinaka earned his Ph.D. from Indiana University and is chair of the Department of Sociology at the University of Hawaii, Hilo, where his interests include social psychology, race and ethnic relations, mathematical sociology, and applied sociology.

Nicholas C. Peroff, Ph.D. is Associate Professor of Public Administration in the Bloch School of Business and Public Administration at the University of Missouri at Kansas City. He has a B.S., M.A., and Ph.D. in political science from the University of Wisconsin-Madison and has taught in South Korea, Taiwan, and South Africa. Peroff has numerous publications in the area of American Indian Studies and is engaged in the development and application of complexity theory in American Indian Policy analysis. He is currently writing a book on Indian gaming policy and the Menominee Indian Tribe of Wisconsin and is president-elect of the Western Social Science Association.

Cheryl Ramos, Ph.D. is an instructor in the Department of Psychology at the University of Hawaii, Hilo. Her research and teaching interests include community psychology, organizational psychology, and program evaluation. She has extensive experience working in local government, nonprofit agencies, and as a consultant. She is active in community organizations.

Sandra J. Reinke, DPA., is Assistant Professor in the Department of Political Science at Augusta State University. She is recently retired from the U.S. Air Force where she served as Executive Vice President of the Air Community College and Commander of the 42d Services Squadron. Her research interests focus on quality performance appraisals and developing a culture of trust in public organizations.

Sharon J. Ridgeway, Ph.D. is Assistant Professor of Political Science and Public Administration at the University of Louisiana, Lafayette. Her research interests include natural resource policy and feminist theory. She worked previously as a community planner and head planner.

Patrick G. Scott earned his Ph.D. from the Maxwell School of Citizenship and Public Affairs at Syracuse University and is Associate Professor of Political Science and Director of the Master of Public Administration Program at Southwest Missouri State University. He formerly served as a management and program analyst at the U.S. Departments of Commerce and Housing and Urban Development. Scott's research and teaching interests include public management, organization theory, and program evaluation. He has published articles in several journals, including the *Journal of Policy Analysis and Management, Journal of Public Adminstration: Research and Theory, Administration and Society, American Review of Public Administration, Public Budgeting and Financial Management,* and *Research in Public Administration.*

Alex Sube Sekwat earned his Ph.D. from Florida Atlantic University and is Associate Professor in the Institute of Government at Tennessee State University and a native of Sudan, where he worked as an administrator in an aid program. He has published a number of articles on economic development in developing countries, budgeting and financial management, and international trade.

Peter T. Suzuki, completed his M.A. at Columbia University, doctoral work at Yale, and his Ph.D. at Leiden University in Holland and is a professor in the Department of Public Administration at the University of Nebraska, Omaha. He completed anthropological field work on administrators in a number of countries including Turkey, Holland, Belgium, and Germany as well as on three Indian reservations in Nebraska.

Clinton P. Taffe, MPA, CGFM is the Administration and Operations Manager for the Leon County Board of County Commissioners in Tallahassee, Florida, and has worked for many years at the county level in Florida in the areas of program budget and policy development, performance measurement, statistical reporting, and quality-diversity initiatives. Taffe earned his MPA from the University of West Florida and obtained his Certified Government Financial Manager designation from the Association of Government Accountants. He is a member of and chapter officer in the Florida Government Finance Officer's Association, the American Society for Public Administration, and the International Personnel Management Association.

James D. Ward, Ph.D. is on faculty at Midwestern State University, where he serves as the director of the Master in the Public Administration Program. He has published several articles on such topics as privatization, affirmative action, and racial profiling. He has served on both the National Board and Planning Committee of the Conference of Minority Public Administrators and on the National Program Committee of the American Society for Public Administration's 1997 national conference.

Robert P. Watson, Ph.D. is Associate Professor of Political Science at the University of Hawaii, Hilo and founding editor of the journal *White House Studies.* He is the author of more than 100 scholarly publications and author or editor of nine books, including *The Presidents' Wives: Reassessing the Office of First Lady* (Lynne Rienner Publishers, 1999, 2000) and *First Ladies of the United States: A Biographical Dictionary* (Lynne Rienner Publishers, 2001).

John D. Wong, Ph.D. is Associate Professor in the Hugo Wall School of Urban and Public Affairs at Wichita State University. Dr. Wong received his B.B.A. and M.A. in economics from Wichita State University, a J.D. from Washburn University, and his Ph.D. from Northeastern University. He has consulted with the Kansas Governor's Tax Equity Task Force, the official Kansas Consensus Revenue Estimating Group, the Kansas Department of Revenue, the Kansas Department of Human Resource, several cities and counties, and is the principal author of the annual *Governor's Economic and Demographic Report.* Wong has written extensively on public finance, revenue forecasting, taxation, electric utility deregulation, health care issues, and policy issues and is co-author of *State and Local Government Capital Improvement Planning and Budgeting and Public/Private Partnerships.*